COMPUTER
BOOK SERIES
FROM IDG

# FoxPro 2.6 For Window~~s~~ ~~For Dummies~~ ~~Cheat~~ ~~Sheet~~

M000096616

## The Catalog Manager (Chapter ~~2~~)

To use it, select File⇨Catalog Manager.

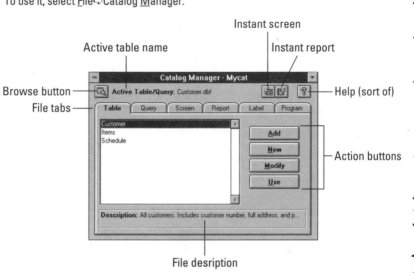

Instant screen

Instant report

Active table name

Browse button — 🔍 Active Table/Query: Customer.dbf

Help (sort of)

File tabs —

| Table | Query | Screen | Report | Label | Program |

Customer
Items
Schedule

Add

New

Modify

Use

— Action buttons

Description: All customers. Includes customer number, full address, and p...

File desription

## Field Types (Chapter 6)

| Field type | Description |
|---|---|
| Character | Anything with letters or numbers; most-common field type |
| Date | Dates (who said this stuff was hard?) |
| Float | Scientific numbers; leave it alone |
| General | Pictures, sounds, and other wickedly advanced stuff; leave it alone |
| Logical | Yes or No; great for simple questions |
| Memo | Long, *long* free-form text field; perfect for rambling notes |
| Numeric | Normal numbers, with or without decimals |

## dBASE to FoxPro Dictionary (Appendix B)

| dBASE Object | dBASE Extension | FoxPro Object | FoxPro Extension |
|---|---|---|---|
| Catalog | .CAT | Catalog | .FPC, .FCT |
| Database | .DBF | Table | .DBF |
| Form | .SCR | Screen | .SCX |
| Index | .MDX | Compound index | .CDX |
| Index | .NDX | Single index | .IDX |
| Label | .LBL | Label | .LBX |
| Query | .QBE | Query | .FPQ |
| Report | .FRM | Report | .FRX |

IDG
BOOKS

Copyright © 1994 IDG Books Worldwide.
All rights reserved.

Cheat Sheet $2.95 value. Item 076-4.

For more information about IDG Books, call
1-800-762-2974 or 415-312-0650

### ... For Dummies: #1 Computer Book Series for Beginners

# FoxPro 2.6 For Windows For Dummies

Cheat Sheet

COMPUTER BOOK SERIES FROM IDG

## Useful Keyboard Shortcuts
### (Chapter 33)

| Command | Key |
| --- | --- |
| Go away! | Esc |
| Undo | Ctrl+Z |
| Cut | Ctrl+X |
| Copy | Ctrl+C |
| Paste | Ctrl+V |
| Add a record | Ctrl+N |
| Look at a memo | Ctrl+PgDn |
| Close the window | Ctrl+F4 |
| Look at windows | Ctrl+F6 |
| Switch programs | Alt+Tab |
| Good-bye, FoxPro | Alt+F4 |

## Creating a Table (Chapters 6 and 8)

1. Write down what you want it to do.

2. List all the things it needs to store (fields).

3. Select Run⇨Wizard⇨Table or File⇨New⇨ Table/DBF.

4. Enter the fields (name, type, and size).

5. Save the new table.

6. Fill in your data.

## Relating Tables (Chapter 12)

- You're relating one table *to* another table. The official lingo says you're *linking* the Parent to the Child.

- Both tables *must* have at least one field in common. That's the *linking field*.

- The linking field *must* have the same name, type, and size in both tables.

- In the Child table, the linking field must be *indexed*. The index has to be active when you set up the relationship.

- Use the View dialog box to build relationships.

- Save your table relationships in View files so that you only have to mess with the process once.

## Best Ready-to-Go Tables in the Table Wizard (Chapter 8)

| Description | Table name |
| --- | --- |
| Customer list | Contacts<br>Mailing list |
| Employee list | Employees |
| Event planning | Events |
| Hotel registry | Guests |
| Household inventory | Household |
| Invoice tracking | Invoices<br>Invoice details |

. . . For Dummies: #1 Computer Book Series for Beginners

# References for the Rest of Us

## COMPUTER BOOK SERIES FROM IDG

Are you intimidated and confused by computers? Do you find that traditional manuals are overloaded with technical details you'll never use? Do your friends and family always call you to fix simple problems on their PCs? Then the *... For Dummies*™ computer book series from IDG is for you.

*... For Dummies* books are written for those frustrated computer users who know they aren't really dumb but find that PC hardware, software, and indeed the unique vocabulary of computing make them feel helpless. *... For Dummies* books use a lighthearted approach, a down-to-earth style, and even cartoons and humorous icons to diffuse computer novices' fears and build their confidence. Lighthearted but not lightweight, these books are a perfect survival guide to anyone forced to use a computer.

> *"I like my copy so much I told friends; now they bought copies."*
>
> **Irene C., Orwell, Ohio**

> *"Quick, concise, nontechnical, and humorous."*
>
> **Jay A., Elburn, IL**

> *"Thanks, I needed this book. Now I can sleep at night."*
>
> **Robin F., British Columbia, Canada**

Already, hundreds of thousands of satisfied readers agree. They have made *... For Dummies* books the #1 introductory level computer book series and have written asking for more. So if you're looking for the most fun and easy way to learn about computers, look to *... For Dummies* books to give you a helping hand.

**IDG BOOKS**

# FOXPRO 2.6

## FOR WINDOWS

## FOR

# DUMMIES™

# FOXPRO 2.6
## FOR WINDOWS
## FOR
# DUMMIES™

## by John Kaufeld

## IDG BOOKS

IDG Books Worldwide, Inc.
An International Data Group Company

San Mateo, California ♦ Indianapolis, Indiana ♦ Boston, Massachusetts

**FoxPro 2.6 For Windows For Dummies**

Published by
**IDG Books Worldwide, Inc.**
An International Data Group Company
155 Bovet Road, Suite 310
San Mateo, CA 94402

Text *and art* copyright ©1994 by IDG Books Worldwide. All rights reserved. No part of this book may be reproduced or transmitted in any form, by any means (electronic, photocopying, recording, or otherwise) without the prior written permission of the publisher.

Library of Congress Catalog Card No.: 94-076887

ISBN: 1-56884-187-6

Printed in the United States of America

10 9 8 7 6 5 4 3 2

1B/RQ/QU/ZU

Distributed in the United States by IDG Books Worldwide, Inc.

Distributed in Canada by Macmillan of Canada, a Division of Canada Publishing Corporation; by Computer and Technical Books in Miami, Florida, for South America and the Caribbean; by Longman Singapore in Singapore, Malaysia, Thailand, and Korea; by Toppan Co. Ltd. in Japan; by Asia Computerworld in Hong Kong; by Woodslane Pty. Ltd. in Australia and New Zealand; and by Transworld Publishers Ltd. in the U.K. and Europe.

For general information on IDG Books in the U.S., including information on discounts and premiums, contact IDG Books at 800-434-3422 or 415-312-0650.

For information on where to purchase IDG Books outside the U.S., contact Christina Turner at 415-286-2747.

For information on translations, contact Marc Jeffrey Mikulich, Foreign Rights Manager, at IDG Books Worldwide; FAX NUMBER 415-358-1260.

For sales inquiries and special prices for bulk quantities, write to the address above or call IDG Books Worldwide at 415-312-0650.

For information using IDG Books in the classroom, or ordering examination copies, contact Jim Kelly at 800-434-3422

**Limit of Liability/Disclaimer of Warranty:** The author and publisher have used their best efforts in preparing this book. IDG Books Worldwide, Inc., International Data Group, Inc., and the author make no representation or warranties with respect to the accuracy or completeness of the contents of this book and specifically disclaim any implied warranties or merchantability or fitness for any particular purpose and shall in no event be liable for any loss of profit or any other commercial damage, including but not limited to special, incidental, consequential, or other damages.

**Trademarks:** FoxPro is a registered trademark of Microsoft Corporation. All brand names and product names used in this book are trademarks, registered trademarks, or trade names of their respective holders. IDG Books Worldwide is not associated with any product or vendor mentioned in this book.

is a registered trademark of
IDG Books Worldwide, Inc.

# About the Author

John Kaufeld got hooked on computers a long time ago. Somewhere along the way, he found out that he enjoyed helping people resolve computer problems (a trait his Computer Science friends generally considered a character flaw, but that everyone else seemed to appreciate). John finally graduated with a B.S. degree in Management Information Systems from Ball State University, and he became the first PC Support Technician for what was then Westinghouse, outside Cincinnati, Ohio.

Since that time, he's logged thousands of hours working with normal people who, for one reason or another, were stuck using a "friendly" personal computer. He's also trained more than 1000 people in many different PC and Macintosh applications. The vast majority of these students survived the experience.

Today, John is the president of Access Systems, a computer consulting firm. He still does troubleshooting, conducts technical and interpersonal skills seminars for up-and-coming computer support gurus, and writes in his free moments.

He's called by a lot of different names, ranging from Hey, It's The Computer Guy to Red (although this last one is a mystery, because he was born, and remains, a blond). His favorite name of all is Daddy, except when the toddlers are particularly grimy. He lives with his wife and two children in Indianapolis, Indiana.

He loves to get e-mail, so drop him a line on CompuServe at 71303.3713. He's also on America Online as JKaufeld (oooh, how original). You Internet surfers can use JKaufeld@AOL.COM.

# ABOUT IDG BOOKS WORLDWIDE

Welcome to the world of IDG Books Worldwide.

IDG Books Worldwide, Inc., is a subsidiary of International Data Group, the world's largest publisher of business and computer-related information and the leading global provider of information services on information technology. IDG was founded more than 25 years ago and now employs more than 5,700 people worldwide. IDG publishes more than 200 computer publications in 63 countries (see listing below). Forty million people read one or more IDG publications each month.

Launched in 1990, IDG Books is today the fastest-growing publisher of computer and business books in the United States. We are proud to have received 3 awards from the Computer Press Association in recognition of editorial excellence, and our best-selling ...*For Dummies* series has more than 10 million copies in print with translations in more than 20 languages. IDG Books, through a recent joint venture with IDG's Hi-Tech Beijing, became the first U.S. publisher to publish a computer book in the People's Republic of China. In record time, IDG Books has become the first choice for millions of readers around the world who want to learn how to better manage their businesses.

Our mission is simple: Every IDG book is designed to bring extra value and skill-building instructions to the reader. Our books are written by experts who understand and care about our readers. The knowledge base of our editorial staff comes from years of experience in publishing, education, and journalism — experience which we use to produce books for the '90s. In short, we care about books, so we attract the best people. We devote special attention to details such as audience, interior design, use of icons, and illustrations. And because we use an efficient process of authoring, editing, and desktop publishing our books electronically, we can spend more time ensuring superior content and spend less time on the technicalities of making books.

You can count on our commitment to deliver high-quality books at competitive prices on topics customers want to read about. At IDG, we value quality, and we have been delivering quality for more than 25 years. You'll find no better book on a subject than an IDG book.

John Kilcullen
President and CEO
IDG Books Worldwide, Inc.

**VIII**
WINNER
Eighth Annual
Computer Press
Awards 1992

**IX**
WINNER
Ninth Annual
Computer Press
Awards 1993

IDG BOOKS

IDG Books Worldwide, Inc., is a subsidiary of International Data Group. The officers are Patrick J. McGovern, Founder and Board Chairman; Walter Boyd, President. International Data Group's publications include: **ARGENTINA'S** Computerworld Argentina, Infoworld Argentina; **AUSTRALIA'S** Computerworld Australia, Australian PC World, Australian Macworld, Network World, Mobile Business Australia, Reseller, IDG Sources; **AUSTRIA'S** Computerwelt Oesterreich, PC Test; **BRAZIL'S** Computerworld, Gamepro, Game Power, Mundo IBM, Mundo Unix, PC World, Super Game; **BELGIUM'S** Data News (CW) **BULGARIA'S** Computerworld Bulgaria, Ediworld, PC & Mac World Bulgaria, Network World Bulgaria; **CANADA'S** CIO Canada, Computerworld Canada, Graduate Computerworld, InfoCanada, Network World Canada; **CHILE'S** Computerworld Chile, Informatica; **COLOMBIA'S** Computerworld Colombia, PC World; **CZECH REPUBLIC'S** Computerworld, Elektronika, PC World; **DENMARK'S** Communications World, Computerworld Danmark, Macintosh Produktkatalog, Macworld Danmark, PC World Danmark, PC World Produktguide, Tech World, Windows World; **ECUADOR'S** PC World Ecuador; **EGYPT'S** Computerworld (CW) Middle East, PC World Middle East; **FINLAND'S** MikroPC, Tietoviikko, Tietoverkko; **FRANCE'S** Distributique, GOLDEN MAC, InfoPC, Languages & Systems, Le Guide du Monde Informatique, Le Monde Informatique, Telecoms & Reseaux; **GERMANY'S** Computerwoche, Computerwoche Focus, Computerwoche Extra, Computerwoche Karriere, Information Management, Macwelt, Netzwelt, PC Welt, PC Woche, Publish, Unit; **GREECE'S** Infoworld, PC Games; **HUNGARY'S** Computerworld SZT, PC World; **HONG KONG'S** Computerworld Hong Kong, PC World Hong Kong; **INDIA'S** Computers & Communications; **IRELAND'S** ComputerScope; **ISRAEL'S** Computerworld Israel, PC World Israel; **ITALY'S** Computerworld Italia, Lotus Magazine, Macworld Italia, Networking Italia, PC Shopping, PC World Italia; **JAPAN'S** Computerworld Today, Information Systems World, Macworld Japan, Nikkei Personal Computing, SunWorld Japan, Windows World; **KENYA'S** East African Computer News; **KOREA'S** Computerworld Korea, Macworld Korea, PC World Korea; **MEXICO'S** Compu Edicion, Compu Manufactura, Computacion/Punto de Venta, Computerworld Mexico, MacWorld, Mundo Unix, PC World, Windows; **THE NETHERLANDS'** Computer! Totaal, Computable (CW), LAN Magazine, MacWorld, Totaal "Windows"; **NEW ZEALAND'S** Computer Listings, Computerworld New Zealand, New Zealand PC World, Network World; **NIGERIA'S** PC World Africa; **NORWAY'S** Computerworld Norge, C/World, Lotusworld Norge, Macworld Norge, Networld, PC World Ekspress, PC World Norge, PC World's Produktguide, Publish& Multimedia World, Student Data, Unix World, Windowsworld; IDG Direct Response; **PAKISTAN'S** PC World Pakistan; **PANAMA'S** PC World Panama; **PERU'S** Computerworld Peru, PC World; **PEOPLE'S REPUBLIC OF CHINA'S** China Computerworld, China Infoworld, Electronics Today/Multimedia World, Electronics International, Electronic Product World, China Network World, PC and Communications Magazine, PC World China, Software World Magazine, Telecom Product World; IDG HIGH TECH BEIJING'S New Product World; IDG SHENZHEN'S Computer News Digest; **PHILIPPINES'** Computerworld Philippines, PC Digest (PCW); **POLAND'S** Computerworld Poland, PC World/Komputer; **PORTUGAL'S** Cerebro/PC World, Correio Informatico/Computerworld, Informatica & Comunicacoes Catalogo, MacIn, Nacional de Produtos; **ROMANIA'S** Computerworld, PC World; **RUSSIA'S** Computerworld-Moscow, Mir - PC, Sety; **SINGAPORE'S** Computerworld Southeast Asia, PC World Singapore; **SLOVENIA'S** Monitor Magazine; **SOUTH AFRICA'S** Computer Mail (CIO), Computing S.A., Network World S.A., Software World; **SPAIN'S** Advanced Systems, Amiga World, Computerworld Espana, Communicaciones World, Macworld Espana, NeXTWORLD, Super Juegos Magazine (GamePro), PC World Espana, Publish; **SWEDEN'S** Attack, ComputerSweden, Corporate Computing, Natverk & Kommunikation, Macworld, Mikrodatorn, PC World, Publishing & Design (CAP), Datalngenjoren, Maxi Data, Windows World; **SWITZERLAND'S** Computerworld Schweiz, Macworld Schweiz, PC Tip; **TAIWAN'S** Computerworld Taiwan, PC World Taiwan; **THAILAND'S** Thai Computerworld; **TURKEY'S** Computerworld Monitor, Macworld Turkiye, PC World Turkiye; **UKRAINE'S** Computerworld; **UNITED KINGDOM'S** Computing /Computerworld, Connexion/Network World, Lotus Magazine, Macworld, Open Computing/Sunworld; **UNITED STATES'** Advanced Systems, AmigaWorld, Cable in the Classroom, CD Review, CIO, Computerworld, Digital Video, DOS Resource Guide, Electronic Entertainment Magazine, Federal Computer Week, Federal Integrator, GamePro, IDG Books, Infoworld, Infoworld Direct, Laser Event, Macworld, Multimedia World, Network World, PC Letter, PC World, PlayRight, Power PC World, Publish, SWATPro, Video Event; **VENEZUELA'S** Computerworld Venezuela, PC World; **VIETNAM'S** PC World Vietnam

# Dedication

To Jenny, for patience, love, and constant support.

To J.B. and the Pooz for staying out of Daddy's office without really understanding why.

To my friends at IDG Books Worldwide for the opportunity of a lifetime.

Thank you, one and all.

# Acknowledgments

First, I want to thank Laurie Smith and Diane Steele, who pushed, prodded, and practically dragged me into the publishing business. Without your gentle persuasions, I'd still be where I was — *eeew!*

This book comes to you through the efforts of many people at IDG Books Worldwide, who collectively work much too hard. Among them (and possibly leading the pack) are Janna Custer and Megg Bonar in Acquisitions; Mary Bednarek, Tracy Barr, and Diane Steele in Editorial; and a mysterious person or group of people known only as *Production* (as in, "These figures have to get to *Production* right away!"). My thanks and enduring gratitude go to you all. It's time to break out the cookies!

The award for Special Patience Beyond the Call of Duty goes to my Project Editor, Greg Robertson, for dealing with me when I was a borderline basket case. My Technical Reviewer, Ray Werner, gets a more detailed trophy, reflecting the marvelous job he did making sure that all the facts in the book were *actually* facts.

Finally, sincere thanks to Patti at Microsoft FoxPro support for her last-minute help in figuring out a fascinating little *feature* in FoxApp. I'd tell you her last name, but Microsoft considers it a trade secret due to her astounding knowledge of FoxPro. If I told you, I'd have to shoot you.

(The publisher would like to give special thanks to Patrick J. McGovern, without whom this book would not have been possible.)

# Credits

**Publisher**
David Solomon

**Managing Editor**
Mary Bednarek

**Acquisitions Editor**
Janna Custer

**Production Director**
Beth Jenkins

**Senior Editors**
Tracy L. Barr
Sandra Blackthorn
Diane Graves Steele

**Associate
Production Coordinator**
Valery Bourke

**Acquisitions Assistant**
Megg Bonar

**Project Editor**
Gregory R. Robertson

**Editorial Assistant**
Laura Schaible

**Technical Reviewer**
Ray Werner

**Production Staff**
Sherry Gomoll
Angie Hunckler
Drew R. Moore
Steve Peake
Patricia R. Reynolds
Kathie Schnorr
Gina Scott
Robert Simon

**Proofreader**
Sharon Hilgenberg
Carol A. Micheli

**Indexer**
Joan Dickey

# Contents at a Glance

# Cartoons at a Glance
### By Rich Tennant

# Table of Contents

xx **FoxPro 2.6 For Windows For Dummies** _____

# Introduction

*T*here's no feeling quite like standing in the open doorway of an airplane at 7,000 feet: clear sky, crisp air, howling wind, jump instructor pushing you to what you're sure is certain death.

Yup, there's no feeling like it at all, unless you're facing FoxPro for Windows without this book.

*FoxPro 2.6 For Windows For Dummies* is your combination jumping buddy, parachute, and emergency chocolate ration. It knows that you have stuff to do, problems to solve, and no time to sit and learn another computer program. You need answers, and you'll find them here, whether it's the basics, the intermediates, or the what-the-hecks.

Better yet, it's all presented for *you,* not some nocturnal, cyborg computer jockey. That means step-by-step instructions, detailed explanations, and illustrations for the stuff that defies normal description. Icons mark text with special interest or meaning. Sidebars protect you from technical slop I had to include. Unlike normal computer books, *FoxPro 2.6 For Windows For Dummies* isn't a shrine to the glory of computerdom. It's your friendly cache of real-world answers — always there, always available, and always reminding you to get the job done but have some fun along the way.

## Who I Think You Are

Books aren't a particularly two-way format. You may be sitting at your computer, lying on the couch, or using this book to prop your eyes open as you stare blankly into your morning coffee. I'm probably out flying kites in central Indiana. Nevertheless, I've thought about you quite a bit.

You work with (and perhaps own) a computer with DOS, Windows, and FoxPro for Windows. You're a beginning or intermediate FoxPro user — perhaps new to the whole database thing. You have things to do, and someone either told you that FoxPro for Windows would help or "that's what we use here, so get to it." You're looking for help, tips, shortcuts, and an impressive-looking ax to wave menacingly at the screen when things don't go well. This book addresses the first three requirements; I tried to do it all, but the marketing department said that the ax presented some packaging issues it couldn't quite resolve.

Because one book can't (alas) cover everything, I assume that you know the basics of DOS and Microsoft Windows 3.1. For Windows, these basics include choosing menu items, using a mouse, knowing mouse terms (click, double-click, click and drag), and manipulating windows (moving, sizing, and closing). Because this book covers a Windows program, you don't have to know much DOS at all. Chapter 4 discusses DOS subdirectories, but I've included extra explanations in case the DOS directory structure isn't your strong suit. If you need additional help with either DOS or Windows, I wholeheartedly suggest *DOS For Dummies* 2nd Edition (by Dan Gookin), and *Windows For Dummies* (by Andy Rathbone), both from IDG Books Worldwide.

# Using This Book

You don't have to sit down and read this treatise from cover to sunshiny yellow cover. If you want to, I guess it's OK, but don't feel obligated. The book is really meant to smuggle you in, brief you on what's happening, and then get you back to work before it's too late for you *and* your data.

This book is organized in sections, with each section focusing on a broad facet of the program. Within sections, individual chapters approach different aspects of the topic. The chapters are littered with icons (which you hear more about later) and cluttered with technical sidebars. Read what you must, and then put the knowledge to work and the book back on the shelf.

Through all these discussions, I mention many different keyboard commands and menu shortcuts. These are the really useful ones, so I think that you'll like them. Menu shortcuts look like this:

   Alt+File⇨Exit

This line means "hold down the Alt key, press F (for File), and then release them both and press X (for Exit)." The F and X are underlined because that's how they appear on the menu.

Keyboard commands look just a little different:

   Ctrl+F4

Here, I want you to hold down the Control (Ctrl) key, press F4, and then release both keys. If you treat the Ctrl and Alt keys the same as you treat the Shift key, you will have no problems with this stuff.

Because this is a Windows program, there isn't much need to discuss DOS commands. FoxPro for Windows has its own command window, however (a throwback to ancient days when Foxes ruled in DOS), and I'm obliged to use it now and again. Things for you to type in the command window are formatted like this:

**@ 2,5 SAY "Why must you type commands in a Windows program?"**

This line means that I want you to switch to the command window, type the entire line (including the quotes and the @), and then press the Enter key.

As you've probably discovered on your own, programs often display messages to you. They complain about this or that, or they inform you that they're shutting down for the night and taking your work along for the ride. Messages such as these are formatted as follows:

```
There must be a reason.
```

These messages often appear along the bottom of the FoxPro window, although sometimes they pop up in dialog boxes to more completely annoy you.

# Looking for Mr. Goodstuff

To make reading easier, the book is broken up into parts, chapters, and smaller things. The parts are boundaries for the large topics the book covers. The chapters focus on a portion of the greater part topic. They contain the fascinating information, the worrisome details, and anything else that stood still long enough to join in the fun. Within the chapters lurk the smaller things. These are the subheadings, bulleted or numbered lists, figures, and sidebars that actually do the dirty work.

Enough explanation. Now for an idea of what awaits you in later pages.

## Part I: Stuff They Think You Already Know

In this part are the tribal secrets the gurus always think that you received at birth, so they never bother to tell you. Starting with the basics of FoxPro for Windows, you continue into problem-solving ideas, through explanations of the whole relational database thing, ending in thoughts about getting your disk organized and backup rituals to ward off the evil spirits of failure.

# Part II: If that's a Table, Where Are the Legs?

The ability to identify a data table correctly is something of a prerequisite to the act of creating one. After you're past this obstacle, you meet the data and learn the finer points of storing, organizing, fixing, and erasing the stuff. This part is the meat of the book — beyond here it's good, interesting information, but it's all about what to do with your tables *after they exist*. In Part II, you bring them to life.

# Part III: Vays to Make ze Data Talk

Genteel society may say "query," but, depending on your mood and patience level, it can turn into "interrogation" in short order. FoxPro for Windows contains a surprising variety of tools for pulling information from reluctant databases. This part helps you select the right implements and provides you with examples of successful extractions.

# Part IV: Presentation Skills for Introverted Databases

Overcoming a table's natural disdain for public speaking requires some careful effort. Again, it's FoxPro for Windows to the rescue. The report and label builders give data some much-needed confidence. Dressing up in a nice, new graph makes your data stand tall and feel proud. All three tools illuminate trends, spice up presentations, and generally prepare your tables for that romp in the public eye. The whats, whys, and how-tos are in Part 4.

# Part V: Things that Didn't Quite Fit Elsewhere

Like any population, a certain number of things, try as they might, just aren't like the others. In FoxPro for Windows, these include the screen builder, application builder, and desk accessories. Even so, they all have important things to contribute and can make a real difference when their special talents are required. Read all about it right here.

# Part VI: The Part of Tens

Finally, the part that makes a ...*For Dummies* book the special literary experience it is: the Part of Tens. Hear about problems, shortcuts, helpful commands, help instructions, and bold new frontiers in just one little part. It's compact, helpful, and fun — you just can't beat that combination.

## Part VII: Appendixes

If you're on your own with an uninstalled FoxPro for Windows glaring at you, this appendix is your salvation in black and white (with pictures). It unlocks the mysteries of installation and generally makes sure that you don't get lost or hung up in the process. FoxPro for Windows really isn't bad, as installations go, but it's easier with this appendix at your side.

Appendix B is just the thing for those of you making the sacred pilgrimage from Borland to Microsoft. It helps you adjust to the new climate and explains what's new, what's different, and where the bathrooms are. As an extra added bonus, there's also a dBASE-to-FoxPro translation chart, so you don't have to guess what FoxPro calls things. If you're switching, you can't afford to be without this appendix.

# Icons Scattered Throughout This Book

Because all words and no pictures makes books dull (heck, any six-year-old knows that), the text is spiced with cool icons. The editors think that I included them to make the book fun to read and the good stuff easier to find, but the truth is, between you and me, they're just so darn cute that I _had_ to put them in. Here's the graphical lowdown:

Points out the easy way to do something. These icons save your time, energy, and hair.

Marks useful reminders and buries them deep in your subconscious. In fact, we haven't discovered how to limit the effect, so you may find yourself dreaming about the book before you're finished.

Like the vertical hairs on a hissing cat's back, friendly warnings about pitfalls, traps, and errors in the making. Please, oh, please pay attention to these and don't do them.

Points you to another part of the book for related information. Many times, the way _this_ is set affects how _that_ works, so explore these cross-references when you can. Like super tips, they save you time, energy, and you know what.

Says "Here's something you can skip, unless you really want to read it, which is OK, but don't get the idea that you have to, because you don't." This icon flags technical information that some people, because of their learning style, like to know. It's not for everybody, so don't get guilt-ridden if you skip a few of these.

# Yelling "Geronimo!" and Jumping on in

That's enough ground school; You're ready to fly. Start with something that annoys you. Or with the table of contents. Or go straight to the important stuff and check out the Cartoons at a Glance page. Just start — somewhere — and yell "Geronimo!" frequently. It keeps people guessing.

# Part I
## Stuff They Think You Already Know

**The 5th Wave**    By Rich Tennant

"WELL, RIGHT OFF, THE RESPONSE TIME SEEMS A BIT SLOW."

# In this part...

The first time you sat down at a word processor, you probably knew how to type and already had written at least a few letters, papers, or other great works of literature in your lifetime. Nobody had to show you how to write a business letter (although you may have needed help finding it on the disk later). You were a beginner, but you knew the basics.

What a different world it would be if databases were like that. Nothing in normal experience really prepares you for a career doing the database thing. To the newly initiated, databases are often confusing, confounding, and completely arcane contraptions that should be consigned to a damp corner of some grimy dungeon (along with their creators). But why am I telling you — you're probably in the midst of just such an experience. (By the way, why *do* you have that big iron door on your basement?)

Part I gives you that all-important background to make the database experience endurable, if not (I know it's a long shot) fun. From starting the program, to making problems go away, right through protecting a southern exposure near you, this Part arms you with the Good Stuff for your journey into FoxPro.

# Chapter 1

# It Looks Pretty Harmless from Way Up Here

*T*here aren't too many cute things to say about an overview. It's a good place to start. It's boring if you already know the stuff. It's the basics wrapped up in a guide to the more advanced stuff yet to come. It's fun if you're beginning. It's scary if you're beginning. It's all that and more. But why take my word for it? Read on and find out for yourself.

# Introducing FoxPro for Windows

And now, a public service announcement explaining what you've gotten yourself into: FoxPro for Windows is a graphical, PC-based, relational database management system suitable for a wide variety of applications for either business or home use. Thank you. You may now run screaming from the room.

"Relational database management system" shortens to an acronym: RDBMS. Yeah, I was surprised, too.

Wait — don't give up already — it's not as bad as it sounds. FoxPro's just putting on airs to impress you. The same thing happens to job titles when you're writing a résumé. After a little while, you get to know the FoxPro behind the acronym, the FoxPro that's a flexible tool for organizing your stuff.

Because it's a tool, *it* adapts to you and your way of doing things, instead of the other way around. It dutifully keeps things in order, sorts on command, and can put one heck of a dog-and-pony show on any piece of paper that sits still long enough. Despite its occasionally terse and nerdy dialog boxes, it's generally friendly and usually means well.

## Database-ics: electronic déjà vu

You are an experienced database user. Surprised? It's true. Strip away the electronic hype, and databases look amazingly like common household objects: recipe boxes, phone books, checkbook registers. They're nothing but glorified *lists*, for goodness' sake. That makes FoxPro for Windows nothing but a super-charged list manager — a cross between pencil and paper, a programmable calculator, and the Terminator.

Here's another shocker: You *already* know how to build databases. Over the years, you learned and practiced classic database design. Remember that first shopping list — the one that just had names because you knew you'd remember the size and quantity you needed? When it didn't

work out as well as you hoped, you changed it. *Shopping List 2.0* captured more data (so the next cake would have flour and sugar in it). Good work, closet data analyst. You designed and then refined your own database system to meet a specific need.

It's scary when I put that way, isn't it? Swallow the computer-induced panic and remember something: *You know this stuff already.* Don't let the computer's flash-and-dazzle freak you out. FoxPro for Windows is just a fancy new way to do something you've been doing for years. The key to using FoxPro well is applying what you already know.

# Starting the Program

Assuming you just walked into the room and suddenly decided that this was the time to work with your database program, here are the steps to jump starting FoxPro for Windows:

1. **Sit down and get comfy.**

   Adjust the chair, monitor, mouse, and general workspace so that you're in ergonomic heaven (or at least not ergonomic Cleveland).

2. **Turn on your computer and monitor.**

   Optional devices you may want to turn on include the printer, modem, fax, CD player, space heater, and lava lamp. Sit patiently while your computer goes through its self-test routine at the speed of light. Breathe a sigh of relief as it passes once more.

3. **Some computers automatically come up into Windows; others don't.**

   You know you're sitting in front of a member of the latter group if you're rudely dropped off at something that looks like this:

   ```
   C:\>
   ```

   That is the *DOS prompt*, a reminder of the old days when DOS ruled the world. To make it go away, type **WIN** and press Enter. WIN is the command that runs Windows.

   If Windows isn't loaded, won't start, or is generally giving you fits, I prescribe a good reading of *Windows For Dummies* from IDG Books. That should do the trick.

4. **With any luck, you'll see Windows and the Program Manager.**

   If you see a window labeled *FoxPro for Windows* that contains a little fox face icon like Figure 1-1, continue to the next step. Otherwise, look for a program group called *FoxPro for Windows*. Double-click it. The missing window (complete with the foxy icon) should appear.

   If you haven't loaded FoxPro, consult Appendix A for a helping-hand approach to installing the software.

**Figure 1-1:**
A foxy little
icon.

**5. Double-click the fox face.**

FoxPro for Windows should blaze into glory on your screen.

If FoxPro for Windows doesn't start, note any error messages that appear, and then exit Windows (press Alt+F4 and then Enter to quit Windows). Once the C:\> prompt appears, restart your computer by pressing Ctrl+Alt+Del (the so-called Three-Finger Salute). When your computer comes back, get back into Windows and try FoxPro again. If it still doesn't work, note any error messages and consult your computer guru. Your computer may need more resources to run the program successfully.

# A Quick Look Around

At this point, your screen should look like Figure 1-2. This is FoxPro for Windows as it rolls out of bed, all sleepy-eyed and in need of a cup of digital coffee. Except for the super-cool fox graphic, there isn't much to it. Table 1-1 gives you the five-cent tour anyway.

| Table 1-1 | FoxPro for Windows Screen Items |
|---|---|
| *Screen Item* | *Description* |
| Control box | The gray box in the upper left-hand corner of the window. Click here once to pull down the window's Control menu. Double-click to close FoxPro for Windows. |
| Title bar | Appears in the dark band across the top of the window. Contains the official name of this window. Click and drag here to move the window. Double-click to maximize the window so that it fills the whole screen. Double-click again to return the window to its previous size. |
| Minimize button | Small triangle pointing down in the upper right-hand corner of the window. Click here to reduce the window to the fox face icon. |
| Maximize button | Currently a small triangle pointing up; may appear as twin triangles pointing up and down. When it's a single triangle, click here to maximize the window so that it fills the entire screen, just like double-clicking the title bar. If it's the double triangle, click it to return the screen to its previous size. |
| Menu bar | Across the top of the window in the light-colored band just below the title, like all good Windows applications. These are the program's controls. From time to time, the menu changes slightly, depending on precisely what you're doing. |

| Screen Item | Description |
|---|---|
| Status bar | The gray band across the bottom of the screen. Messages from FoxPro for Windows show up here. On the right side of the bar are three boxes that show how Insert, Num Lock, and Caps Lock are set. If the key is on, the appropriate box reads Ins, Num, or Caps. |
| Command window | Prominently displayed near the cool fox graphic. As you work with your database, lots of arcane text appears in here. These are the commands that you had to remember when using older versions of FoxPro. FoxPro for Windows provides infinitely easier menus that accomplish the same thing. For now, you may want to double-click in the Command window's Control box and watch it vanish into the ether. |

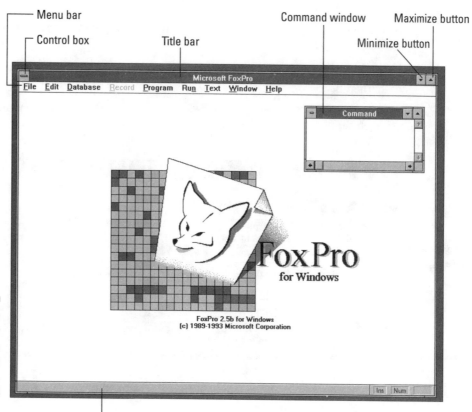

**Figure 1-2:**
FoxPro for Windows, first thing in the morning.

Like all good windows, you can resize FoxPro for Windows by clicking and dragging any corner or side of the window. If Windows tricks like this are new to you, please take a moment to buy *Windows For Dummies* from IDG Books. Doing so will make your life with FoxPro for Windows *much* easier. Really — I mean it. I'm not just pushing books.

# Opening a Table

The next question is, "What now?" — and it's perfectly valid. Word processors usually start you in a new document. Spreadsheets give you a fresh sheet to play with. FoxPro for Windows kind of unceremoniously dumps you into a blank screen. No new documents, no obvious next steps, no instructions. What now?

Because most of your time in a database program is spent fiddling around with tables, how about opening a table? Here's how:

1. **Select Database⇨Browse. If you're keyboard-centric, press Alt+D, and then B.**

   Because a table must be open before you can browse it, the Open dialog box appears, just like Figure 1-3.

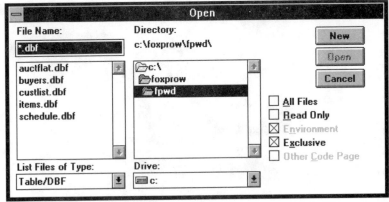

**Figure 1-3:**
The Open dialog box shows you to your tables.

2. **If the table you want to open appears in the list on the left side of the dialog box, go to Step 4.**

   Otherwise, you may have to change disk drives and/or directories to find it. My tables happen to be on my hard disk, drive C, but if yours are on some other disk drive, it's no problem. Just use the drop-down list labeled Drive to change disk drives. Click the down arrow and then select the drive you want from the list.

**3. You may also need to change directories to find your table.**

Do so with the directory box in the center of the screen — the one with all the file folders in it. Double-click a directory name to change to that directory. In Figure 1-4, FoxPro tells me I'm in C:\FOXPROW\FPWD. That's the FPWD subdirectory, inside the FOXPROW subdirectory, inside the *root*, or main, directory of drive C. To get here from the root directory, I double-clicked FOXPROW and then double-clicked FPWD again.

**4. In the file list on the left side of the box, double-click the name of the table you want to open.**

Poof! Your table appears in the middle of the screen, just as in Figure 1-4. Not a bad result for four easy steps, is it?

If you want to open a second, third, or umpteenth table, check out Chapter 7 first. There's more to it than meets the eye.

| Items | | | | | | |
|---|---|---|---|---|---|---|
| **Item_id** | **Item_name** | **Item_value** | **Item_minb** | **Item_desc** | **Ownr_last** | **Ownr_first** |
| A12256 | Racing Chariot | 3000 | 500 | Memo | Leslie | Edward |
| A12257 | Chandelier | 5000 | 1000 | Memo | Fant | Thomas |
| A12258 | Race Car - #16 | 20000 | 5000 | Memo | Candling | PJ |
| A12259 | Race Car - #24 | 21000 | 5000 | Memo | Candling | PJ |
| A12260 | Director's Chair | 100 | 10 | Memo | Kitchen | Carole |
| A12261 | Script - 29 Steps | 50 | 3 | Memo | Kitchen | Carole |
| A12262 | Prison Uniform | 250 | 100 | Memo | Sentence, Jr. | Max |
| A12263 | Walking Stick | 100 | 15 | memo | Trama | Elavial |
| A12264 | Suit, Black | 500 | 100 | memo | Rogers | Nex |
| A12265 | B&W Promotional Photos (100) | 400 | 150 | Memo | Pazzi | Mal & Mack |
| A12266 | B&W Promotional Photos (100) | 350 | 100 | Memo | Pazzi | Mal & Mack |
| A12267 | B&W Promotional Photos (100) | 300 | 100 | Memo | Pazzi | Mal & Mack |
| A12268 | One Sheets (20) | 275 | 85 | Memo | Gambol | Alex |
| A12269 | One Sheets (20) | 320 | 100 | Memo | Renet | Ellen |
| A12270 | Premiere Three Sheet | 500 | 350 | memo | Saturnae | Marvin |
| A12271 | Swiss Space Army Laser | 15000 | 5000 | Memo | Mentitalll | Andy |
| A12272 | Background Painting | 2760 | 985 | Memo | Lewison | Randi |
| A12273 | Model Ship | 850 | 300 | memo | Trieta | Sara |
| A12274 | Pants (30) | 50 | 5 | Memo | Schlegel | Edwin |
| A12275 | Shirts (50) | 60 | 5 | Memo | Schlegel | Edwin |

**Figure 1-4:** A table in Browse mode, with its records, fields, and data shamelessly on display.

# The Two Ways of Looking at Your Stuff

Your table is currently in Browse mode, as is the one in Figure 1-4. Each line contains one record, with the fields laid out side by side. By looking across the line, you can see all the information about one particular item. This mode is great when you're just cruising through your tables (browsing?), looking here and there to see what you can see.

So, is Browse mode the *only* way to see your stuff? No! The great thing about computers is their flexibility. They're like a combination burger joint and 162-flavor ice cream parlor; you can have things whatever twisted way you want them right now. *Of course,* FoxPro for Windows has two ways to look at tables. Browse is only the first; the other one is called *Change* or *Record* (like an album; not the act of saving something for posterity) mode. In the name of simplicity, I'll just call it Change mode.

To flip your table into Change mode, select Browse⇨Change. Not too tough, eh? Your table is now officially in Change mode and should look something like Figure 1-5. To go back to Browse mode, select Browse⇨Browse (Browse replaced Change as the first item on the menu).

**Figure 1-5:**
The same table in Change mode. Now you can see the whole record at once.

Use PgUp, PgDn, the right-arrow key, and the left-arrow key to frolic among your fields in whatever mode you choose.

As you've no doubt noticed, Change mode lets you see your information in complete records. Granted, this display style takes more space, so you only see one or two (maybe three) records at a time, but now you can see *all* the fields instead of just the first few. Compare Figures 1-4 and 1-5. Before looking at Figure 1-5, you didn't know the person's address was stored, did you? On the other hand, it's easier see a spectrum of records in Figure 1-4.

This is just the tip of the whole Browse and Change thing. Chapters 7 and 9 delve into the depths of these mysterious and powerful tools.

## The anatomy of a table: the electronic birdz and beez

Now that you've seen one and I'm obviously too late, it's time for that little talk about the birds, the bees, and the data. All tables are basically alike; they all have the same parts. So do humans, but that's for when you're older.

Put briefly: A *table* is a group of *records* made up of *fields* that describe *stuff*. Not just miscellaneous stuff, though — this stuff must be similar. It may be recipes, receipts, receivables, pictures, pitchers, or pinch-hitters, but it *must* have a common theme. Now for the details.

It all starts with *stuff*. Unorganized stuff. Stuff piled everywhere. Stuff tipping over onto the cat, getting the toddlers in trouble, and generally being a pain. Then the idea: Store the stuff in your computer. Now, you can just tip the computer onto the cat. What a timesaver!

Next come the *fields*. Looking at some sample stuff, you determine what you want to remember about it. Is the color important? Its size? What about the quantity you have stacked in the corner? Each individual piece of information about the stuff gets its own field. For each piece of stuff, a number of fields describe it.

All the fields describing one piece of stuff make up a *record*. One record, one — well — stuff. Looking at a whole record tells you everything interesting about one piece of stuff.

Records are grouped into *tables,* or *databases*. The terms are used interchangeably, so don't get hung up on one or the other. These days, it's fashionable to say "table," but nobody calls you a nerd if you use "database." I say it and they don't call me a nerd. At least, not often.

So what about files? In the largest sense, *files* contain *tables*. When you open a table, you're actually opening a file on a disk somewhere. When you save a table, you're creating a file. Tables, just like documents and spreadsheets, live in files.

There's much more to know about fields, records, and tables, but this gets you started. If you want more right now, see the section about fields in Chapter 6.

# Quick and Simple Searching (Not!)

Browsing through your data is nice, but when you're looking for something in particular, wouldn't it be great if the computer did the looking for you? No sooner said than done, as FoxPro for Windows proudly presents the *Find* command.

Find requires that you know only two things: what you're looking for and where you want to look. In database terminology, the "what" is the data and the "where" is the field it's in. This combination of "what" and "where" is called an *expression,* which is why you use the Expression Builder to create it.

Sometimes, it makes more sense if you write down your search goal on paper before trying to build the expression for FoxPro for Windows. For my example, the "search sentence" would be: *Show me a record in the Items database with an Item_id of A12271.* Isn't it funny how antique devices like paper and pencil help you understand the miracles of modern technology?

With that in mind, here's the how behind the Find.

The following is both graphic and shocking. Readers who flip out when faced with complex dialog boxes or five-way intersections should proceed cautiously. Get a buddy to read with you if necessary. Drink lots of fluids and spend the day in the bathroom. Eat your greens; they're good for you.

1. **With your table in either Browse or Change mode, choose Record⇨ Locate.**

   The Locate dialog box appears. It has three different options, of which you are going to ignore two.

2. **Click the For button.**

   This brings up the Expression Builder, which you see here in Figure 1-6.

**Figure 1-6:**
The
Expression
Builder,
the evil
offspring of
a dastardly
programmer.

| Expression Builder | | |
| --- | --- | --- |
| **Functions** | | OK |
| String / Logical | Math / Date | Cancel |
| Locate Record For: <expL> | | Verify |
| **Fields:** | **Variables:** | |
| item_id C | _alignment C | |
| item_name C | _box L | |
| item_value N | _indent N | |
| item_minb N | _lmargin N | |
| item_desc M | _padvance C | |
| ownr_last C | _pageno N | |
| | _pbpage N | |
| From Table: Items | _pcolno N | |

3. **After recovering from the shock, find the name of the field you want to search in the Fields area of the dialog box.**

   Ignore everything else for now. Double-click the field name. It should now appear in the cleverly titled `Locate Record For: <expl.>` box. Don't panic if it looks funny: FoxPro for Windows wrote it in the form of *tablename.fieldname* (Items.Item_id, for example).

4. **Notice the blinking vertical cursor at the end of the field name.**

   That's your signal to type. Press the "equals" key (=). An equals sign appears behind the field name. Keep going — you're nearly there.

5. **Now type what you're looking for, in quotes if it contains any letters (a part number, word, name, or something like that).**

   For my example, I typed **"A12271."** See Figure 1-7 for a look at the final expression.

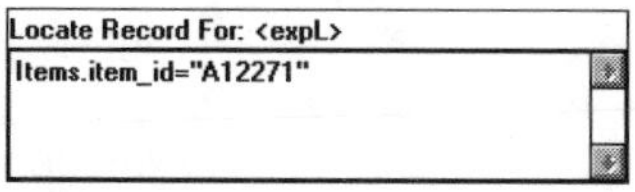

**Figure 1-7:**
The
completed
expression.

```
Locate Record For: <expL>
Items.item_id="A12271"
```

6. **Prepare to feel joy and boundless excitement as you click OK and get the heck out of the Expression Builder.**

   If you get the message Boolean expression required, make sure that you put an equals sign in your expression. If you're searching for a number, try putting the number in quotes. Some numbers, like ZIP codes, are stored as letters in the database. I know it sounds strange, but just put in the quotes and trust me for now.

7. **The Locate dialog box thankfully reappears. Note that your hard-won expression is in the dotted box next to the <u>F</u>or button. That's a good sign.**

8. **Click the Locate button.**

   Those of you who don't have a mouse must press Tab until the Locate button is highlighted; then press Enter. Sorry, but there's no keyboard shortcut for this one.

If you don't have a mouse, please go get one. Mark your place in the book, get in the car, and go buy a mouse. Don't wait — do it now.

After all that effort, FoxPro for Windows now highlights the first field of the first record it found matching your criteria. If that's not the record you were looking for, choose <u>R</u>ecord⇨<u>C</u>ontinue or press Ctrl+K to find the next match. If there are no more matches, FoxPro for Windows highlights the last record in the database.

Find is a swell command, but there are many other ways to seek out things in your tables. Start in Chapter 13, and then continue through all of Part III to discover the secrets of searching.

# Changing What's There

After the trauma of looking for something in your table, imagine your chagrin at finding an error. Changing data in a table is easy, which is good, because I could really use a break after that whole Locate/Continue thing.

First, your table can be in either Browse or Change mode — it doesn't matter which. When you find that little something that needs repair, put the I-beam cursor right on top of it and click. A box appears around the field, and the blinking vertical bar shows up right where you clicked. Use your right-arrow, left-arrow, Backspace, Del, and spacebar keys to fix whatever ails the data. When you're finished, just press the up-arrow key or down-arrow key to leave the field. Your changes are saved automatically.

Your changes are saved *when you leave the field.* Look at what you've done carefully before pressing that next key — there's no undo once you're out. Be careful!

# Creating, Saving, and Printing Quick Reports

Having data in your tables is great. Looking at it on-screen is swell, too. And — hey — that whole Locate thing is a real blast. But what about printed output? Doesn't this super-deluxe Windows package comprehend the world of a paper-more, not paper-less, office? Of course it does; and you can do it right now.

FoxPro's "Quick Report" feature builds the report automatically, while-u-wait. You choose the general layout, destination (screen, file, or printer), and give it a name. FoxPro for Windows does the rest. For overview purposes, here's the quick scoop on Quick Reports for the printed page or your screen viewing pleasure:

1. **First, make sure that you have a table open. Refer to "Opening a Table" earlier in this chapter if you need help.**

2. **Choose Database⇨Report.**

    This pops up the Report dialog box, looking for all the world like Figure 1-8.

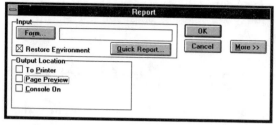

Figure 1-8:
The Report
dialog box,
ready for
some Quick
Report
action.

3. **In the Report dialog box, click the Quick Report button. This pops up, yes, another dialog box: the Quick Report dialog box, to be precise (as we computer types always are).**

4. **Quick Report has two main options — the big buttons under the title Field Layout — for your quick report.**

   The button on the left makes a report like Browse mode; the one on the right arranges things like Change mode. FoxPro automatically chooses the Browse mode arrangement. If that's what you want, don't change anything; just click OK, and you're finished. If you want your fields arranged the other way, simply click the right button (selecting the Change mode layout); then click OK. That exits the Quick Report dialog box and returns you to the Report dialog box.

5. **It's time to choose your destination.**

   The default sets the report for screen viewing. If that's your choice, click OK and continue with the next step. For printing, click the Page Preview check box off; then click the To Printer check box. Finally, click OK. The Save As dialog box appears.

   If you accidentally forget to change your destination and end up with screen view when you meant to print, you can either recreate the report or refer to Chapter 20 for information about changing what you've created.

6. **Give the report a name but *NO* extension; FoxPro for Windows provides that automatically.**

   Just type your chosen name into the Report File space and click Save. FoxPro for Windows automatically saves the report in the current directory. If you want it stored elsewhere, select the appropriate directory in the dialog box. You can refer back to "Opening a Table" earlier in this chapter for the details of operating the directory and drive controls.

7. **If you chose the print option, the Print dialog box pops up.**

   Click OK to print the report. If you left the Page Preview check box turned on, the report is displayed in a cool browsing window. When you've finished browsing your masterpiece, click OK or press Esc to close the report and return to FoxPro.

As always, there's more to come. In fact, Part IV is all about reports (graphs, too!) and the myriad funky and amazing things you can do with them.

# Closing Things When You're Finished

When your day is done and it's time to bid a fond farewell to all things FoxPro, be sure to close everything *before* turning off the computer.

To quit FoxPro for Windows, choose File⇨Exit or press Alt+F4. Likewise, close all other Windows applications (most use the same keystrokes as FoxPro). Finally, close Windows itself the same way. Pick up your stuff, turn off your office light, and go to the mall for a while. You've earned it.

Turning off the computer without closing FoxPro for Windows (or any application, for that matter) can cause file corruption, software errors, data loss, hair loss, plus some really **serious** problems. Just close all the windows (including Windows) before hitting the power switches, okay?

# Chapter 2

# Solving Problems with (or without) Your Computer

································································

## In This Chapter

▶ The joy of turning off your computer

▶ In the problem, there was a beginning

▶ Breaking the big problem into little problems

▶ Think big, solve small

▶ The second (or third) right answer

▶ Knowing where "There" is

································································

*1* want to tell you a secret: I'm a heretic. Contrary to millions of dollars in industry propaganda, I don't think every informational problem should be solved with a computer, with FoxPro, or with any particular software package. Wicked, individualistic thinking, isn't it?

Don't get me wrong — I'm not saying anything bad about FoxPro for Windows or computers or electronic encyclopedias or anything like that. Heck, I love 'em. All I'm saying is, different problems require different solutions. Ever hear the quote, "In a world of hammers, everything looks like a nail"? (No? Well, you have now.) Put succinctly, this chapter is about having a screwdriver outlook in a hammer world; about solving problems with, or without, your computer.

## The Joy of Turning Off Your Computer

The first of my Great Steps to Great Solutions is simple: Turn off your computer. Okay, you don't have to turn it completely off, but just don't pay any attention to it right now.

Setting aside the electronic ball and chain frees your imagination. It's one less constraint on your creativity. Now you can look for the *best* solution and worry later about what form it takes. If that form happens to be a FoxPro for Windows database system, that's great. If you wind up with a $5.00 editor's spike for storing your loose ideas, that's fine too. Either way, it's not something you need to worry about now. Right now, focus on the problem.

# In the Problem, There Was a Beginning

Since you have to start somewhere, start with the problem. Or, more precisely, start by determining what the problem *is*.

This is another place I've made a fine fool of myself. "Aha — a problem!" I would say. "I shall ride forth and subdue it, returning peace and productivity to the office!" Yeah, right. In reality, I wasted half the morning chasing the problem's third cousin (once removed). Yup, some knight in shining armor this digital warrior turned out to be.

So, Step #2 in the Great Solutions series is this: Know thy Problem. Understand why it's there and why it annoys you. Find out where it came from. Ask questions about it. Are you the only one who sees it, or does it bother other people too? How will solving it make things better, life smoother, or business more profitable? Is your problem someone else's old solution? Beware the advice, "It's okay — we've always done it this way."

The single most important question to ask is this: Is it a problem or a symptom? Treating a symptom doesn't change the underlying problem, except to blunt its effect for a while. Your time is limited enough; spend it squashing problems instead of nailing symptom jelly to the solution tree.

# Breaking the Big Problem into Little Problems

Remember sentence diagramming? The teacher would write long, convoluted thoughts on the chalkboard and you were supposed to waste the better part of a sheet of paper drawing a tortured etymological family tree explaining the whole thing. It didn't make much sense to me either, at least not then. But now, today, this shared experience haunts us again to form the basis for the next step toward better solutions: Break big problems into little ones, and then attack.

Big problems, you see, can lead to even bigger solutions (see the next section for more about this problem-within-a-problem). Small problems, on the other hand, are often solved small. By looking at the pieces instead of the puzzle, you learn more about your goal. Is it truly one problem, or is it several small things going collectively wrong?

Understanding size leads to the right solution. The next step is to size the solution correctly.

# Think Big, Solve Small

I've seriously fractured a famous quotation to open this section. I hope you appreciate the sacrifice. The quote: "Any sufficiently complex solution is indistinguishable from a problem."

All that fanfare for a simple truism: Keep it simple, solver. Tear the problem apart and find out what makes it tick. Stomp *that piece* and leave the rest alone. Create just enough solution to solve the problem.

Now's the time to worry about what form of solution you need. If your solution is "create a flexible phone list," you might print one with your word processor (it's easy to change), build one with the Windows Cardfile accessory (it's fast and free), or develop a phone-tracking system in FoxPro for Windows (it's anything you want it to be). How flexible and full-featured a solution do you want? Is the problem big enough to warrant a big solution? If it is, then go for it — create The Solution That Ate Manhattan. If not, don't get hung up. Just because your answer is smaller than the national debt is no reason for shame.

The best solutions are often the simplest.

# The Second (or Third) Right Answer

Brainstorms are a good thing. I've been caught in a few without an umbrella, and, let me tell you, there's nothing like it. Ideas here, ideas there, potential solutions right and left. It's like being Rodin's "Thinker" on a Mensa cruise.

But danger lurks within! With so many ideas coming so fast, the temptation is to grab the first one that looks good and focus on it. It may be a truly great idea, the precise solution you're looking for. Or it may be the *almost* right solution to a problem *kind of* like yours. Worse yet, it may be a problem in drag.

When a perfectly good answer pops into your mind from nowhere, write it down. Test it. Try it from different angles. But don't close your mind to other possibilities. Look for the second right answer. Maybe even the third. Keep turning things around in your mind until you're satisfied that *this* is the right solution. Even then, let part of your brain keep doubting.

Regardless of the deadlines, there is *always* time to do it right the first time. There is *never* time to do it again.

## Knowing Where "There" Is

Here's one final I-knew-that-already thought: Know where you're going before you leave. Years of programming, system analysis, and getting woefully lost in the car have burned that into my psyche.

Know where you're going before you leave. Applied to the whole problem-solving discussion, it becomes "know what comes out before worrying about what goes in." If you're creating a new report, determine what the report should say before building the database to support it. If your customers want a price list, ask whether they want catalog numbers, descriptions, and stock status, too. When you know what's expected, it's time to implement your answer. Doing so any earlier almost guarantees that you're busily creating another problem.

## Why experts don't always give good answers

Experts, by definition, are *experts*. They're really, really good at something. They know everything about their topic (or at least they're *supposed* to know it all). They're focused. And *that*, I submit, is their problem.

An expert looks at your problem *through his (or her) expertise* and is liable to solve it that way. Database experts see database answers; computer experts see computer answers. Unfortunately, you need *problem* answers — you know, answers that solve your problems. Experts, alas, aren't really equipped to handle things like this.

Your best defense against an expert is another expert. When you face a challenging problem, get input from several experts. The variations in their solutions often shed new light on the problem and lead to a truly cool resolution. Sometimes, you even find the rare expert who knows when the problem is *outside* her specialty and *tells you*. Keep people like this available. Take them to lunch. They are true experts.

# Chapter 3

# The Relational Thing: It Followed Me Home

*L*ike a dewy-eyed, digital puppy dog trotting adoringly at your heels (or more likely, running madly down the interstate behind your car), the relational capabilities of FoxPro for Windows followed you home from the software store. What a deal — millions of people in this world looking for a good relationship and you just nip off to the shop and bring one home in a box. Some people have all the luck.

Puppies and relational databases need lots of care and attention (and guess who has *that* job). With puppies, you have no choice: If you ignore them, they cry, chew, whine, yelp, and then claim physical and emotional hardship while suing you for every cent you own.

FoxPro for Windows would never do that, particularly because it knows that you don't *have* to build relational databases if you don't want to. It's true — the Relational Data Cops are a myth, and digital freedom is the law. Freedom brings responsibility, so the relational-or-not question now hangs precariously over your head.

This chapter is your hard hat in case the question descends on you unexpectedly. It introduces the two organizational models and explains what's at stake for you and your data, depending on the one you choose. Don't wait another minute — that thing could fall at any ti — (FOOMP —wobble, wobble, wobble-squeak).

# Deciding on Organization

There's a choice to be made. Before touching your keyboard, even before starting FoxPro for Windows, you must select an organizational model for your impending creation. Don't get all stressed out, though. The decision's not that tough, and it's no big deal if you change your mind later.

Ah, the beauty of electronic databases; almost *nothing* is ever final. Make your choice, create the table (or tables), and then try them for a while. If you don't like the way everything works, change it. A click here, some typing there, and then — poof! — it's new and improved. The best part is that your data comes along without a hitch (at least most of the time).

You have only two organizational choices: flat file and relational. These models represent quite different approaches to the whole database process. The next two sections give you a working knowledge of each one, describe some features and benefits, and point out the potholes in the electronic road.

Regardless of which model you choose now, you can usually convert to the other model later. Really. I'm not kidding.

# Anyone Can File Flat

*Flat file* is the "original" database model. When PC database programs first came out, flat file was the only choice. It's still the simplest model to understand. Think "phone book," and you have it clearly in mind.

- ✔ Everything is in a single table. It's one-stop shopping.

- ✔ Each line contains all data for the record. There's nowhere else to look — ever.

- ✔ Flat file is great for such things as phone lists (where did I get that idea?), videotape collections, and product catalogs. Any simple list is a prime candidate for flat file.

- ✔ When in doubt, start with a flat file. If you realize later that it's just not working, you can easily convert it to a relational system.

- ✔ In my experience, 60 to 70 percent of everything people like you and me do with databases works fine in flat files. Come to think of it, the number may even be higher.

- ✔ With too many fields, flat files become unwieldy and hard to work with. Limit yourself to 25 fields or fewer; 10 to 15 is great.

# Relating to Relational Databases

In real life, relationships are complicated. It's the whole "people" thing: If you could just have relationships without getting *people* involved, the process would be much smoother. It's the people that keep mucking everything up.

Relationships are easier between databases, but they never go on dates, either. *Relational databases* are groups of tables that work together. Instead of one table playing Oz, you have a committee. Depending on your needs, this concept can be a good thing or a wicked you-know-what of the west reunion. Business invoices are the classic relational example because each transaction includes customer information that is seriously duplicated every time the customer comes back to buy something else.

The relational model splits data among different tables. An auction company, for example, might keep names and addresses in the CUSTOMER file, consignment records in ITEMS, and purchases in SALES.

Keeping this whole thing together are *links,* or *keys.* These items connect the different tables and relate them to each other. When you buy something at the auction, the system stores in one record of the SALES file your customer number, the item number, the seller's number, and the price you paid. The customer numbers link SALES to CUSTOMER; the item number links SALES to ITEMS.

- ✔ Keys must be unique. Two records cannot share the same key. If they could, you might find yourself billed for the gold leaf and walnut veneer kitty litter box someone else took home. This is the reason that your life is cluttered with so many customer numbers, Social Security numbers, and account numbers: it's easier for computers to track us with nice, neat keys like these than with our woefully non-unique names.

- ✔ The terms *link* and *key* mean the same thing. Remember, this *is* software you're dealing with, so it just wouldn't acceptable to have only *one* term. Having two lends the proper air of confusion and befuddlement to the situation.

The relational model hates duplicated data. It likes for stuff to be entered once and only once. After that, *refer* to it, soldier — don't reenter it! When you buy two or three hundred more things at the auction, only your customer number is repeated for each SALES record. Your CUSTOMER record already has your name, address, credit card number, and pain tolerance (in case you go over your credit limit), so there's no need to reenter it every time you buy something.

Relational systems work best for lots and lots of data. It's an economies-of-scale thing: hundreds of customers, thousands of products, billions served (oops). If your requirement is smaller than that, reconsider using the flat-file model instead.

Multitable systems mean keeping track of several tables at a time. If you lose one, the others don't make sense. The moral of the story: If you want to be relational, you have to be organized.

# *What Flat Versus Relational Means to You*

Now, the $64,000 question: Why should you care about all this flat file and relational stuff? The straightforward answer: because your database is a tool that helps you do a job. The right tool can make or break the job, so there's something to be said for taking the time to choose wisely.

A database that's cumbersome, cranky, and frustrating costs both you and your company. Time spent fiddling around with fields, jerry-rigging tables, and generally patching things with digital chewing gum means time away from your job. Although the "break" from real work may be fun at first, depression and homicidal thinking set in shortly.

Taking the time up front to think about your requirements is vital. Go thou and think.

## The not-really-relational database

According to the purists, there is no such thing as a relational database system. None. Not even FoxPro for Windows, in all its glory, is a *truly* relational database. Note the use of the word *truly* — it's important.

To be a *truly* relational database, a program must pass a series of 12 tests called the *relational model,* much like Pinocchio's quest to become a *real* boy. This dream-world model was developed more than 20 years ago by a man who had too much time to think about such things. His rules define a system so frustratingly complex and rigid that any program that succeeds in being named a *truly* relational database would be promptly laughed off the market.

Back here in the real world, FoxPro for Windows is considered a relational database. It follows the important parts of the relational model. The parts it blows off are, frankly, not that important to those of us with work to do.

# Choosing One or the Other

BEEP BEEP BEEP BEEP — it's the Decision Alarm and it's calling your name. Time to make that first big choice of the data day, the electronic equivalent of correctly differentiating between the toothpaste and the athlete's-foot cream first thing in the morning. The wrong choice just puts a bad spin on your whole day.

You know the options, and you know your needs. If you don't, now is *not* the time to decide on your organizational model. Brush up on what you're lacking and then come back.

Don't get all hung up on the decision. It's not a right-and-wrong thing; it's more like optimal and less than optimal. If you later conclude that you blew this step, switching to the other model is no big deal. Make the best choice you can and run with it.

If your project description looks like a list, look at a flat file for the job. Possible uses include the ones in this list:

- Mailing list
- Phone list
- Seminar attendance sheet
- Customer information
- Product catalog

When the key word in your project is *more* — more fields, more records, more complexity — the relational model may be the better choice. Classic examples are contact management, accounting, inventory, and sales records.

✔ If you're undecided about which way to go, choose flat file and get started. It's the simpler of the two systems, requires less work up front, and readily converts to a relational system.

✔ Overanalyzing, overorganizing, and overstructuring is overkill. 'Tis a gift to be simple; 'tis a gift to get it done.

# Chapter 4
# The Art of Organizing Your Stuff

There's never enough room for your stuff. Your office is too small, your house is too small, and your disk is too small. Even this chapter isn't very big. Your only hope for sanity is to make the best of whatever space you have. It may be too late for your home and office, but there's still hope for your computer. FoxPro, Windows, and DOS provide all the organizational tools you need, but it's your job to use them.

## Think First

I organize the way I think. Because that's a pretty random and chaotic process, my wife handles the files. My computer, though, is a marvel of rational order, because I organize it the way I *work*.

That is the gist of my advice to you: Consider what you do with your PC and then organize appropriately. Granted, this method involves thinking about your job, but now is as good a time as any to start.

Here are some ideas for keeping your electronic life in some semblance of order:

1. **Use subdirectories that make sense to you and your work flow.**

   For instance, if your work is project oriented, give each project its own directory. If you deal with a small group of clients, every client gets a directory.

   - Create your directories with FoxPro for Windows' Filer (available under Help⇨Filer), the Windows File Manager (an icon somewhere in your Program Manager window), or DOS commands (but people might laugh and point).

   - For help with Filer, see Chapter 27. Assistance with File Manager is available in *Windows for Dummies* by Andy Rathbone (IDG Books Worldwide). If you want to use DOS commands, contact a good psychiatrist, and then pick up *DOS for Dummies,* 2nd Edition, by Dan Gookin (also from IDG Books Worldwide) after your appointment.

2. **Put related things together.**

   If you constantly switch back and forth between a few tables all day, put them in the same directory. Do the same with a multitable relational database — it makes the little monsters a little easier to handle.

3. **Make the stuff you use most often easy to find.**

   Don't bury it under seven layers of subdirectories — keep it handy. Otherwise, you spend all your time trying to type the path correctly in hopes of finding your files again.

   I have a directory called \SAFEPLAC for things that don't fit anywhere else in my structure but that need a place to live. The secretary at my first job taught me this trick. It's for those times when you think, "I need to put this stuff in a safe place." Laugh if you want, but it works.

# The Question of Where

Planning a directory system is similar to planning a house: You have to keep the building site in mind; otherwise, you might end up with a tree in your bathroom. The dog might be ecstatic, but your parents would *have* to say something. Directories live on disks, so that's a pretty good starting point.

If you need help with the concepts behind disk drives and subdirectories, see *DOS for Dummies,* 2nd Edition, by Dan Gookin (IDG Books Worldwide).

# Pick a disk — any disk

Odds are that you either have a hard disk in your computer or you're connected to a network and share a huge, communal disk drive. Your computer probably has at least one floppy drive also.

Never, never, *never* keep your original databases on a floppy disk. Floppies die if you even look at them wrong. It's OK to use them for backup copies of your stuff (the next chapter gets into that subject), but they're absolutely out of the question as a permanent home for your valuable tables.

You probably store data right there on your computer's hard disk. Most people do, myself included. It's quick and easy, and it's always at your fingertips.

If keeping things on the network is an option, take it. Most networks have lots of space, respond quickly, and are backed up every night. The most important of these advantages is the last one, because it lifts the responsibility from your shoulders. If your information is *particularly* valuable, you might want to keep an extra copy anyway.

For the true technoparanoid, a removable disk drive is an option. You pop these high-capacity disks (some are more than 150 MB in size) out of the computer and take them with you. You often see them in big corporations, defense industries, or anywhere else that people worry on a large scale. The most common systems are Bernoulli and Syquest.

# One directory isn't enough

People take two extremes with directories: they either doggedly bury themselves under hundreds of them or use just one and pack it with everything they own. Neither of these approaches is particularly helpful. Fringe behavior isn't healthy in real life; it's not any healthier with computers.

Having too many directories drives you nuts. Every task becomes a miniature "In Search Of" episode, as your data eludes you like Nessie of the Loch.

Likewise, please don't put all your files and tables in one directory. Pretty please? Such schemes quickly degrade into a swampy morass of moth-eaten stuff — some forgotten, some lost. As more files pile in, response time gets slower because of all the junk FoxPro for Windows has to sift through. Come on, live on the edge a little. Try two directories. Please?

Start with a few directories and see how it goes. You can always make changes later.

Keep a printout of your directory structure handy. Jot down on it some notes that describe which files, tables, and kinds of information live where. This documentation is invaluable for training new people or helping you through one of those brain-dead days. In DOS 6, type **TREE/A > LPT1** (substitute your printer port name if it's not LPT1). The printout's not beautiful, but it's better than nothing. If you're using something earlier than DOS 6, contact your support guru or call Microsoft for some help printing your directory structure.

# *Putting the What Where*

Now that the structure is in place, it's time to populate it with your stuff. This is a time for great care and attention, because errant actions can leave you scratching your head, wondering why you ever got into this organization thing in the first place.

When you move a table, make sure that you copy *all* the associated files to the new directory. If your table is called ALLOFIT.DB, copy every file that begins with ALLOFIT, whether you recognize the file or not. To do that, tell Filer or File Manager to copy ALLOFIT.* to the new directory. FoxPro for Windows creates these "extra" files behind the scenes and uses them for secret, nefarious purposes. Don't leave any of them behind, or else FoxPro may declare that your table is corrupted.

Leave the originals in place until you try out the newly moved copies. After you're convinced that everything is fine, go ahead and delete the ill-organized originals.

When you create something, think about where it needs to go *beforehand,* and then put it there when you're ready.

# FoxPro Filer, File Manager, or DOS?

Does it make a big difference which tool you use for all this moving, creating, copying, and such? Not really. All three accomplish the same end.

Filer is OK, but its main virtue is that it's right there under the Help menu in FoxPro for Windows. For ease of use, Filer's no beauty queen. I'm not saying that it's hard to use; it's just not particularly intuitive.

File Manager is arguably your best choice, because doing the file management kind of thing is its life. The commands are easy to find, and the display is understandable. It's even pretty good on the ease-of-use scale. Plus, you don't have to have FoxPro for Windows running to use it.

Doing directories and such at the DOS prompt is no big deal for a wacko computer hack like me, but even I, in my advancing age, am growing accustomed to graphical programs such as File Manager and Filer. The days of the DOS prompt are numbered anyway. I suggest investing the time to learn File Manager and making it your tool of choice.

The 5th Wave          By Rich Tennant

"I ALWAYS BACK UP EVERYTHING."

# Chapter 5
# Protecting Your Gluteus Datamus

- - - - - - - - - - - - - - - - - - - - - - - - - - - - - - - - - - - - - - - -

- - - - - - - - - - - - - - - - - - - - - - - - - - - - - - - - - - - - - - - -

There's nothing particularly mystical about a backup. In fact, it's pretty mundane — until the fateful day you need it, that is. Then it's Lancelot, complete with white horse, riding forth to save your fair data from the digital dragon at the door. Sometimes it's even that theatrical.

You may wonder why I stuck a whole chapter about backup smack-dab in the middle of a database book. (Goodness knows, my editor did.) It's here because bad stuff happens sometimes — even to people who use FoxPro for Windows. Databases keep the most important information you have: customer lists, home inventory, and sales transactions, to name a few. Losing your computer before you began using FoxPro for Windows would have been a bother. Losing it now could cause permanent damage to your psyche. This chapter prepares you so that when catastrophe strikes, it isn't all that catastrophic.

## Backup Defined

Backups are the straight men in a world of computer comedy. A *backup* is a copy of your files. Boring. Depending on your needs, it may be a complete copy of everything on your computer, copies of the really important stuff, or just what's new since the last time you saved everything. It's usually done on floppy disks or special tapes. Whoopee.

This list presents some techno-term drivel about different kinds of backups to impress your impressionable friends:

- *Full backup:* Just that — a complete backup of everything on your computer, programs and all. This backup is the best kind to have because it's your entire computing world wrapped up to go.

- *Partial backup:* Just the important stuff. It's usually done once or more each day to protect data that changes continually (if you have any).

- *Incremental backup:* Copies everything that either changed or was created since your last full backup. It's faster than a full backup, but obviously not as complete.

I won't get into a whole academic diatribe about backup. I'm *for* it. I do it myself, primarily because I *wasn't* doing it, knew better, and lost an entire hard drive (data files, too) because of it. If you do it, at worst, people will think that you're a nerd. If you do it and disaster strikes, you may get a promotion. Then you can invite the people who called you a nerd into your new corner office and laugh back at them.

## Computers fail whenever they can

No truer statement ever made print. For all their speed, accuracy, and swell company, computers live to fail. That's their goal in life. "One more day toward my next crash," they think proudly in the morning. Loutish little creatures.

Failure can be foreseen, though. To provide a frame of reference for your worry, I humbly submit John's Approximations of Product Life Span. Read this part carefully, because it's not in the warranty:

*Computer:* If it survives the first 30 days, it's a keeper. If it's properly protected from power problems and treated with general care, expect a long, 7-year life. After that, it will still work, but nobody will care.

*Hard drive:* This is a moving, mechanical part, so it's more prone to death than simple solid-state electronics. Start worrying at the 5-year mark — it's due to die shortly thereafter.

*Floppy drive:* Another mechanical part, like the hard drive. Because it doesn't see as much use as the hard drive, it may live longer. Then again, if it dies, it's not that big a deal. Expect three to six years, depending on use and abuse.

*Monitor:* The wild card of the equation, your monitor might last forever or die tomorrow. If you're lucky, it will outlast your PC. If you're like me, a brief prayer each morning when you turn it on certainly doesn't hurt. On the average, it will outlive your hard drive.

*Modem:* Of the hundreds I've worked with, I've seen only two modems die in the past 12 years. Because they're almost all circuitry, they last forever. Really.

# The Central Questions

Pop quiz time! This is an open-brain test, so there's no need to stop thinking. Now that you're sure that everything will die tomorrow (or perhaps today, if you're lucky), take this quiz to frame your backup needs. Answer the questions completely. Please use a number 2 pencil.

## How important is your stuff?

Does your business live and breathe through the computer? Or was it out of service for a week before anyone noticed? Score ten points if the thought of life without your data makes you pass out completely, five points if it gives you the shakes, and one point if you don't know whether you *have* any data.

## How often does it change?

Some data, like sales-history information, doesn't change. After all, it's history, and this isn't *1984*. Other things, such as stock prices, change practically before you're finished typing them. Think about what's important to you. Does it change by the month, week, day, or hour? Receive ten points for constant change, seven for daily differences, three for weekly updates, and one for owning the electronic Rock of Gibraltar.

## How much can you afford to lose?

The amount of data you can afford to lose is a different angle on the preceding question about how often your data changes. Here, consider how important those changes are. What would happen if you lost, for example, all the changes that happened last week. Hey — HELLO in there. Come on, it's OK. All I asked was — well, never mind what I asked. You get ten points for a beautifully executed full faint. Score five points for brief heart palpitations. If you're still thinking about the question, take one point and go on.

## Why should you care?

Hopefully, I've beaten this question into the ground by now. You should care. Trust me. Here's a free ten points.

You're finished! Total the points to find your official PCs Are My Life backup score. The interpretation is easy: the higher the score, the more important good backups are to your life.

# Developing the Plan

The questions in the preceding section have a purpose apart from the sheer fun of taking a pop quiz: They're the things you must consider when you're developing a backup plan for your computer. What's important, how often it changes, and how much you can lose without losing your shirt dictate how and how often you need to back up.

If you're using a computer in business or just want the best protection, a full backup is the best and simplest bet. You're covered whether one file freaks out or the entire disk drive goes bad. On the down side, full backups take the longest amount of time to perform and usually require a *tape drive*. In the past few years, though, tape drive prices have dropped incredibly. You can get a good one almost anywhere for less than $300, including software. Depending on the size of your disk drive and speed of your computer, a full backup takes anywhere from 20 minutes to an hour. The best thing is that you don't need to be there while it's running. Start it and go have lunch. When you come back, it's finished and you're protected again.

To cover just your data, a partial backup is the way to go. I use this method to make sure that my chapters are safe as I write. Depending on the amount of data you need to save, you can use floppy disks or a tape drive. You need some backup software, such as Central Point Backup, Fastback, or the Norton Backup, if you're planning to use floppies. If you have DOS 6.2, use the MSBACKUP program that comes with DOS.

If your computer and data are *very* important to your life or business, get some professional guidance. Talk to your local guru and follow her advice.

# Sticking with It

It's unfortunate, but doing backups is similar to being on a diet: It makes a difference only when you do it. Skip a day here, eat some cake there, and pretty soon you're out of shape, cake, and time. I guarantee you, that's when disaster strikes.

Make a commitment to your plan and keep it. Do it when you feel like it and when you don't; *particularly* when you don't. Write it down in your calendar; keep the appointment. This is how you pay the data insurance premiums. Don't let the policy lapse.

# Part II
## If that's a Table, Where Are the Legs?

**The 5th Wave**          **By Rich Tennant**

"MISS LAMONT, I'M FILING THE CONGREGATION UNDER 'SOULS', MY SERMONS UNDER 'GRACE' AND THE FINANCIAL CONTRIBUTIONS UNDER 'AMEN.'"

# In this part...

**D**ata tables and regular tables have little in common. For one thing, data tables don't have legs, and regular tables don't fit on your average disk drive. Real tables are great for meals and card games, but you can't even balance a bowl of soup on a data table. Some data tables fit on a single floppy disk, but some real tables won't even fit in your house.

Having clearly made that distinction, let me say that Part II is about data tables, not real tables. It covers creating, populating, sorting, indexing, and teaching your table some entertaining tricks. You won't find out how to set out a formal dinner, but you may pick up a thing or two about putting the guest list in order.

# Chapter 6
# Basic Table Carpentry

• • • • • • • • • • • • • • • • • • • • • • • • • • • • • • • • • • • • • • • • •

## In This Chapter

▶ Designing a table on paper

▶ Field types for every need

▶ Common fields and sizes

▶ Creating a table on-screen

▶ Saving your new table in the right place

▶ To enter or not to enter data

• • • • • • • • • • • • • • • • • • • • • • • • • • • • • • • • • • • • • • • • •

*B*uilding a table isn't hard. It doesn't even have to be complicated, despite FoxPro for Windows' best efforts to the contrary. With some planning and forethought, it can be — dare I say it? — easy. The first time is always nerve-wracking, but the next time isn't. The more tables you build, the easier it is to wonder why you have so many.

## Designing a Table on Paper

Do your thinking and planning on paper; leave the computer alone until it's time to create your masterpiece. This approach takes some getting used to, but your hairline will thank you in the long run. Get out a sharp pencil, a clean sheet of paper, and your brain. Although your brain is optional for some things in this book, you definitely need it right now.

These steps show you how to plan the grand plan:

1. **Write down everything you can think of.**

   Use an extra sheet of paper, if necessary.

2. **Go back and limit your list to things you want to store in the new table.**

   Five to 15 items is a good start.

   You can't run around in mixed company (meaning normal people and nerds) and say *items* — remember, they're called *fields.*

3. **Come up with a clever name for each item on your list.**

   This name is the actual field name. See the sidebar "The rules of the name" so that FoxPro for Windows doesn't yell at you about invalid entries. Write down the names on your increasingly scribbled-up piece of paper.

4. **Think of the longest possible entry for each field and write it down. (You may need a new piece of paper for this step.)**

   Count the number of characters (letters, numbers, and spaces) the Great Sample Entry contains. Write that number next to the field name from Step 3. It's no big deal to change this number after you create the table, so don't worry if something bigger comes along.

That about does it. The big precreation step left is scratching your head over the field *type,* but that subject is covered next. Is this great or what?

# *Field Types for Every Need*

FoxPro for Windows has a field type for literally every occasion. With seven different kinds available, you have more flexibility than a contortionist on muscle relaxants (and that's a *lot* of flexibility). All you have to do is figure out which one best describes the data in question. As long as you approach it from that angle, type selection is a cinch.

✔ Choosing the field *type* is more important than when you guestimated its *length.* You can change the field type, but it can be risky for your data. Swapping among some types causes data loss, which is the polite way to say that your data is trashed. Consider your options well before proceeding.

✔ Now that I've put the fear of Type into you, here's the silver lining: About 80 percent of the time, you use only the Character or Numeric field types. Most of the remaining 20 percent is split between the Date, Logical, and Memo types. Float and General types are strictly programmer toys. Freely aspire to using them, but don't expect me to help you.

# The rules of the name

It wouldn't be software if there wasn't something waiting to trip you up and then yell at you for falling. Today's tripwire is the innocent topic of naming your fields.

FoxPro for Windows has some specific rules on this subject that Must Be Obeyed. What a surprise. Put succinctly, *field names* must operate within the following constraints:

✔ Have to begin with a letter, darn it, not a number

✔ Can contain any letter, number, or clever combination of letters and numbers

✔ Cannot have spaces in them

✔ May also use the underscore (_) character

✔ Are limited to ten letters, numbers, and underscores in length

Don't even *try* capitalizing a field name. FoxPro for Windows does whatever it wants to about that, which happens to mean capitalizing the first letter of the name. No other capitalization options are permissible. So there.

Here are some examples to drive home the point:

| | |
|---|---|
| Firstname | A perfectly good name. |
| 1993_net | \<BEEP> It starts with a number. |
| NetSales1993 | \<BEEP> The number problem is fixed, but now it's too long. |
| NetSales93 | All is good with the name. FoxPro for Windows is appeased. |
| M/F | \<BEEP> Nobody said *anything* about using slashes in field names. |
| R_u_hungry | Legal, valid, and conversational. |
| R_u_single | Syntactically OK, but not quite the sensitive field name of the '90s. |
| Item Value | \<BEEP> A good idea completely ruined by a space. |

*Character fields* are the most common field type. Use them to store anything that contains letters or a mix of letters and numbers. Some examples are names, addresses, ZIP codes, Social Security numbers, and phone numbers.

*Numeric fields* are a distant second on the hit parade, but valuable nonetheless. This type works for any field that's *really* a number — something you might use in a calculation. Price, quantity, discount, and driver's license points all qualify as real numeric numbers.

✔ If you calculate with it, it's numeric. If it couldn't cipher its way out of a paper bag, it's character. If it tells bad jokes and dons lampshades at parties, it's "a character." The difference can be important.

✔ Another surefire way to tell a numeric number from a character number is to ask this question: Does the data ever *start* with a zero? If so, is the zero important to the data — would it mean something different if the zero weren't there? A "yes" means that you have a character number on your hands; a "no" is more of an abstention than a vote one way or the other. In that case, refer to the "calculation" test.

*Date fields* are a no-brainer. Use them for, uh … dates. Yeah, that's it — dates.

*Memo fields* are the epitome of free-form, go your own way flexibility. Memo fields hold anything — that's right, anything — you care to put in them. They expand to accommodate your largest dreams. Use them for notes, thoughts, haiku poetry, and anything that's bigger than the average character field. They have a significant drawback, though: You can't use a Memo field in a query. That means FoxPro can't answer any serious questions about the text in your memos. You *can* search for specific text in memo fields with the Locate command (the details are in Chapter 13), but that's the extent of your questing options.

*A logical field* stores only two possible values: T (true) or F (campaign promise). It's used for simple yes-or-no question fields, such as "prepaid," "commission," or "re_elect."

The final two field types are special-use-only power tools. Odds are that you won't ever need them, so skip them if you want. Otherwise, hold on tight and prepare for a wild, sleep-inducing ride.

*The float field* is the first cousin of the numeric field, except float has a floating decimal place. Does this mean that the numeric decimal sinks? Beats me. Allegedly, float fields exist for the realm of scientific calculation for reasons normal people can't comprehend. Leave them alone and then they won't come home dragging researchers behind them.

The preceding sentence reads better if you mentally picture the final line of "Little Bo Peep" while reading it.

*General fields* are truly amazing and powerful; they're literally a digital magic wand. A general field stores anything you can cut and paste from another Windows application, including pictures, documents, and sounds — even video clips. If you ever have a few stray hours on your hands, create a table with a general field and see what you can do with it. For now, just remember that it's out there somewhere.

# Common Fields and Sizes

In a continuing effort to save you time, energy, and money (mainly so that you can fiddle around with more programs and buy more ...*For Dummies* books), I offer you Table 6-1, the best in ready-to-use fields. They're guaranteed fresh and useful, and they come complete with name, type, and size. Most are self-explanatory, but I've included descriptions for everything, just to be on the safe side.

Use these suggestions as a springboard for your own thoughts, or just take them as they sit. They cover the gamut of common data, with some specialized ones thrown in at no extra charge. Feel free to mix and match to your heart's content.

✔ Some fields, particularly those for address and phone number, are duplicated — and with good reason. These days, one person can have four (or more) phone numbers without trying too hard: voice, fax, cellular, and home are just the beginning. Likewise, "One Worthaton Pointe Centre, P.O. Box 2800" doesn't exactly fit in a single address field. Consider the data you're storing and allow extra fields to avoid nasty surprises later.

✔ If you have the newest version of FoxPro, the Table Wizard offers lots of help and sample fields. Check out Chapter 8 to put some magic in *your* table.

| Table 6-1 | Fields for Every Occasion | | |
|---|---|---|---|
| *Name* | *Type* | *Size* | *Notes* |
| Greeting | C | 4 | Mr., Ms., Mrs., Miss |
| First_name | C | 15 | First name |
| MI | C | 4 | Middle initial; allows for two initials |
| Last_name | C | 20 | Last name |
| Job_title | C | 25 | Job title |
| Company | C | 25 | Company name |
| Address1 | C | 30 | First of two address lines; see preceding tip for details |
| Address2 | C | 30 | Second of two address lines; see preceding tip for details |
| City | C | 20 | City name |
| State | C | 4 | State or province |
| Zip_code | C | 10 | ZIP or postal code; stored as character data, not as numbers |

*(continued)*

### Table 6-1 *(continued)*

| Name | Type | Size | Notes |
|------|------|------|-------|
| Country | C | 15 | Country; necessary if you deal with other lands |
| Voice | C | 12 | Voice phone number; use size 17 to include extension |
| Fax | C | 12 | FAX phone number |
| Home | C | 12 | Home phone number |
| Cellular | C | 12 | Cellular or car phone number |
| Email | C | 30 | E-mail address; long enough for most complex addresses |
| Telex | C | 12 | TELEX number; use size 22 to include answerback |
| Assistant | C | 25 | Name of assistant or secretary |
| SSN | C | 11 | Social Security number |
| Referred | C | 25 | Who referred this person to you |
| Notes | M | 10 | Free-form notes; size entry is automatic; can be any length |
| Terms | C | 12 | Net 10, Net 30, 2/10 Net 30 |
| Check_no | N | 6 | Check number |
| Card_no | C | 18 | Standard credit card number; handles VISA and MasterCard |

# Creating a Table On-Screen

It's time to do the dirty deed and turn your paper plan into digital reality.
Good luck.

1. **Make sure that your computer is on and FoxPro for Windows is running.**

   If your apparatus is off or your software is standing still, fix the problem
   and continue.

2. **Select File⇨New, and the cool dialog box in Figure 6-1 appears.**

   The New dialog box has lots of choices, but don't get carried away. The
   one you want, Table/DBF, is already chosen. If something really odd
   happened and it isn't selected, click the circular button next to it.

3. **Click New to forge ahead.**

4. **The workhorse of database creation, the Table Structure dialog box, makes its appearance.**

   It's empty, just like Figure 6-2, but you're about to change all that.

5. **Type the first field name into the Name entry box. Press Tab when you're finished typing.**

**Figure 6-1:**
The New dialog box, with the Table/DBF option highlighted and ready.

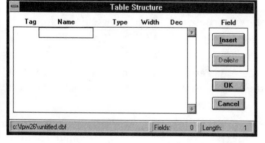

**Figure 6-2:**
The Table Structure dialog awaits your command.

Remember the naming rules discussed earlier; otherwise, FoxPro for Windows becomes annoyed and beeps loudly at you.

- When you begin typing, other controls and doohickeys pop into existence. Don't fret over all the options — take things one step at a time.

- For now, don't worry about the Tag button to the left of the field name. If you want, try clicking in it a few times. An up arrow appears, and then a down arrow, and then it's blank again. Leave it that way for now. This button sets up an index for your table, which is woefully outside the current discussion. See Chapter 11 for a complete treatise on the emotional peaks and valleys of indexing.

- No, your Shift key isn't broken. FoxPro for Windows has an authoritarian control thing about capital letters. In this dialog box, FoxPro lets you enter field names only in all lowercase. It's not that big a deal — just humor the software and get on with it.

6. **The default entry in the Type box is Character. If that's what you want, silently rejoice and press Tab to cruise on to the Width entry.**

   If you had a different type in mind, press the first letter of your choice and watch it appear before your eyes. Then act surprised when FoxPro for Windows tabs to the next section by itself. It's *helping,* you see.

   If you chose the Date, Logical, Memo, or General type for your field, the cursor automatically jumps down to the next field name. The Width entry for these types is automatic and not open for discussion. Continue with the next field in your table — this one's finished.

7. **Enter the Width of your new field (the default is 10).**

   Either manually type the new number or mouse-ually change it by clicking the cool little up and down arrows. Press Tab when you're satisfied (with the field width, that is).

8. **Numeric and float fields require one more setting: the decimal size. It works just like the Width entry — either type a number or mouse around until it's right.**

   If you specify decimal places, increase the Width entry by the number of decimals plus one for the decimal point itself. To build a field that can hold 876.92, give it Width 6 and Dec 2 — three "widths" for the 876, one for the decimal point, and two for the decimal places.

9. **Continue the process until all your fields are in or until some biological need rears its ugly head.**

   Address biological issues immediately. There's no sense in dirtying up the carpet, regardless of how much fun you're having building the table.

10. **When your table design is finished, like the one in Figure 6-3, click OK and bid a fond farewell to the Table Structure dialog box.**

    The first two fields I entered in the figure scrolled off the top of the list, but they're still there. I have faith.

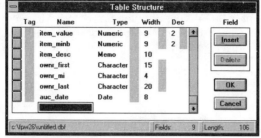

**Figure 6-3:**
The Table
Structure
dialog box
with a
complete
table
design.

# Saving Your New Table in the Right Place

Hot on the heels of creating the table structure, FoxPro for Windows demands
to know where you want to put it. Unsaved tables make the software nervous
and, goodness knows, you don't want nervous software running amok on your
computer. FoxPro asserts its informational demand in the form of the Save As
dialog box, displayed for your enjoyment in Figure 6-4. The name I entered is in
the Save Table As box; the chosen destination is highlighted under Directory.

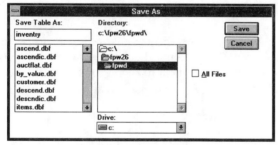

**Figure 6-4:**
With the
layout
complete,
save the
table with
the Save As
dialog box.

Here's how to get the Save As dialog box to go away and leave you alone:

1. **In the Save Table As box, type the DOS name for your table.**

    As usual, you're limited to eight characters; letters, underscores, or
    numbers only, and no spaces — period. And no periods, either.

2. **If you want to change disk drives or directories, double-click your way
    to the new destination in the Directory box.**

3. **When all is said and you're done, click Save.**

    FoxPro saves your table with its given name in the appropriate place.

If you need help working the drive and directory controls, refer to the "Opening a Table" section in Chapter 1. For more about subdirectories in general, get your hands on a copy of *DOS For Dummies,* 2nd Edition, by Dan Gookin (IDG Books Worldwide). It's written so well that your mind will absorb the information by touch alone.

# To Enter or Not to Enter Data

No sooner is that dialog box gone than another one obnoxiously takes its place: Figure 6-5, the whining child of FoxPro dialog boxes. Can't you see it there, ice cream dribbling down its chin, jumping up and down, and shouting, "Can we do the records now? Please? Can-we can-we can-we, please? Oh, puhleezze?"

**Figure 6-5:**
FoxPro can't
wait to fill
the table.

No matter what happens, remember who's in charge. Behavioral issues *can* be overcome with enough time and patience. Luckily, FoxPro for Windows is a patient disciplinarian and will do its best to keep you in line until you learn what it expects from you.

The data-entry choice is yours. If you have more tables to build, tell the dialog box No and it will go off to sulk in some dusty corner of system memory. Otherwise, grudgingly click Yes and let FoxPro for Windows gleefully lead you ahead.

Figure 6-6 shows what clicking Yes and typing for a while gets you. Your table pops into a new window, fashionably displayed in Change mode. Below it is the Item_Desc memo window, used to deal with large amounts of free-form memo text. I sized the windows so that they're most aesthetically pleasing, and then entered my first record. Here are the steps:

This is just a quick overview to get you started. For information about full-blown data adding, changing, and deleting, see Chapter 7.

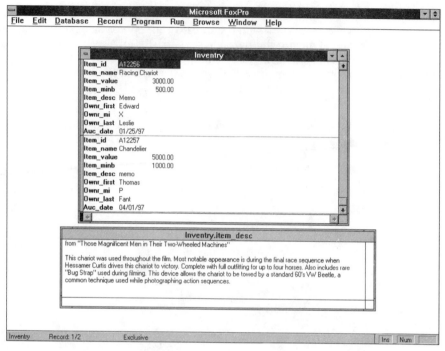

**Figure 6-6:**
With the
table
structure
ready,
FoxPro
needs data
to satisfy its
voracious
appetite.

1. **When your empty Change window pops into place, the cursor lands in the table's first field.**

   Your job: type. Yup, type to your heart's content. Complete each field (or skip some if you please); press Enter or Tab to go on to the next one.

   If FoxPro beeps at you while you're typing and moves itself to the next field, it's *not* poltergeists. That's FoxPro's special way to say that you filled up the field and that it's time to move on.

   - It's easy to go back and reenter or fix something. Pressing Shift+Tab or Shift+Enter moves you back up to the field in disrepair. After you're there, type the new entry. It automatically replaces what was there before.

   - At last, something that works more or less the way you expect it to.

2. **Putting text into memo fields is a little different. Use Ctrl+PgDn to open the memo window, type your stuff, and then press Ctrl+F4 to close the memo window and keep going.**

Since they're like little files unto themselves, FoxPro gives you a special window to work with them. With your cursor on a memo field, press the secret memo window code key: Ctrl+PgDn. A new window, with your table and field name in the title bar, pops up on-screen. Type all the text you want and then press Ctrl+F4 to close it and return to the Change window when you're finished.

3. **Keep going until you're plum tuckered out and data-dry. To finish the session and save your changes, select File⇨Close.**

Everything goes away and leaves you in peace. Ahhh.

# Chapter 7

# Adding, Deleting, and Fixing the Whoopsies

. . . . . . . . . . . . . . . . . . . . . . . . . . . . . . . . . . . .

. . . . . . . . . . . . . . . . . . . . . . . . . . . . . . . . . . . .

This is where the nose meets the grindstone, where the rubber meets the toad. Dimensionally challenged amphibians aside (yech), a lot of your time is devoted to changing this data, adding that data, or deleting the stuff over there. Editing a database is a never-ending job, but with this chapter in hand, you're up to the task.

## Open First, and Then Browse

Which came first, the chicken or the egg? My guess is quiche. Eggless quiche would inspire someone at almost any mental level to design and build a good egg, which, in turn, requires a good chicken. There are further philosophical and culinary points to this discussion, but I'm not going to get into them right now.

The FoxPro for Windows version of the question is easier, although less appetizing. Which comes first, opening the table or browsing the data? It shouldn't surprise you that opening the table is your initial job. After it's open, you can peek inside, change what you see, put more stuff in, and wonder where it all came from in the first place. But more about that later. The task at hand is prying the little bugger (or, if you're using more than one table, buggers) open.

## Viewing for Fun and Profit

In Chapter 1, you learned a shortcut to open and browse a table in one step. It's a good trick, but it *only* works for the first table you open after starting FoxPro. You're beyond that now, so stretch those mental muscles and say hello to the View dialog box, the wise sage and Senior Administrator of the FoxPro for Windows virtual office. Here's how it works:

1. **Open the dialog box by selecting Window⇨View.**

   Provided you don't have any tables open yet, your View dialog box looks just like Figure 7-1. For now, you're interested in the numbered space titled Work Areas and the buttons in the middle of the dialog box (Setup, Browse, Open, and such). These are the tools that open, close, and generally wield power over the tables of your life.

   - The Work Areas are like office cubicles for your data. When you open a table, FoxPro for Windows assigns it to one of the 255 possible work areas. The table stays there until you close it. There's nothing special about one work area or another — they're all alike. The only important rule is that each table must have its own private work area — no sharing. Sorry, but that's just how it is.

   - The Open, Browse, and Close buttons are your friends. Remember that for now and hang loose for more details shortly.

   - The Setup button is covered later in this chapter under "Restructuring Tables." The Relations and 1-To-Many buttons receive their due in Chapter 12.

   - Don't worry about the buttons on the left of the box. They're covered at length in Chapter 28, which is a good place to leave them for now.

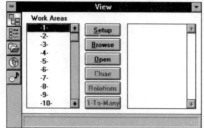

**Figure 7-1:**
The View
dialog box,
master of all
it surveys —
nothing in
this case.

2. **Highlight an empty work area by clicking the number.**

   • When you open the dialog box, work area 1 is already highlighted, so you can skip this step if that area is okay with you.

   • If a name appears instead of a number, a table is already assigned to that work area. Select another area or click Close to evict the table.

3. **Click Open, and the Open dialog box appears. Select your table, and then click OK.**

   The name of the table appears in the Work Areas box. Notice that the table itself still doesn't appear anywhere. Frustrating, isn't it?

4. **Click Browse, and the table blazes into life, much like Figure 7-2.**

   Finally, your table arrives. Feel free to express your joy with a little victory jig or a big victory polka, depending on your elation, free space, and privacy.

   • To open another table, go back through the preceding steps. Remember to click a different work area than the one you just used. If you don't, the table you worked so hard to see will go *poof!* and disappear once again.

   • If the newly opened table covers up part of the View dialog box, as it does in Figure 7-2, click on whatever small portion of the View dialog box you can still see. If the table completely covers it up, either press Window⇨View or press Ctrl+F1. Sooner or later, the View dialog box reappears.

   • If you don't know what to do next or are so taken by the sheer beauty of your data that all productivity has ceased, stay tuned for the next section's exciting episode of *Browse vs. Change: The Two Faces of Your Table.* That should snap you out of it.

| Item_id | Item_name | Item_value | Item_minb | Item_desc | Owner_last |
|---------|-----------|-----------:|----------:|-----------|-----------|
| A12256 | Racing Chariot | 3000 | 500 | Memo | Leslie |
| A12257 | Chandelier | 5000 | 1000 | Memo | Fant |
| A12258 | Race Car - #16 | 20000 | 5000 | Memo | Candling |
| A12259 | Race Car - #24 | 21000 | 5000 | Memo | Candling |
| A12260 | Director's Chair | 100 | 10 | Memo | Kitchen |
| A12261 | Script - 29 Steps | 50 | 3 | Memo | Kitchen |
| A12262 | Prison Uniform | 250 | 100 | Memo | Sentence, Jr. |
| A12263 | Walking Stick | 100 | 15 | memo | Trama |
| A12264 | Suit, Black | 500 | 100 | memo | Rogers |
| A12265 | B&W Promotional Photos (100) | 400 | 150 | Memo | Pazzi |
| A12266 | B&W Promotional Photos (100) | 350 | 100 | Memo | Pazzi |
| A12267 | B&W Promotional Photos (100) | 300 | 100 | Memo | Pazzi |
| A12268 | One Sheets (15) | 275 | 85 | Memo | Gambol |

Items      Records: 25

**Figure 7-2:**
Like
Dorothy's
house, the
Items table
lands on the
wicked View
dialog box.

# Browsing's Two Modes

FoxPro for Windows, being a computer program and thus enraptured with the concept of a million ways to do things, offers you not one, but *two* different ways to wander through your data. Actually, there are three or four ways, but the others aren't important right now, so we can ignore them. They get what's coming to them later in the book.

Back to the matter at hand. Browsing has two distinct modes: Browse and Change. Each has its own pluses, minuses, and appropriate uses, all of which are outlined in this chapter. Don't get all hung up on one or the other — it's easy to switch back and forth between them, so try both and see what works for you.

To flip between the two modes, select Browse⇨Change or Browse⇨Browse, depending on what mode you're in to begin with.

## "Browse" browsing

The first of the two modes, Browse mode, organizes your data as a table. Figure 7-2 (yes, he's referring to it *again*) displays the Items table this way. Each record is on a row; the fields are columns. This layout is good for comparing a number of records or visually scanning through your data.

Its main drawback is the width of the screen. Looking at the Items table, you don't know whether you're seeing the whole record or other things are hiding outside the window. If your records have many fields, and thus are very wide, you find yourself constantly scrolling back and forth across the table. This can be frustrating, so don't do it unless things have gone really well today and you want to address that issue.

## "Change" browsing

Change mode, put simply, is the opposite of Browse. In Figure 7-3, the Items table returns for a second big appearance, decked out in a fashionable Change mode window. This is a new look for the table, a fashion statement emphasizing completeness over sheer data volume. Note particularly the visual display of the full record — it just takes your breath away. Companion pieces and accessories to complement the look are available in fine stores everywhere.

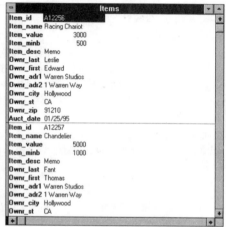

**Figure 7-3:**
The Items
table
modeling
this year's
finest
Change
mode
display: the
"full record"
look.

Of course, it's not for everyone. All fashions have their place — the same holds true for the avant-garde Change mode look. Apart from personal comfort considerations, Change mode only shows one, perhaps two, records at a time. This just won't do for getting a "big picture" look at your data. Likewise, smaller tables with few fields simply look better in the simple lines of Browse mode.

# Adding and Editing Records

Compared to many database programs in the world today, FoxPro for Windows is pretty lenient about adding new records and changing existing ones. In fact, it doesn't even matter whether you're in Browse or Change mode. The basic steps are the same; only the hard parts were changed to protect the faint of heart.

## Adding records

1. **Open the table you're intent on enlarging.**

2. **Pick your preferred mode of display: Browse or Change.**

Again, this really doesn't matter. Even though one *is* called "change" mode, there's no rule that says you have to use it when you're changing your data. Use whichever one makes you feel most comfortable, most productive, or most like you're on a sunny beach instead of holed up in front of your computer with a book as your primary companion.

3. **Press Ctrl+N to create a blank record at the end of the table.**

Visually, this can be a shock — particularly if you're in Change mode. The window suddenly goes blank and it looks like you just killed the whole table. Nothing of the sort actually occurred. You're now at the bottom of the table, looking at a blank record. That's why everything is blank. If you don't believe me, press PgUp and see for yourself. Thus comforted, press PgDn and set about to the task of entering data.

The effect in Browse mode isn't very thrilling: the cursor jumps to a blank record at the end of the table, perhaps accompanied by a brief, frenzied scrolling of your data. Yawn.

4. **Enter your data.**

   - Use the Tab key to move from field to field. To go backwards through the table, use Shift+Tab.

   - If you have a memo field in your table, tab to it and press Ctrl+PgDn or double click the word Memo. This opens a window for the memo text. When you're finished, click on the table window and continue typing. If you don't remember precisely what a memo field is, but think you found one in your mailbox this morning, refer back to "Field Types for Every Need" in Chapter 6 for a quick refresher.

   - If FoxPro for Windows beeps at you and moves the cursor to the next field without asking, it means you filled up the field you were working on. If your data is bigger than your field, see the "Restructuring Tables" section later in this chapter.

5. **Repeat the process if you have more to add.**

## Changing a record or two

1. **Open the table that's in need of change.**

2. **Set the display mode to your choice of Browse or Change.**

These steps shouldn't be news. If you're keeping score, they're the same ones you use when adding records to the table. The difference starts in the next step.

3. **Scroll through the table to the record that needs a dose of electronic castor oil.**

If your table isn't too big or you know what you're looking for, it's easiest to just scroll through the table with PgUp and PgDn until you find your target. It saves wear and tear on you, plus gives you another opportunity to avoid the Expression Builder dialog box (always an important consideration).

Refer to the "Quick and Simple Searching (Not!)" section of Chapter 1 if your table is too big to sift through manually. Also check out Chapters 12 and 13 for advanced — well, at least physically farther into the book — stuff about finding things lurking within your tables.

4. **Click the offending data and make your change.**

- The blinking vertical cursor appears wherever you click. Use your arrow, Backspace, and Del keys to fix the problem. Continue until you're satisfied with the surgery.

- If you're changing a memo field, double click the word Memo to see your text, and then make your changes. If you have more memo fields to edit, you can click the table, move to another record, and leave the window open. As you move from record to record, the Memo window always shows you the current record's text.

After you leave the field, there is no easy way to repair a change that went wrong. I repeat: After you leave the field, there *is no easy way* to repair a change that went wrong. The key phrase in the warning is *after you leave the field.* Before leaving, you can undo the change quite easily. Press Edit⇨Undo or Ctrl+Z; the old data comes back and you start breathing again. If you change your mind *after leaving the field,* I hope you remember what was there, because you have to type it back in.

With the preceding pleasant thought smoldering in your psyche, consider a brief browse through Chapter 5. Reading about backups may calm you down.

5. **If you're up to it and have more to change, repeat the process.**

# Changing Lots of Records

If you need to make the same change to a lot of records, this section is for you. No, you don't have to manually type in 478 new ZIP codes — you can make FoxPro do it for you with Record⇨Replace. There are several steps, but it's one of those "long to explain, quick to do" things. Here's the lowdown:

1. **On a piece of paper, write down the change you want to make.**

   Write a sentence (even a fragment is fine) describing your change. This helps immensely when you're explaining the change to FoxPro. Here's a sample change sentence: "change all the records with ZIP code 99778 to ZIP code 96778." Not too tough, is it?

2. **Open the table destined for massive change. Choose Browse or Change mode for comfortable data viewing.**

3. **Select Record⇨Replace. The Replace dialog box pops up.**

   This is a pretty friendly dialog box, as FoxPro for Windows dialog boxes go. Be nice to it, and it returns the sentiment.

4. **In the field list on the left side of the dialog box, click the field you want to change.**

   You may have to scroll through the list to find the field you're interested in. When you click the field name, FoxPro highlights it so you know that's what you selected. Figure 7-4 shows the Replace dialog box with the ZIP code field thus highlighted.

**Figure 7-4:**
After
scrolling
through the
list, the ZIP
code field is
at last
found.

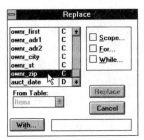

5. **Click the Scope checkbox. In the Scope dialog box, click the All radio button, and then click OK.**

   In this step, you're telling FoxPro for Windows how much of the database you want to change. Most of the time, you'll include the entire database — why correct *some* of the records but not all? Clicking the All button includes every record in your table.

   If you want to limit your changes to a smaller group of records, use one of the other Scope options: Next to change only the following so-many records, Record to change a single record number, or Rest to include all records from the current one to the end.

6. **Click the For checkbox to start the Expression Builder.**

- Don't panic yet — you're almost finished.

- Remember the "change sentence" you wrote down in step 1? Here's where it comes into play. You're telling FoxPro "change all the records that are like this."

**7. Scroll through the Fields box and double-click the field you want.**

This is your first step toward freedom from the Expression Builder dialog box. The field name appears in the intuitively named FOR Clause box. The field name may look strange at first glance, but the software knows what it's doing. FoxPro puts the table name in front of the field name, that's all.

**8. Press the "equals" key (=). An equals sign appears behind the field name.**

You can use any "logical" condition here: greater than, less than, not equal to, and all the others. If you're not sure how they work, get a guru to help. Logical operators can be tricky — you can quickly find yourself with a whole table of changes if you apply one incorrectly.

See Chapter 30 for a tour of the logical operators living in FoxPro's neighborhood.

**9. Finally, type what you're looking for. Remember to put quotes around it if it's a word (or a number masquerading as a word). Click OK to save your expression.**

Figure 7-5 shows the completed masterpiece. So much work, so little expression.

If you get the message Boolean expression required, make sure that you put an equals sign in your expression. If you're searching for a number, try putting the number in quotes. For example, even though ZIP codes are numbers, the ZIP code field stores them as letters, so FoxPro demands quotes around the sample. Chapter 6 explores the twisted world of numbers that act like words, so flip there briefly if your data is giving you fits.

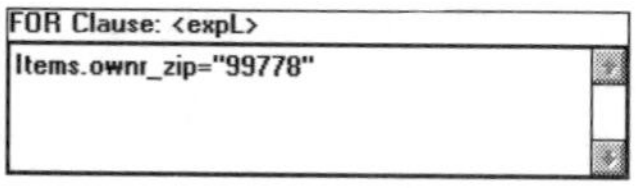

**Figure 7-5:**
The results
of the quest.

| FOR Clause: <expL> |
|---|
| Items.ownr_zip="99778" |

10. In the box next to the With button, type the replacement text.

11. Feel overwhelming joy as you double-check your dialog box and click Replace.

Finally, the end of the journey. Figure 7-6 displays the culmination of the effort: a completed Replace dialog box.

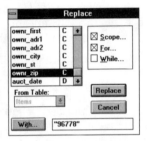

**Figure 7-6:**
The finished Replace dialog box gives you a warm, fuzzy feeling.

# Deleting, Undeleting, and Really Deleting

The FoxPro for Windows approach to deleting records is too easy. Granted, there are a few steps, but it still ought to be harder than this:

1. With the table open and in your choice of Browse or Change mode, find the record whose time is up.

2. Click the open rectangle on the left of the window, between the window border and the left side of the first field.

This is *deleting*. Luckily, it's harder to explain than do. Figure 7-7 shows the mouse pointer in position; Figure 7-8 shows the post-click results. Notice that there isn't much difference between the two figures — just the addition of a black box where a gray one used to be. Congratulations, you just marked a record for deletion. Not quite the "jungle beast stalks and kills noble prey" thing, is it?

*Undeleting* is a cinch. If you change your mind or mark the wrong record, click the same place again. The record is instantly reprieved from an uncertain future. The mark is a toggle switch, so clicking again turns it off. Breathe a sigh of relief for me, too.

3. Repeat the process for any other records you want to rub out.

4. **Once all the condemned records are marked, select Database⇨Pack and click Yes in the ensuing dialog box.**

   Now, finally, the moment of *really deleting*. This step does the dirty deed. All the records you marked are gone. Permanently. As my three-year-old son says, they went "poof-away." See the sidebar about socks and tables for a complete, although almost technical, explanation of what the heck you're doing.

   Think before you pack. This is called the *really deleting* step for a reason. I think you catch my drift.

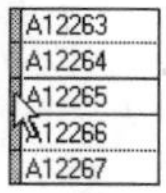

Figure 7-7:
Crouched
for the click

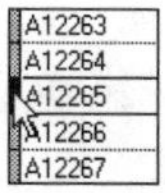

Figure 7-8:
...and its
marked
prey.

# Deleting Lots of Records

If you want to delete the records for California, every customer who lives in the 04882 ZIP code, or only people named Eddie, FoxPro for Windows can do it for you. The key thing to remember is that all the records must have something in common, some characteristic that describes the whole group.

If you can't think of anything that describes the entire group, try breaking the group into smaller pieces that *do* share something. Repeat the deletion process for each subgroup until all the records are marked. See, there's always a way.

## Packing your socks, packing your tables

There's an art to packing socks. Whether you're just putting them in the drawer or preparing for that long-awaited trip to the exhilarating southern reaches of rural Nebraska, socks are not things to deploy randomly.

Take care in their placement, lest a pair should begin quarreling and decide to part company on the next wash day. Should that unfortunate event occur, you're left with a morose foot covering languishing about in your drawer, pining away for its mate as only a forlorn textile can. This is not a pretty sight. I've seen it and can speak with some authority on the matter.

Packing a table, on the other hand, is infinitely easier, but fraught with the same kind of peril. In the beginning, all is well as you enter record after record into your new table. As time goes on, some records grow tired, argumentative, obsolete, or irrelevant. Their time is nigh; they must be deleted.

Deleting alone doesn't send them to the Great Data Table in the Sky, though. FoxPro makes you go through one more step: a good old-fashioned table packing. This physically rebuilds the table and any open indexes, removing each and every trace of the quarrelsome records. Like spring cleaning, when you bless some charitable organization with all the things that are "too nice to throw away" but too useless to keep around, packing is an electronic housecleaning, a final disposing of everything that's marked for the digital donation box. You're left with a squeaky clean table that's just like new and lots more space to fill up with stuff for future deletion.

That covers flat-file tables, but a relational system is a little different (what a surprise). Here, records work in teams: One obnoxious record in table A relates to a group of equally disagreeable records in table B. Make sure that you mark all the associated records in both tables before packing them — unrelated records really muck things up. After everything is marked, pack both, not just one, of the tables. Please take extra care and caution if you do this. Your data will thank you.

1. **Using the most low-tech tools possible (flint and wood are fine), describe the records you want to delete.**

   If this sounds like the first step of the previous "Changing Lots of Records" section, you're right — it's the same concept applied to deleting records instead of changing them. On a piece of paper, write out a sentence that identifies the records for extermination. Something like "delete all records for the state of California" is fine. Set it aside where you can find it again.

2. **With the table open and in one view or another, select Record⇨Delete. The Delete dialog box pops up.**

   This dialog box bears a striking resemblance to the Locate dialog box discussed at length in Chapter 1. When you think of it that way, it's a rather sickening resemblance.

3. **Click the Scope button to see the Scope dialog box. In there, click the All radio button, and then click OK to return to the Delete dialog box.**

   This tells FoxPro to consider all the records in the database when looking for ones to delete.

The other options limit FoxPro to only looking at some of the records. Next includes only the number of records you specify (the following 30 records, for example). Record considers a single record number. Rest comprises all records from the next one to the end of the table.

4. **Click the For button to bring forth the Expression Builder. Use it to create the official FoxPro version of your "delete sentence" from Step 1. Click OK when you're finished.**

   Doing the Expression Builder thing is covered in detail under "Changing Lots of Records," so we'll not go through it again here. The technique is the same for both changing and deleting.

5. **Click the Delete button. Look at your records, raise your hand, and wave good-bye (but do it quickly).**

   Figure 7-9 shows the finished Delete dialog box, complete with the record-killing For clause.

**Figure 7-9:**
The armed
Delete
dialog box.

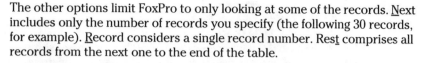

# Saving Your Changes

There's nothing to say here except that FoxPro for Windows does it for you. This is both a blessing and a curse.

✔ It's nice because you never worry whether you saved that last change just before quitting time Friday. An old spreadsheet program was notorious for letting you exit without so much as a reminder to save your work. FoxPro takes the opposite approach: It never asks whether you even *want* to save the changes; it takes the initiative and does the save.

✔ It's frustrating as heck if your fingers slip and then your cat jumps on the down arrow key. That record, the one that now says "wilfiuow" in the Name field, is part of your table. Permanently. Be careful when browsing through a database. There's no way to turn editing off, so it's up to you to not accidentally hack up the data.

# *Restructuring Tables*

Despite your best planning, yesterday's table may need some (*ahem*) adjustments to meet today's needs. Maybe a field is too small, too large, or missing entirely and you want to fix that. Luckily, FoxPro for Windows provides an easy way to redesign, or *restructure,* your table to correct its shortcomings.

Restructuring can be a completely painless experience or the computer equivalent of surfing in a lava flow. There are several pitfalls to watch for, so read this entire section *before* starting to restructure your table. It's for your own good — I promise.

1. **Decide on your changes before even *thinking* about going any further.**

   Determine what's wrong with the table now and how best to fix it. If you're adding a new field, decide on the type and size. If you're changing an existing field, finish your internal debate over the details and finalize everything in your mind. Commit your decisions to paper, if it helps.

2. **Open the View dialog box by selecting Window⇨View. The dialog box appears on-screen.**

3. **If your table isn't listed under Work Areas, click Open and assign it to one. If it's already there, go to the next step.**

4. **Click the Setup button. The Setup dialog box pops into view.**

   There are many wonderful and mysterious things you can do in here, but for now, keep your mouse focused on the task at hand.

5. **In the Structure box, click the Modify button.**

   Welcome to your destination: the Table Structure dialog box, as shown in the warm and welcoming Figure 7-10. If you have some plastic leis handy, place them around your neck to enhance your arrival experience.

If you find yourself instead in a dialog box titled Index, you took that left turn at Albuquerque. Click Cancel in the lower right-hand corner of the dialog box to get out of there, and then try for the Modify Structure button instead of the Modify Indexes button.

**Figure 7-10:**
The Table
Structure
dialog box
welcomes
you.

| Tag | Name | Type | Width | Dec | Field |
|-----|------|------|-------|-----|-------|
| | item_id | Character | 10 | | Insert |
| | item_name | Character | 30 | | |
| | item_value | Numeric | 7 | 0 | Delete |
| | item_minb | Numeric | 7 | 0 | |
| | item_desc | Memo | 10 | | OK |
| | ownr_last | Character | 20 | | |
| | ownr_first | Character | 12 | | Cancel |
| | ownr_adr1 | Character | 20 | | |

c:\foxprow\fpwd\items.dbf    Fields: 13   Length: 172

**6. Click a field name — any field name.**

This may seem vague, but when FoxPro for Windows dumps you into this dialog box, you need to click *somewhere* to get things started. I recommend just picking a field at random and clicking its name — just the name; nowhere else. From there, you can use the arrow, PgUp, PgDn, Tab, and Shift+Tab keys to move among the fields at will. But you have to start somewhere or you won't get started at all.

The change of 1,000 records begins with a single click.

**7. Carry out your changes.**

There are four things you can do to the fields in a table: add, delete, change, or move them. Each of these is covered in the following sections. Refer to the section you need, and then come back here when you're ready to finish.

If you want to modify some field names *and* make other changes, perform these as *two separate steps.* The order isn't important; just change the names and save the structure; then go back to add, delete, and move to your heart's content, and save the structure a second time. *If you don't do this, you may lose the data in the fields you renamed.* FoxPro for Windows uses either the field name or position to figure out where to move existing data after a restructuring. If the field's name *and* position are different, FoxPro gets confused and *throws away the data.* This is not a good thing, particularly if it happens to you.

**8. Click OK when you're finished. If you're sure you like the changes, click OK when FoxPro asks whether it should make the changes permanent. Finally, click OK in the Setup dialog box, and you're home free.**

This sounds a little more dramatic than it is. Even if something terrible goes wrong, the "Recovering with the Automatic Backup Files" section digs you out of it. Just sweat a little bit during the second click and FoxPro for Windows is happy. By the third click, you're a pro.

## *Adding a field*

**1. Decide where to put the new field.**

- If you want it at the end of the table, press PgDn until you get to a blank name box at the bottom of the field list.

- If you want it between two existing fields, use your arrow keys to highlight the *second* field name, and then click Insert. A field cleverly named "newfield" appears.

**2. Type the field name, type, and width.**

If you need help with these entries, refer to the "Creating a Table On-Screen" section in Chapter 6.

**3. Continue with any other changes.**

## Deleting a field

1. **Highlight the name of the field you want to delete.**

   It's easiest to use the arrow keys to move vertically through the list.

2. **Click <u>D</u>elete.**

   The highlighted field vanishes both from view and from your table structure.

   It's not completely gone yet — not until that fateful moment when you answer <u>Y</u>es to the `Make structure changes permanent?` question. If you just made a *huge* mistake and deleted the wrong field, click Cancel. Answer <u>Y</u>es when FoxPro asks `Discard structure changes?` and your field is safe again.

3. **Continue with any other changes.**

## Changing a field

1. **Highlight the field you want to change.**

   As mentioned earlier, it's easiest to use the cursor keys for this kind of detailed list wandering.

2. **Using the Tab or Shift+Tab keys, move to what you want to edit.**

   Your choices are field Name, Type, Width, and Decimal size.

   It's important to use the Tab or Shift+Tab key combination for this step. Using the cursor keys with the Type field highlighted doesn't move you elsewhere — it *changes* the field type. You can do some awful damage before you know it, so stick with Tab and Shift+Tab.

3. **If you're changing the field Type, press the first letter of the new type or use the mouse to select your choice from the drop-down list. For any other change, type the new entry or value.**

4. **Continue with any other changes.**

   If you changed a field name and plan other structure alterations as well, you could lose some of your data. *Please* read the warning text in Step 7 of "Restructuring Tables" so this won't happen to you.

## Moving a field

1. **Highlight the field you want to move.**

   Is this news or what?

2. **Move your mouse pointer over the double-headed arrow button on the left side of the window.**

   The pointer itself turns into a double-headed arrow. That lets you know you're on the right track.

3. **Hold down the mouse button and drag the field to its new position.**

   As you drag the field, a dotted gray box shows where you currently are.

4. **When you have the field right where you want it, release the mouse button.**

   The field lands unceremoniously in its new position.

   Do not change the name of a field you just moved. Doing so causes FoxPro for Windows to become quite upset and delete all the data in that field. Don't say I didn't warn you.

5. **Continue with any other changes.**

## Recovering with the Automatic Backup Files

Change can be scary, particularly really *big* change. Tweaking the genes of your favorite table falls into this category, particularly because you can't preview the manipulations; you can only measure their effect after the fact. This is fine if it all works right, but when things go wrong, we're talking about major *change stress.*

Once again, those clever people at Microsoft packed a surprise in your lunch: FoxPro for Windows *automatically* backs up your data *before* mutating the table. It stores the backups in the same directory as your new, hopefully improved table. The backup table has the same name, but ends in .BAK instead of .DBF. If the table contains a memo field, the associated memo file is backed up as well. Its backup extension is .TBK; the original memo file ends in .FPT.

The automatic backup *only* happens when you change the structure of your table — not when you're just hacking around and most likely to need it. It's like major medical insurance: It's there if something incredibly bad happens, but doesn't cover the thousands of cuts, scrapes, and other small-scale body breakages that happen all the time.

If the restructuring goes awry and your table ends up like a cross between Tron and the Swamp Thing, here's how to make things right:

1. **Make sure that the backup files exist.**

It never hurts to check. Look for one or two files with the same name as your rampaging monster table, but ending in .BAK or .TBK. Figure 7-11 shows an example of what you see by using Filer.

For reasons I don't completely understand, you can run Filer by selecting Help⇨Filer from the main menu. Why is Filer under Help and not under File, where it might logically go? Because this is *software,* darn it; since when do the engineers make software *logical?*

Filer, in its glory and power, is detailed in Chapter 27.

If you find them, life is cool. If you don't, make sure that you're in the right directory. FoxPro for Windows really *does* create them, so keep looking.

**Figure 7-11:** The FoxPro Filer, with the grace- saving backup files highlighted.

| Name | Size | Last Modified | | Attr |
|------|------|---------------|---|------|
| custlist.dbf | 966 | 19-Feb-94 | 6:53a | .... |
| custlist.fpt | 896 | 19-Feb-94 | 6:52a | .... |
| items.dbf | 4750 | 26-Feb-94 | 5:44p | .... |
| items.fpt | 4032 | 26-Feb-94 | 1:49p | .... |
| items.frt | 2296 | 26-Feb-94 | 8:23p | .... |
| items.frx | 9527 | 26-Feb-94 | 8:23p | .... |
| schedule.dbf | 161 | 11-Mar-94 | 6:32a | .a.. |
| thething.bak | 554 | 08-Mar-94 | 6:18a | .a.. |
| thething.dbf | 514 | 11-Mar-94 | 6:27a | .a.. |
| thething.fpt | 1088 | 11-Mar-94 | 6:27a | .a.. |
| thething.tbk | 1216 | 08-Mar-94 | 5:57a | .a.. |
| x.frt | 2296 | 26-Feb-94 | 10:26p | .... |
| x.frx | 9527 | 26-Feb-94 | 10:26p | .... |

Drives: c:

Directories: fpwd

Files Like: *.*

Tag All  Tag None  Invert

Find  Copy  Move  Delete  Sort

Edit  Attr  Rename  Size  Tree

**2. Delete the mutants with Filer, File Manager, or DOS.**

First, kill the .DBF file. If the table has a memo field, delete the .FPT file as well. If you're using Filer to deal with THETHING, click THETHING.DBF, and then click Delete. Optionally, do the same thing to its associated memo file, THETHING.FPT.

**3. Restore the backups to their rightful names.**

Either copy or rename the backup tables so the .BAK table is now .DBF and the .TBK table becomes .FPT. Click THETHING.BAK, click Copy or Rename, and then change the name to THETHING.DBF. Repeat the process for THETHING.TBK, changing it to THETHING.FPT.

I suggest copying instead of renaming, because that *still* leaves you with a backup in case something else goes wrong. Call me paranoid, but I'd rather be two noids than lose my stuff.

# Chapter 8

# Table Building at the Wave of a Wand

. . . . . . . . . . . . . . . . . . . . . . . . . . . . . . . . . . . . . . .

### In This Chapter

▶ Hundreds of fields for your shopping convenience

▶ Using the Table Wizard to build tables

. . . . . . . . . . . . . . . . . . . . . . . . . . . . . . . . . . . . . . .

**D**esigning a useful table isn't easy. FoxPro expects you to include a place for everything you can think of, come up with clever names for all the fields, and then remember to type in all the stuff you thought of. And all *FoxPro* does is sit there and beep if you mess up. It's hardly a fair and equitable arrangement, if you ask me (which nobody has).

As part of their ultimate goal of Better Living through Better Software, those sensitive folks at Microsoft heard the sound of ripping hair roots and muttered curses. In the latest version of FoxPro (version 2.6), they offer you the Table Wizard, an automated helper for the field-challenged. All-seeing, all-knowing, and *still* fun at parties, it may actually make table designing (dare I say it?) *easier*.

# Hundreds of Fields for Your Shopping Convenience

When you use the Table Wizard, you're not so much *creating* a table as you are *assembling* one. Instead of designing all your own fields (a sometimes harrowing task if ever there was one), you get to pick and choose from hundreds of ready-made ones. It's unique, it's novel, and it's only in FoxPro 2.6.

To those of you with the old version of FoxPro, I say a heart-felt, "I'm sorry, but you can't do this — it's not in your program."

Finding the right fields is reasonably simple. The fields are arranged in more than 40 sample tables. Each table is a ready-to-use database tailored to a specific need: contact management, customer lists, recipes, photographs, and much more. You pick the table that sounds closest to what you're building, and then choose what you need from that table's available fields. If there's a field that's *almost* what you want, you can customize it later. Table building just doesn't get better than this.

Microsoft really went overboard with the applications. Almost anything you can think of building a database for is in there. From Accounts to Authors, Events to Invoices, and Photographs to Film, you're covered. Following is a brief list of my top picks:

| | |
|---|---|
| Contacts | Good starting point for customer lists. Includes standard contact information and spaces for multiple phone numbers. Also see Mailing List. |
| Employees | All the info you need to track your workers: employee ID, name, address, hire date, and work information. |
| Events | Great for meeting or training organizers. Covers event dates, venue, space, and more. |
| Guests | An all-in-one guest register for any kind of hostelry. Even includes fields for special guest needs and after-stay follow-up. |
| Household | Very robust group of fields for a household inventory. An insurance adjuster's dream. |
| Invoices | Straightforward invoice tracking table. Pairs up with the Invoice Details application for a linked-table solution. |
| Mailing List | Excellent for a customer or phone list. Includes name, address, phone, and more. Also check out Contacts. |
| Photographs | The ultimate database for prints. Stores subject, location, and technical information. |
| Video | If your tape collection exceeds your annual salary, this application is for you. Find films by cast member, title, producer, review, or original retail price. |
| Wine List | Stuff for the wine connoisseur. Includes fields like variety, vintage, color, and origin. |

## Good Wizard or Bad Wizard? It depends

I suppose the question isn't really *good* versus *bad* — it's more like *helpful* versus *annoying*. It's that fine line that separates good waiters from the bothersome ones you want to throw your dinner at. I'm not sure that the Table Wizard quite has the concept figured out yet.

The Table Wizard works just great if you want exactly what it has to offer. It's even passable if your goal is *close* to something it has in stock —

minor modifications are no problem. Unfortunately, it comes up short if what you want isn't anything close to what it provides. Granted, there are ways to add fields manually, but that kind of defeats the purpose of the automated table-creation process.

The moral of the story: build your tables with whatever tools make the most sense. Then eat a brownie.

# *Using the Table Wizard to Build Tables*

As with the other Wizards, there's not a whole lot to making the Table Wizard do its thing. Mostly, it's a follow-your-nose process, so hook up your proboscis and prepare for towing.

1. **Decide which crisis you're addressing and write up a list of the fields you need.**

    This is the basic table design step. Even the Table Wizard hasn't changed it.

    Check out Chapter 6 for everything you need to know about designing useful tables (with or without the Table Wizard).

2. **Select Run⇨Wizard⇨Table from the main menu to invoke the Table Wizard.**

    The first Table Wizard screen appears. Unless something goes dreadfully wrong, your screen should look remarkably like Figure 8-1.

3. **Scroll through the Tables list to find a sample table that sounds like the one you're building. When you ferret it out, click it.**

    The Fields list immediately displays that table's available fields.

4. **Choose the fields for your table. Click Next when you're finished.**

    • To include a field, double-click it in the Fields list.

- If you find a field that's almost, but not *quite* what you want, double-click it anyway. Next, click the Modify Field button to bring up the Modify Field dialog box. In this box, you can change anything about the field, including its name, type, and size. To change the name or size, press Tab until that box is highlighted, and then type the new entry. To give it a different type, click the down arrow next to Data Type and pick from the drop-down list. Complete your changes by clicking OK. Figure 8-2 shows a common change in the making: I originally grabbed a Wizard-provided field called OrgName and changed its name to Company.

- If you want all the fields for this application, click the >> button. That moves all the fields in one easy step (instead of lots of slightly more difficult steps).

- Remove a field from the Selected Fields list by double-clicking it.

- Eliminate the entire Selected Fields list by clicking the << button.

- Do you ever think about why it's easier to destroy things than to build them? I just wondered.

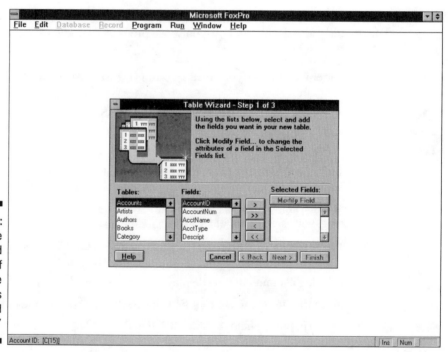

**Figure 8-1:**
The Table
Wizard
peeks out of
its castle
and wishes
you "good
day."

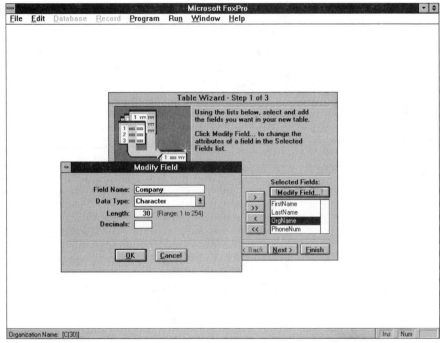

**Figure 8-2:**
I didn't like
OrgName so
I changed it
to Company.
Let's hear it
for the
Modify Field
button!

5. **To build an index for the table, double-click the appropriate field in the Available Fields list. Click <u>N</u>ext to finish the job.**

   Figure 8-3 shows this dialog box in action, creating an index on the AccountID field.

   - You likely need just one index field. Pick something that's unique — you don't get extra brownie points for a table with duplicate entries.

   - If you're unsure whether an index is a good idea (or, for that matter, why unique fields win you extra brownie points), seek guidance in Chapter 11.

6. **Your table is finished (but you already knew that from the screen, you sly thing). Pick your save option and click <u>F</u>inish to take the checkered flag.**

   There are four different options on-screen. You have three, because you shouldn't need the last one (Modify Structure of Table) until you're far too dangerous for this book. Your remaining choices are:

Save table        This saves your new table structure and lets you
                  get on with other things.

Save and browse   Often, you want to start stuffing stuff into the new
                  table right  away. (After all, the stuff's lying around
                  everywhere and you're probably tired of it clutter-
                  ing up your existence.) This option saves the table
                  and then takes you directly into the classic FoxPro
                  Browse mode, where you can perform the ritual
                  stuff stuffing until the table's stuffed to the brim.
                  Given the capacity of tables in FoxPro for Windows,
                  that may take a long time.

Save and create   Since this *is* software, they couldn't just say *run the
                  AutoScreen Screen Wizard.* Instead, they came up
                  with  this AutoScreen business. They're talking
                  about the Screen Wizard. Choose this option (just
                  like Figure 8-4), and FoxPro saves the new table and
                  fires up the other Wizard to build a pretty interface
                  for the new table. It runs the new screen automati-
                  cally, so you can add data if you want. It's a pretty
                  good deal.

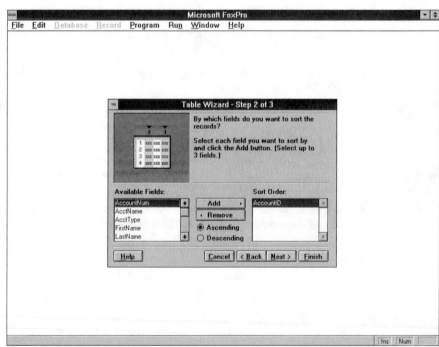

**Figure 8-3:**
That'll be
one index
on the
AccountID
field, hold
the onions.

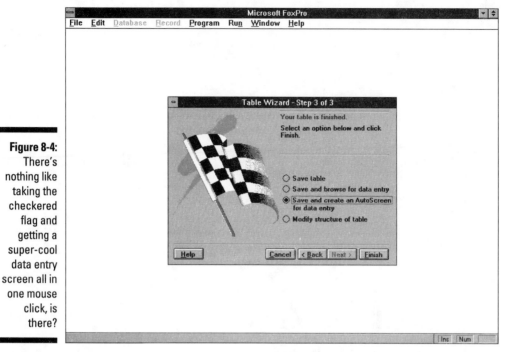

File   Edit   Database   Record   Program   Run   Window   Help

Table Wizard - Step 3 of 3

Your table is finished.

**Select an option below and click Finish.**

○ Save table
○ Save and browse for data entry
◉ Save and create an AutoScreen for data entry
○ Modify structure of table

Help          Cancel   < Back   Next >   Finish

Ins   Num

**Figure 8-4:**
There's nothing like taking the checkered flag and getting a super-cool data entry screen all in one mouse click, is there?

If you haven't met him before, see Chapter 25 for a polite introduction to the Screen Wizard.

**7. Enter a name for your creation in the Save As dialog box. Click Save to keep your work.**

Depending on what you chose in Step 6, a variety of things happen after clicking Save. They're explained in Step 6, so we'll not march through them again.

"HOW'S THAT FOR FAST SCROLLING?"

# Chapter 9
# The Ultimate Browse Experience

"*W*ouldn't it be nice if . . ." — what magical words. They carry a lilting quality, even in your mind's voice. Wouldn't it be nice if there were world peace? Wouldn't it be nice if no one was hungry? Wouldn't it be nice if FoxPro would work *with* you instead of condemning you to do things the way some demented software engineer thinks they should be done? {sigh} Truly, that would be nice — something to wish for.

Hey — your wish is my command.

## Changing the Order of Fields

Wouldn't it be nice if . . . you could change the order in which fields are displayed in the Browse window without mucking around with the table structure? (Poof!)

1. **Open your table. View it in either Browse or Change mode — it doesn't matter which.**

2. **Put your mouse pointer on a field name. Press and hold down the mouse button.**

    The field name changes color, just like the Last_Name field in Figure 9-1. It means the field is ready to move.

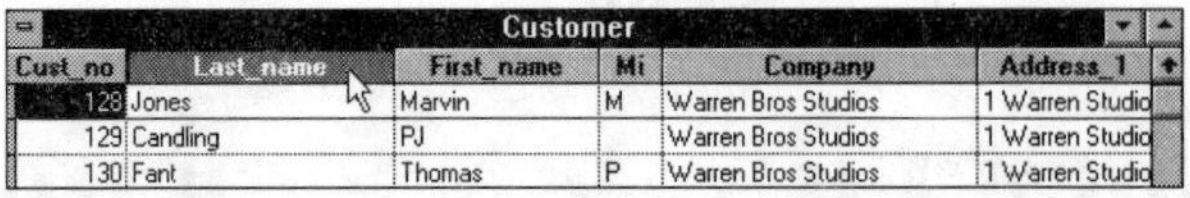

**Figure 9-1:**
Preparing to
drag away
the Last
Name field.

| Cust_no | Last_name | First_name | Mi | Company | Address_1 |
|---|---|---|---|---|---|
| 128 | Jones | Marvin | M | Warren Bros Studios | 1 Warren Studio |
| 129 | Candling | PJ | | Warren Bros Studios | 1 Warren Studio |
| 130 | Fant | Thomas | P | Warren Bros Studios | 1 Warren Studio |

Customer

### 3. Slide the field across the window until it's where you want it.

Figure 9-2 shows the field in motion across the table. Yikes! Why is the data all gray?

Don't worry that the data turns light gray after you start moving the field. That's perfectly normal. It changes back when you drop the field into its new location. Really — it does.

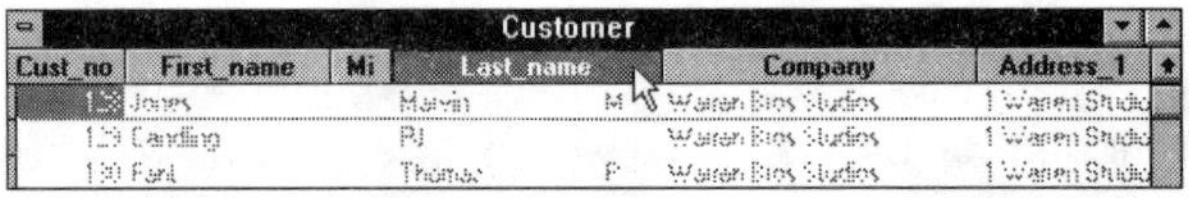

**Figure 9-2:**
The data is
grayed out
during
dragging.

Customer

| Cust_no | First_name | Mi | Last_name | Company | Address_1 |
|---|---|---|---|---|---|
| 128 | Jones | | Marvin | M Warren Bros Studios | 1 Warren Studio |
| 129 | Candling | | PJ | Warren Bros Studios | 1 Warren Studio |
| 130 | Fant | | Thomas | P Warren Bros Studios | 1 Warren Studio |

### 4. When it is where you want it, release the mouse button.

There it is — your field has landed and all the data is back to normal.

You changed the field order in the Browse window *only*. You haven't changed the table's structure at all.

### 5. Move some more fields, if you want.

Reorganize the whole window if you want. Heck, have a good time. Call me when you're finished.

If you don't have a mouse, Tab to the field you want to move, and then select Browse⇨Move Field. Use the arrow keys to reposition the field. Press Enter when it's in place.

# Changing Field Width, Sort of

Wouldn't it be nice if . . . you could tweak the field widths to get more fields on-screen in Browse mode? (Poof!)

1. **Open your table and view it in Browse mode.**

   This is a Browse mode-only trick. Don't try it in Change mode, or weird stuff happens.

2. **Put the mouse pointer on the bar at the right side of the field name. Press and hold down the left mouse button.**

   Your mouse pointer changes to a two-headed arrow, just like the one in Figure 9-3. The black line coming down from the arrow appears when you begin the next step.

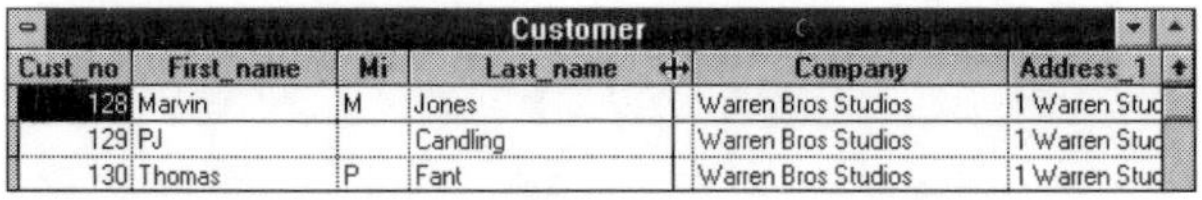

**Figure 9-3:**
The pointer as a two-headed arrow.

| Customer | | | | | | |
|---|---|---|---|---|---|---|
| Cust_no | First_name | Mi | Last_name | Company | Address_1 | |
| 128 | Marvin | M | Jones | Warren Bros Studios | 1 Warren Stud |
| 129 | PJ | | Candling | Warren Bros Studios | 1 Warren Stud |
| 130 | Thomas | P | Fant | Warren Bros Studios | 1 Warren Stud |

3. **Move the mouse from side to side to change the field width. When it's just right, release the button.**

   The aforementioned black line tells you how wide you're setting the field. When you release the mouse button, the field resizes itself to the line. Figure 9-4 shows the super-cool results. Is this a great country or what?

   You didn't change the amount of data the field can hold; you changed the amount of space the field uses to display its contents.

4. **Change any other fields you want.**

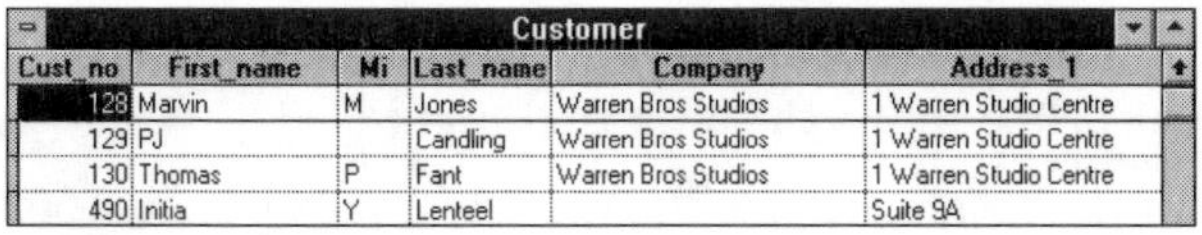

**Figure 9-4:**
The Last_Name field's new size.

| Customer | | | | | | |
|---|---|---|---|---|---|---|
| Cust_no | First_name | Mi | Last_name | Company | Address_1 | |
| 128 | Marvin | M | Jones | Warren Bros Studios | 1 Warren Studio Centre |
| 129 | PJ | | Candling | Warren Bros Studios | 1 Warren Studio Centre |
| 130 | Thomas | P | Fant | Warren Bros Studios | 1 Warren Studio Centre |
| 490 | Initia | Y | Lenteel | | Suite 9A |

If you're doing this without a mouse, I feel sorry for you. My empathy aside, tab to the field you want to resize. After you're there, select Browse⇨Size Field. Use your right- and left-arrow keys to adjust the field width. When it's perfect, press Enter.

# Making the Grid Go Away

Wouldn't it be nice if . . . the Browse mode grid would go away once in a while? (Poof!)

1. **Open a table and set it for Browse mode viewing.**

   This is a Browse mode trick, so make sure that you're in Browse mode before trying it. Okay?

2. **Select Browse⇨Grid.**

   Grid is a toggle: it's *on* if there's a check mark next to it in the menu, *off* if there isn't.

# Splitting the Browse Window — The Best of Both Worlds

Wouldn't it be nice if . . . you could see your data in Browse and Change mode at the same time? (Poof!)

1. **Open the table and set it for either Browse or Change mode.**

2. **Place your mouse pointer in the lower left corner of the table window, over the solid black rectangle at the end of the scroll bar. Press and hold down the mouse button.**

   When properly positioned, the simple arrow pointer turns into a wild looking two-headed arrow and parallel line affair. Pretty neat stuff.

3. **Move the mouse toward the middle of the window.**

   Figure 9-5 shows the mouse in motion, busily splitting the window. The double vertical line shows the proposed split.

   It usually works best if you split the window 30/70 instead of 50/50, since Change mode doesn't need as much horizontal space as Browse mode does.

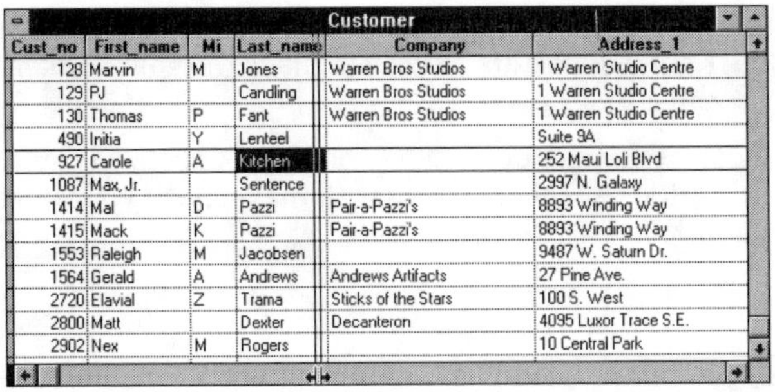

**Figure 9-5:**
The mouse
pointer,
caught in
the act of
splitting the
Browse
window.

| Cust_no | First_name | Mi | Last_name | Company | Address_1 |
|---|---|---|---|---|---|
| 128 | Marvin | M | Jones | Warren Bros Studios | 1 Warren Studio Centre |
| 129 | PJ | | Candling | Warren Bros Studios | 1 Warren Studio Centre |
| 130 | Thomas | P | Fant | Warren Bros Studios | 1 Warren Studio Centre |
| 490 | Initia | Y | Lenteel | | Suite 9A |
| 927 | Carole | A | Kitchen | | 252 Maui Loli Blvd |
| 1087 | Max, Jr. | | Sentence | | 2997 N. Galaxy |
| 1414 | Mal | D | Pazzi | Pair-a-Pazzi's | 8893 Winding Way |
| 1415 | Mack | K | Pazzi | Pair-a-Pazzi's | 8893 Winding Way |
| 1553 | Raleigh | M | Jacobsen | | 9487 W. Saturn Dr. |
| 1564 | Gerald | A | Andrews | Andrews Artifacts | 27 Pine Ave. |
| 2720 | Elavial | Z | Trama | Sticks of the Stars | 100 S. West |
| 2800 | Matt | | Dexter | Decanteron | 4095 Luxor Trace S.E. |
| 2902 | Nex | M | Rogers | | 10 Central Park |

**4. When the split is where you want it, release the mouse button.**

A new scroll bar appears at the cursor, and the window splits into two views. Figure 9-6 displays the totally useful outcome.

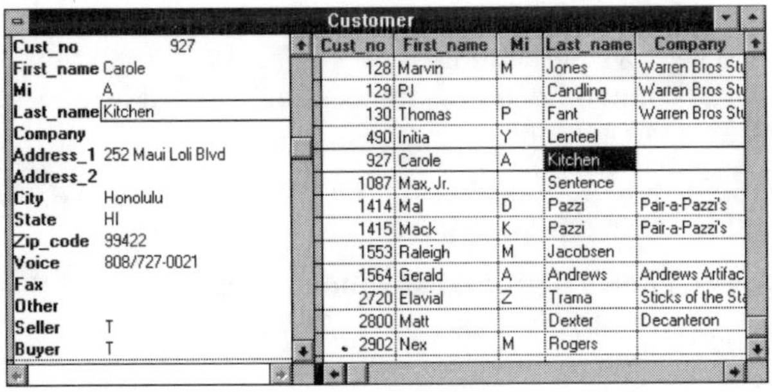

**Figure 9-6:**
The new,
improved
window,
featuring
not one but
two modes
of view.

| Customer | | | | | | | | |
|---|---|---|---|---|---|---|---|---|
| Cust_no | 927 | | | Cust_no | First_name | Mi | Last_name | Company |
| First_name | Carole | | | 128 | Marvin | M | Jones | Warren Bros St |
| Mi | A | | | 129 | PJ | | Candling | Warren Bros St |
| Last_name | Kitchen | | | 130 | Thomas | P | Fant | Warren Bros St |
| Company | | | | 490 | Initia | Y | Lenteel | |
| Address_1 | 252 Maui Loli Blvd | | | 927 | Carole | A | Kitchen | |
| Address_2 | | | | 1087 | Max, Jr. | | Sentence | |
| City | Honolulu | | | 1414 | Mal | D | Pazzi | Pair-a-Pazzi's |
| State | HI | | | 1415 | Mack | K | Pazzi | Pair-a-Pazzi's |
| Zip_code | 99422 | | | 1553 | Raleigh | M | Jacobsen | |
| Voice | 808/727-0021 | | | 1564 | Gerald | A | Andrews | Andrews Artifac |
| Fax | | | | 2720 | Elavial | Z | Trama | Sticks of the St |
| Other | | | | 2800 | Matt | | Dexter | Decanteron |
| Seller | T | | | 2902 | Nex | M | Rogers | |
| Buyer | T | | | | | | | |

**5. To switch back and forth between the views, click the side you want or press Ctrl+H.**

**6. To look at a different view of the table in each part of the window, select Browse⇨Link Partitions.**

By default, the two sides of the window are linked together. When you move the cursor in the Change mode side, the Browse mode window plays Monkey See, Monkey Do and gamely follows along.

The Link Partitions setting controls this behavior. If there's a check mark by it, it's on; otherwise, it's out taking a break. Turning it off frees the two windows to explore completely different parts of the table at the same time. This can be fun or annoying, depending on your outlook. Play with it and see what works for you.

- For the rodent-phobics out there, select Browse⇨Resize Partition. Use the right- and left-arrow keys to move the split marker, and press Enter when it looks good.

- If you can't see quite everything you want, double-click the table window's title bar (emblazoned with the name of your table). That should take care of the problem.

# A New Font for a New Look

Wouldn't it be nice if ... you could pick the font FoxPro for Windows uses to display your table? (Poof!)

1. **Open the table you want to customize and pick either Browse or Change mode to view it in.**

This change transcends the arbitrary, temporal constraints imposed by language and sensory perception as they affect the interaction of human and automated communication systems at the current level of psychic and technological development.

Translation: The font setting affects both Browse and Change mode, so it doesn't matter which one you choose.

2. **Select Browse⇨Font. The Font dialog box appears.**

Figure 9-7 shows what you've gotten yourself into.

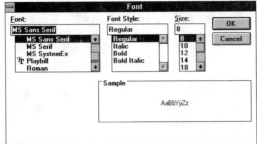

**Figure 9-7:**
The Font
dialog box.
Promise to
not choose
Wingdings,
okay?

**3. Choose the appropriate <u>F</u>ont, Font St<u>y</u>le, and <u>S</u>ize. Click OK when you're finished.**

The Sample box gives you a sneak peek at the outcome of your settings. Scroll through the options in each section and click your choice to highlight it. The OK button saves your settings when you're ready.

If you don't have a mouse, Tab between the areas and use the up- and down-arrow keys to make your selection.

✔ Don't get too wild with your selection. The goal is usually to make the table easy to read, so don't pick something so fancy that the table becomes artwork instead of real work.

✔ Entries with the cool TT logo next to them are TrueType fonts. These are *scalable*, which means Windows can display them in any size. They also print just like they look on-screen, which is a big plus if you're doing some serious table publishing.

✔ If other people use your table on their computers (via a network or some other way), stick with common fonts like MS Sans Serif, MS Serif, Arial, Times New Roman, or Courier New. Your table may not look quite the way you intended if the other people don't have the font you specified. Since almost every Windows system has these fonts, they're pretty safe choices.

✔ Use MS Sans Serif or MS Serif with text between size 8 and 10. These are *bitmapped* fonts, specially designed to look right on-screen in very small sizes. TrueType fonts look great when they're big, but sometimes don't work well small.

✔ When things go wrong and you want to forget that you tried the font thing in the first place, click Cancel. FoxPro for Windows obligingly ignores your dialog box ramblings and pretends it never happened.

## *It Remembers Just How You Like Things*

Wouldn't it be nice if . . . FoxPro for Windows remembered how you liked everything to look and set it up that way automatically? (Poof!)

FoxPro for Windows automatically saves all these settings when you close the table and then uses them when you open it. You don't have to do anything special — truly something to wish for.

# Chapter 10
# Being In and Out of Sorts

## In This Chapter

- ▶ What it does and when to use it
- ▶ Sorting on one field
- ▶ Sorting on multiple fields
- ▶ Naming the sorted database
- ▶ Why did "Zebra" come before "apple"

*T*here's a natural trait in humans for collecting stuff. I don't know why, but people seem compelled to gather things together whenever possible. Once the stuff is together, a secondary trait kicks in and they start organizing it. The really interesting thing is that no matter which way they organize it, they always end up needing it organized some other way.

Databases aren't immune to this. In fact, they're probably *more* susceptible than most things. There seems to be a correlation between the quantity of stuff in a given collection and the ways it must be organized. The more stuff, the more ways you want to look at it. And the more ways you want to look at it, the more time you spend organizing instead of collecting new stuff.

Quite a vicious cycle, wouldn't you say? Luckily, FoxPro for Windows breaks the cycle with the Database⇨Sort command. It lets you look at almost any amount of stuff in nearly any way you want with a minimum of heartache and mental loss.

## What It Does and When to Use It

The Sort command does what it says: It sorts the records in the order you specify. Of course, since this *is* a computer program, it's not quite that simple. There are a few pitfalls, limitations, conditions, requirements, stipulations, caveats, qualifying factors, and such that you should to be aware of (see the sidebar "Pitfalls, free-falls, and Niagara Falls" for full details).

By default, records appear in a table in the same order you entered them. If you patiently typed them in classic third grade alphabetical order, that's how you see them. On the other hand, if you applied politically correct rules of alphabetizing while typing the data, they're in no order at all so that none of them is offended by its position relative to the others.

Either way, sorting reorganizes your records in a new order according to your instructions.

✔ You can sort a table by only one field or a combination of fields — even all the fields in the table. Why you'd *want* to sort on every field in a table, I don't know, but it's nice that the option is available.

✔ For each field you sort by, FoxPro lets you choose ascending order (smallest to largest, or A to Z) ) or descending order (largest to smallest, or Z to A). You can specify a different order for each field you choose. This means that with one sort command you can organize a national customer list alphabetically by state (ascending order) and, within each state, by total purchases from largest to smallest (descending order).

✔ You can't sort on the contents of memo or general field types. I'm sorry, but those are the rules.

✔ You can select which records to include in the sorted table. You can specify records for a certain state, include customers above a given spending level, or exclude certain ZIP codes.

✔ Sorting physically reorganizes the records and creates a new table, completely separate from your original. To see the records in sorted order, you must use the new table.

✔ The new table can include all the fields from the original table or just some of them. The choice is completely yours.

✔ All the preceding features work together for maximum power and flexibility. If you're doing a bulk mailing with your word processor, you can sort your customer database by ZIP code, and then include only address-related fields in the newly sorted table. Feed the sorted table to your word processor. When it creates the letters, they'll already be in ZIP code order because the table was sorted that way. Too cool.

✔ Despite the ravings of the paranoid sidebar, sometimes sorting *is* the best answer to a particular need. But, like the last squirt of sunscreen on a bright day at the beach, apply it wisely and sparingly for the best results.

## Pitfalls, free-falls, and Niagara Falls

Some things sound great at first blush, but take on a certain rotten-egg quality under the light of further scrutiny. For me, this includes free-fall parachute jumping, going over Niagara Falls in anything that isn't flying at least 1000 feet over the water, and the sorting capabilities of FoxPro for Windows. Sorting, you see, has some pitfalls.

**Sorting creates a new, separate table.** You knew that already, but the significance takes some time to sink in. Imagine this: One original table begets several sorted tables, which begets supreme confusion on your part when . . .

**Sorted tables aren't automatically updated when the original table changes.** They're separate tables, so nothing happens to them when your master table is updated, corrected, or completely

trashed. You must recreate the sorted tables each time you update the original, to keep the sorted versions current.

**Sorted tables take disk space.** Back to the original example: One original table of, oh, 500,000 characters (or 500K) is sorted three different ways. This yields three new tables, each 500,000 characters strong. You now have a total of 2,000,000 characters (or 2 MB) parked on your hard disk, all in the name of seeing your data in three new ways.

What's the answer to these dilemmas? Sort when you must, update, and then recreate—and erase when you're finished. Or just chuck the whole thing, skip ahead to Chapter 11, and learn about the true wonders of indexing.

# *Naming the Sorted Database*

Because every sort produces a new table, you need to come up with lots of clever, creative names to keep these unruly children in order (and so you'll know what's cool to delete when things get too cluttered). Here's a sanity-saving idea: Start each sorted database with "S_" and use the remaining six letters for some exceedingly brief description of the sort. Here are some examples:

| | |
|---|---|
| S_STATE.DBF | Records sorted by state. |
| S_CUSTNO.DBF | Records sorted by customer number. |
| S_5ZIP.DBF | Records sorted by five digit zip code. |
| S_S_S_S.DBF | Records losing air and sinking fast. |

# Sorting on One Field

The most common sorting job is the simple "organize this table by {insert your field name here}." You're sorting the table according to the values in a single field. Here goes:

1. **Open the table by selecting File⇨Open or Window⇨View⇨Open (whatever suits your fancy).**

   Change the view if you want, but being in Browse or Change mode doesn't affect sorting.

2. **Select Database⇨Sort to open the Sort dialog box.**

   The all-powerful, ever-fun-to-be-around Sort dialog box, as seen in figure 10-1, pops into existence.

| Sort | | |
|---|---|---|
| All Fields: | | Sort Order: |

**Figure 10-1:**
The jam-packed Sort dialog box awaits your instructions.

| | | | | |
|---|---|---|---|---|
| item_id | C | 10 | | |
| item_name | C | 30 | | |
| item_value | N | 7 | 0 | |
| item_minb | N | 7 | 0 | |
| item_desc | M | 10 | | |
| ownr_last | C | 20 | | |
| ownr_first | C | 12 | | |
| ownr_adr1 | C | 20 | | |

Move  Remove

Field Options
● Ascending
○ Descending
☐ Ignore Case

From Table: Items

Input
☐ Scope...
☐ For...
☐ While...

Output
Save As...  ☐ Fields...

OK  Cancel

3. **In the All Fields box, click the field you want to sort by.**

   This highlights the field name in the list. If your field is buried somewhere in the table, use the scroll bar to cruise through the field list until you find it.

   You can't sort with the contents of memo or general fields. In fact, FoxPro won't even let you click on those fields in the All Fields box — the names appear in gray text to remind you that they're off-limits.

4. **In Field Options, choose Ascending or Descending.**

   Ascending sorts from smallest to largest; Descending from largest to smallest. Since this is an either-or choice, choosing one option automatically turns off the other.

5. **If you want FoxPro to treat uppercase and lowercase letters equally, click Ignore Case.**

   This setting is important if you're sorting Character fields containing mixed-case words. If you're sorting numbers (regardless of field type), it doesn't make a difference. Refer to the upcoming "Why Did 'Zebra' Come before 'apple'" section for examples of the Ignore Case option.

6. **Now that all the field options are set, click Move.**

   The field name now appears in the Sort Order box with an arrow right next to the name. For now, pay no attention to the double-headed arrow farther to the left of the field name. It comes into play in the next section, "Sorting on Multiple Fields."

   The single-headed arrow next to the field name visually shows the sort order you selected: an up arrow for Ascending, a down arrow for Descending. There is no indicator for Ignore Case, so you have to remember that by yourself. Back in the All Fields box, notice that the field name is now gray. Since you already chose it, FoxPro won't let you choose it again.

   If you moved the wrong field or just want to change your mind, click the field name in the Sort Order box, and then click Remove. The errant field beats a hasty retreat.

7. **To limit the records included in the sorted table, click the For checkbox inside the Input box.**

   The Expression Builder pops up (I know — I should've warned you about that) and invites you, in its ever-friendly way, to create the expression of your dreams. If you want to include all the current records in your sorted table, skip this step entirely.

   The art of creating expressions with the Expression Builder is wrestled to the ground in several sections of the book (Chapters 1 and 7 come to mind first), so I won't get into the gory details here. The basic steps are: double click on the appropriate field name in the Fields box, type an equals sign (or whatever logical operator you're using) after the field name in the FOR Clause: <expl> box, and then type whatever you want to match or avoid. Remember to put the *whatever* in quotes if you're working with a character field or if FoxPro yells at you about it. Click OK to make your escape.

8. **Click Save As and enter a name for the new sorted version of your table. Select a new disk drive and directory as well, if you so desire.**

   The classic Save As dialog box appears. Type your table name in the Sort Destination File box. If you want to change directories, mouse around in the Directory box. Disk drive choices live in the Drive box near the bottom of the dialog box. When you're finished with your selections, click Save or press Enter.

9. **If you want to include only certain fields in the sorted table, click the Fields button in the Output box.**

The Field Picker dialog box pops into view, looking better in real life than it does in Figure 10-2. This looks a lot like a simplified version of the Sort dialog box (and it is). The goal is to move fields from the All Fields box on the left to the Selected Fields box on the right. Do this by clicking a field and then clicking Move, or just by double-clicking the field name to move it in one easy step. Select as many fields as you want to include. Click OK or press Enter when you're finished.

- This really is a different step than number 7. There, you are including certain *records* in the new table. Here, you're limiting the *fields* included in each record.

- The All button moves all the available fields into the Selected Fields box.

- If you selected an incorrect field, click its name in the Selected Fields box, and then click Remove. It hops back to the All Fields side of the dialog box.

- To trash the whole Selected Fields list and begin anew, click Remove All.

- The fields you choose appear in the sorted database in the order you *selected* them, so think about your choices and their order carefully.

10. **Click OK to do the sort and create the new table.**

| **Field Picker** | | | |
|---|---|---|---|
| **All Fields:** | | | **Selected Fields:** |

| item_id | C | 10 | |
| item_name | C | 30 | Move |
| item_value | N | 7 | 0 |
| item_minb | N | 7 | 0 | All |
| item_desc | M | 10 | |
| ownr_last | C | 20 | Remove |
| ownr_first | C | 12 | |
| ownr_adr1 | C | 20 | Remove All |
| ownr_adr2 | C | 20 | |

From Table: Items     [ OK ]   [ Cancel ]

**Figure 10-2:**
The Field
Picker
dialog box.

# Sorting on Multiple Fields

Sometimes, sorting with a single field just doesn't cut it. It's great if you want to sort your customers by state, but what if you want them listed by state *and* total spending? That's a multiple field sort — and FoxPro for Windows does those, too.

✔ You use the same process to create a multiple field sort as a single field sort, except you repeat Steps 3 through 6 for each field you want to sort by. Every field gets its own sort order (ascending or descending) and ignore case setting, so you can mix and match to meet whatever need you have.

✔ Pick the fields in order of importance, with the most important ones first. When FoxPro is sorting your table, it organizes everything based on the first field. So, what about the other fields? Well . . .

✔ If there are any ties (records with the same entry in the first field), FoxPro looks at the second field of the records to figure out what order they should be in. If that field is the same too, it looks to the third field you included in the Sort Order box (if there is one). If it's *still* the same after three fields, FoxPro throws up its paws and leaves them in whatever order it found them.

✔ Specify as many fields as you need to make the sort work. If your goal is sorting the customer list by state and spending level, you would include at least the state and total spending fields. You might include the customer name or number as a third sorting field, in case two customers in the same state spent the same amount of money with you.

# Why Did "Zebra" Come before "apple"?

Alphabetizing is nothing but a series of rules. You learned this years ago when you were little (and wanted to get big) and computers were big (and wanted to get little). Apply the rules correctly, and the words come out in perfect alphabetical order every time; mess up the rules, and you're condemned to repeat third grade until you get it right. FoxPro, I'm afraid, is still working toward fourth grade admission. I'm not saying that FoxPro for Windows can't alphabetize — I'm saying that it *can,* but according to its own rules. Unfortunately, those rules don't completely conform to traditional alphabetical constraints:

✔ Spaces come first, followed by numbers, capital letters, and lowercase letters.

✔ Capitalization counts. Capitalized words come before lowercase words, even if this makes them *alphabetically* out of order.

✔ Numbers in a character field are treated as letters and are sorted in order from 0 to 9. Numbers in a numeric or float field are sorted in standard numerical order — thank goodness.

✔ If all this stuff about character fields, numeric fields, float fields, and football fields isn't ringing any bells in your mind, stick your finger in the book and flip back to Chapter 6 for a quick refresher.

Figure 10-3 shows five windows, each containing a list of words and numbers. The window on the left, titled SORTDEMO, is a list of random words and numbers typed in no particular order. Notice that some words are duplicated, but with different capitalization. The other windows are grouped into two pairs: ASCEND and ASCENDIC are ascending sorts of the SORTDEMO word list, and DESCEND and DESCNDIC are descending sorts. The ASCENDIC and DESCNDIC files used FoxPro's "ignore case" option (thus the IC ending on the filenames). Now for the detailed analysis of the experiment:

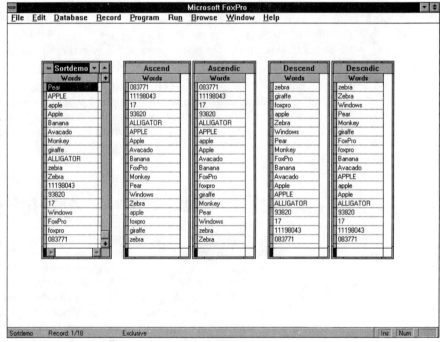

**Figure 10-3:**
A list of words (SORTDEMO) and the results of four different sorts. See the text for a detailed analysis.

| Ascending | The standard ascending sort looks almost normal, except for the fact that "Zebra" comes before "apple." The sort was case-sensitive, so anything in uppercase received preferential treatment. Also, since the numbers are in a character field, they didn't sort in *numerical* order — FoxPro treated them like words, not numbers. |
|---|---|

| | |
|---|---|
| Ascending, ignore case | This looks more like it! It's still not perfect, though, as evidenced by the three "apples" near the middle of the list: FoxPro left them in the same order it found them inside SORTDEMO. This sort *wasn't* case-sensitive, so FoxPro couldn't make out any differences between the three words. Lacking any other relevant thoughts on the matter, it made no changes and went on to something more interesting. The "zebras" and "FoxPro"s met the same fate. |
| Descending | The world is upside down and a "zebra" is reigning. DESCEND is a perfect mirror image of the Ascending sort, which is what you should expect. Kinda nice to actually *get* what you expected, isn't it? |
| Descending, ignore case | It's almost a mirror image of ASCENDIC, but not quite. Something interesting happened with the duplicated words. Compare the two "zebra" entries in this table and ASCENDIC: they're in the same order in both tables. If DESCNDIC was just a mirror image of ASCENDIC, "Zebra" would be first, not second. FoxPro found the two zebras in a particular order and, since "ignore case" is turned on, can't tell the two apart. FoxPro isn't about to muck up a good thing, so it left them in that order in the new table. Descending with ignore case turned on *doesn't* simply make a mirror image of an Ascending sort. |

TIP

🢒 FoxPro is rather twisted about the sorting stuff, isn't it?

🢒 To get the hang of this, try sorting a small table in several different ways. Compare each result to get a feel for what FoxPro is doing.

🢒 If FoxPro's way of sorting begins to make *too* much sense, call it a day and visit an eigth grade grammar class for an hour or two. It may not be too late to salvage those years of public education.

🢒 The preceding examples are only for a single field sort. Adding a second or third field changes things, particularly when case isn't a factor. Sorting with two fields in the "ignore case" examples might change the order of the duplicated entries ("apple," "FoxPro," and "zebra"). Since FoxPro couldn't tell the difference between the three "apple" records, it would go on to the second field. If that field was different, FoxPro would sort the records accordingly. If not, FoxPro would become frustrated, decide the records were sour anyway, and go off in search of some fresh ones.

# Chapter 11

# Then Again, Why Sort When You Can Index?

That sorting stuff is all well and good, but you just have to wonder if there's a better way. As luck would have it, there is. It requires less disk space, works quicker, is more flexible and reliable, and emits floral hydrocarbons (that's the technical term for "smells like a rose"). It's even new and improved. You can't ask more than that from even a laundry detergent. So, what is it?

# It's, Well, an Index

So what *is* an index? Good question — thanks for asking. If you picture a "book index," you're on the right track. A book has all this stuff in it and it's organized in some arbitrary way that made sense to the author but maybe not to you. Luckily for both you and the author, the publisher included an index in the book. The index organizes everything in the book alphabetically so that you can jump right to what you're interested in without wading through half a dozen things you aren't. It doesn't restate the whole book, it just has a key word or phrase, and the page numbers to point you in the right direction.

A FoxPro for Windows index does much the same thing. It's a list of where to find records that contain certain data. You might index a customer table by ZIP code to look for geographical trends. Unlike sorting, indexing doesn't physically change the order of the records. It just gives you a new way to look at them. One database can have many indexes, each giving you a different perspective on the table.

The index is a separate file — it's not part of the database itself. There are single indexes, compound indexes, even the ominous-sounding Compound Structural Index. Oooh. Don't worry, because this chapter covers them all.

## To Index or to Sort: That is the Question

It's a great big world, and there's room in it for sorting *and* indexing. Each one solves different problems, so pick your weapon based on the crisis at hand. Here are the ups and downs:

- ✔ Indexes make queries faster and finding records a breeze. They take little disk space, regardless of how big your table is. The speedy Seek command only works with indexed tables. Indexes don't physically change your table, though — they just make your existing table do tricks.

- ✔ Sorting makes a full (or partial, if you desire) copy of your table with all the records physically listed in the order your want. Mashing or mangling the sorted table has no effect on the original — they're completely separate entities. Sorted tables also take disk space, so if your table was big to begin with, having three different sorted versions is seriously eating your disk.

- ✔ The real power of sorting is the capability to organize data by different fields with different orders *at the same time.* With sorting, you can organize a table in ascending order by state *and* descending order by year-to-date purchases. Indexing lets you organize on the two fields, but you can only pick one order for both.

- ✔ With people who have things to do, it's indexing 2:1. Sorting is great for special situations, but indexing is the overall way to go.

## Filing the Index

Before delving into the Better Fields and Tables' *Do-It-Yourself Guide to Data Indexing,* I must pen a few words about index files themselves. A sort is a sort, you see, but an index file can be compact single, non-compact single, compound independent, or compound structural. Options always clear things up, don't they?

*Single index files* contain (surprise!) one index per file: one index on one or more fields for one database. For a long time, this was the only indexing option available. Having lots of indexes meant cluttering up your disk with lots of index files. On top of all that, single indexes don't update automatically; you have to *manually* open them so that they stay up to date. How frustrating.

The most common flavor of single index file is the *compact single index,* which is smaller and faster than the aging, moldy *non-compact single index.* The only reason non-compact files are still an option today is that some folks out there still cling to FoxPro 1, which only understands this quaint form of data organization. Single indexes are good as a temporary thing — the "disposable index" concept — but should generally be avoided as a long-term fix. Unfortunately, you're stuck with them if you're sharing data with people using FoxPro 1. I hope this won't happen to you.

*Compound index files* first appeared in FoxPro 2 — and what a grand entrance it was. Unlike their restricted cousins, compound index files hold multiple indexes. Now you can have your cake and index it 16 ways too. Just think: all this flexibility without scattering scads of single index files around your disk. What would you pay for functionality like this?

But wait — there's more, namely, the *structural compound index file.* This special file, included at no extra charge to you, opens automatically each and every time you use your table. It updates itself with every change and springs into action at a moment's notice. It takes care of itself so you don't have to. Every table can have one — but *only* one — of these wonderful files. If you need still more flexibility than this, consider an *independent compound index.* A table can have several of these, each one holding lots of interesting, flexible, and fun indexes. Get yours today. Don't wait, do it now — FoxPro is standing by.

 ✔ Both compact and non-compact single index files have an .IDX extension.

 ✔ All compound index files end in .CDX. Structural compound index files have the same name as the table they're indexing, so the structural index file for Customer.DBF is called Customer.CDX.

 ✔ If you have trouble coming up with good filenames, keep a copy of *1,286 Names for Your Baby* on hand.

TECHNICAL STUFF

## Technical stuff about new indexes and old FoxPros

Unless you have a compelling reason (read on to find out if you do), stick with the structural compound index file for all your indexing needs. It's flexible and all that other stuff and really should be more than any three people could want in an index.

There are reasons to stick with single indexes (specifically noncompact single indexes). The reasons can be summed up in one word: compatibility. If you're swapping stuff with some wretched souls condemned to FoxPro 1, FoxBASE+, or FoxBASE+ for the Macintosh, ease their pain by coming down to their technological level. They cannot employ the wonders of the compound index, nor can they use even the tiniest compact single index. Treat them with compassion and patience, in the hope that a few years from now someone using UltraFoxExpert 8 for SOI (Symbiotic Organic Implant) will treat you the same way.

# Indexing on One Field

So much for the expository remarks — time to get on with business. The gentle art of creating an index on a single field unfolds as follows:

1. **Make sure that the table you want to index is open for use.**

   You can open a table by selecting File⇨Open, Window⇨View⇨Open, or any of several other clever ways you've likely devised by now. How you do it is your decision; the point is to get the darn thing open.

2. **Get into Setup mode by selecting Database⇨Setup or Window⇨View⇨Setup.**

   The Setup dialog box pops up to let you know you've succeeded.

3. **Click the Add button in the Indexes box. When the Open dialog box appears, click New.**

   Sometimes, working with FoxPro is like running a marathon where the finish line keeps moving away from you. After successfully selecting and clicking your way through all the checkpoints, you've achieved the destination: the Index dialog box, as pictured in Figure 11-1.

   It's only this bad the first time. In the future, you can come back with a (relatively) few clicks and mousings. I wouldn't lie to you about something like this.

If someone (perhaps you) already created an index for this table, its name appears in the big list box next to the buttons. Don't worry if a little picture of a key appears next to the index name. That just means FoxPro is using the index right now. See the "Choosing and Using Indexes" section later in the chapter for more information.

**Figure 11-1:**
FoxPro has
taken the
liberty of
suggesting
an index on
the first field
in the table
(Cust_No, in
this case).

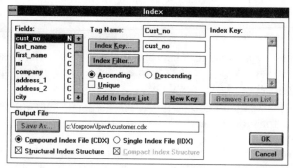

4. **Before going any further, decide what kind of index file to use.**

Unless you have a compelling reason to use some esoteric kind of index file, leave these settings alone and go ahead to Step 5. Needing compatibility with an older version of ForPro *does* constitute a compelling reason.

The following information is rather frighteningly technical, so please feel free to skip it. If you *must* do this terrible thing, direct your attention to the Output File area in the lower left of the Index dialog box.

- To make a *structural compound index file,* make sure that both the Compound Index File (CDX) radio button and the Structural Index Structure checkbox are on. FoxPro does this for your automatically, so you should be able to leave all the settings alone and continue with Step 4.

- To make an *independent compound index file,* click the Structural Index Structure check box off so that the box is blank. When you do, the Save As button and filename box are activated. In the filename box, type a new name for the index file. The easiest way is to double-click the current name — it's the same as your table — and then type your replacement. The other way involves clicking Save As and then using the Save As dialog box to specify the filename and directory. Go whichever way you want.

- To make a *compact single index file,* click the Single Index File (IDX) radio button. This activates the Save As button and filename box. To name your index file, follow the steps for the independent compound index file.

- To make a *non-compact single index file,* click the Single Index File (IDX) radio button, and then turn off the Compact Index Structure check box. Follow the naming steps in the independent compound index file paragraph.

**5. In the Fields box, click the field name you want to index.**

This highlights the field name. If necessary, use the scroll bar to see the rest of the field list. When you click the field name, it automatically appears in both the Tag Name and Index Key boxes.

- FoxPro for Windows automatically gives a single field index the same name as the indexed field. Leave the name alone for now.

- If you're creating a multiple field index, pay no attention to the Fields box and take this exit instead. Go down the ramp and make a left into the first section marked "Indexing on Multiple Fields". The directions are pretty clear from there, so you shouldn't get lost.

**6. Click either the Ascending or the Descending radio button to choose the sorting order.**

Since the goal here is some form of organization, all indexes have a sort direction.

Ascending is smallest to largest (1, 2, 3); descending is largest to smallest (100, 99, 98); rescinding means taking something back ("I rescind your driving privileges"); receding describes my hairline ("I had hair there yesterday").

**7. To ignore any duplicate records, click the Unique checkbox.**

For single field indexes, it's best to leave this box unchecked. If you're indexing a customer on ZIP code, for example, you probably wouldn't want to see only unique records — most of your file would be missing!

Unless you have a specific, well-thought-out reason for turning this on, leave it off.

**8. Click Add to Index List to create the index.**

Figure 11-2 shows a completed index using the ZIP code field. You know it's done because the field name is hanging out in the Index Key box (indexed fields hang out there all the time). The little up arrow next to the field name means the index sorts in ascending order.

Notice that the zip_code field in the Fields box is grayed. FoxPro does that to remind you that an index based on that field already exists. Notice also that FoxPro automatically highlighted the next field in the list (Voice) when I officially added the ZIP code index.

- You *can* create another index with that field, but there's a trick to it. See the sidebar "You *can* have it both ways" for the electronic sleight-of-hand involved.

- If you accidentally add an index for the wrong field, click the field name in the Index Key box, and then click Remove From List.

**Figure 11-2:**
The Customer table has its first bouncing baby index (and it's the Zip_Code field!).

```
                              Index
 ┌──────────────────────────────────────────────────────────────┐
 │ Fields:              Tag Name:  │Voice    │   Index Key:       │
 │ mi           C ▲                                │↑zip_code  ▲│ │
 │ company      C    [ Index Key... ] │voice   │                 │
 │ address_1    C                                                 │
 │ address_2    C    [ Index Filter...] │        │                │
 │ city         C     ● Ascending   ○ Descending                 │
 │ state        C     □ Unique                              ▼│   │
 │ zip_code     C                                                 │
 │ voice        C ▼  [Add to Index List] [New Key] [Remove From List]│
 │                                                                │
 │ ┌─Output File────────────────────────────────────┐           │
 │ │ [ Save As... ]  c:\foxprow\fpwd\customer.cdx    │  [  OK  ] │
 │ │ ● Compound Index File (CDX) ○ Single Index File (IDX) │     │
 │ │ ⊠ Structural Index Structure  ⊠ Compact Index Structure │ [Cancel]│
 │ └────────────────────────────────────────────────┘           │
 └──────────────────────────────────────────────────────────────┘
```

**9. Repeat Steps 5 through 8 for each additional index.**

- If you're using a compound index file, you can create as many indexes as you have fields, so make all the indexes you want.

- Those of you building single index files are finished and may continue with the next step. To build another index, finish Step 10, and then begin again at Step 3.

**10. When you're finished, click OK in the Index dialog box, and then click OK again in the Setup dialog box.**

## You *can* have it both ways

Here's a tricky scenario: You're creating a compound index file and want to build indexes in both ascending and descending order for the same field. After setting up the ascending index, you select the same field and create a descending one. FoxPro declines, saying `Tag name already in use`. What's your next step (before throwing FoxPro out the window)?

Click in the Tag Name box and change the name. That's all FoxPro is complaining about. If the field is called Cust_No, change it to Cust_No2. Anything will work, as long as the new tag is different from all the other tags. After it's changed, click Add to Index List, and your new descending index appears in the Index Key list.

# *Indexing on Multiple Fields*

Sometimes, one field just isn't enough index for your job. That's why FoxPro for Windows can create indexes based on more than one field. It gives you the flexibility to tackle whatever comes your way.

- ✔ You can make an index that organizes by two or more fields in your table.

- ✔ The fields must be the same *type* to work together in an index. They can be any field type (except memo and general), but they all *must* be the same to form an index.

- ✔ As with all good rules, there's a way around the above requirement. It's revealed later in the chapter.

- ✔ Multiple field indexes contribute their share of confusion to the FoxPro world. If you have problems creating the index or get strange results when using it, invest in a bag of snack chips and lure into your office the next FoxPro-savvy guru that wanders by for a quick help session. If you're guru-less, get on the phone with FoxPro support at Microsoft. You can eat the snack chips yourself (it may be all you can afford after the call).

Building multiple field indexes is just like building single field indexes except for the parts that are different. Here's how to do the super-cool multiple field index thing:

Don't be scared because of the number of steps in this section — I took extra care and broke things into small increments to increase your comprehension and the page count of the book.

1. **Pretend you're creating a single field index and go through Steps 1-4 of that section.**

   See — I told you the process was mostly the same.

2. **Click New Key for a clean start.**

   The New Key button clears out anything already in the Tag Name or Index Key boxes. It gives you a fresh foundation to build on.

3. **Click or Tab your way to the Tag Name box and type a name for your new index.**

   Since all indexes must have a Tag, this is the most logical place to start.

   If you're creating a single index file, the Tag Name box isn't available. To get around this "feature" of FoxPro for Windows, click the first field you want in your index. FoxPro automatically names the tag after the field. Now that the tag's in place, you can get on with the process of building the index.

4. **Click Index Key to summon forth the Expression Builder.**

   What would a pleasant trip through FoxPro be without a visit from the abominable Expression Builder? Who knows — it keeps turning up. There's nothing left to do now but deal with it.

5. **In the Fields box, double-click the first field of your index.**

   The field you select appears in the `INDEX ON: <expr>` box.

   If you're doing the single index file thing, your first field is already in the `INDEX ON: <expr>` box and highlighted. Click anywhere in the box to remove the highlight, and then go on to the next step.

6. **Type a plus sign (+) after the first field name in the INDEX ON box.**

   You're telling FoxPro for Windows to use a combination of the fields for the index.

7. **Back in the Fields box, double-click the next field for the index.**

   The new field name appears after the plus sign in the INDEX ON box. Figure 11-3 shows the finished expression for an index by state and ZIP code.

8. **Repeat Steps 6 and 7 for any other fields you want to include in the index.**

   You can include lots of fields in an index, but don't do it. Include enough fields to make your index useful, and stop there.

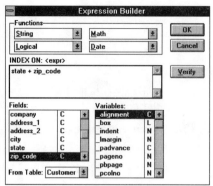

**Figure 11-3:**
Sweet
success at
last, as the
expression
for my state
and zip code
index is
done.

9. **Click OK when your index is complete.**

   FoxPro for Windows returns you to the Index dialog box. Your hard-won expression appears in the Index Key box, right where it should.

   You're out of the multiple field woods now. The remaining steps are old hat — you did them all in the single field index section. If you temporarily forget some of the details, take a brief gander there to refresh your memory.

10. **Click either the Ascending or Descending radio button to select the sort order.**

11. **Click the Unique checkbox to ignore any records with duplicate index values.**

12. **Click Add to Index List to save your new index.**

    So much work, so little feedback. Figure 11-4 shows the Index dialog box with the state and ZIP code index at home in the Index Key box. Seems like there ought to be more celebration, doesn't it?

13. **Repeat the steps to build other indexes, if you want.**

14. **When you're ready, click OK in the Index dialog box, and then click OK again in the Setup dialog box to save all your work.**

    FoxPro assumes that you like the last index you created the best, so it starts using that one automatically. To select a different index, see the next section.

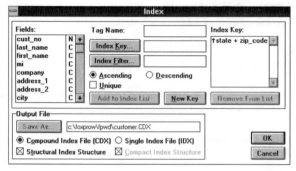

**Figure 11-4:**
One figure
ago, it was a
youthful
expression;
now it's a
full-grown
index.

# Really technical stuff about multiple field types in indexes

If you absolutely *must* build an index with fields of different types, there is a way to do it. This isn't for the faint at heart, so please sit down if you're prone to fainting (or just faint and then you're prone anyway).

Usually, you need to combine a character field and either a numeric or date field, which FoxPro normally won't let you do. The secret is to disguise the date or numeric field as a *character* field so that FoxPro won't know the difference. Pretty tricky, isn't it?

When you're in the Expression Builder, use the super-secret FoxPro functions STR and DTOS to carry out the deception. STR (for STRing) con-

verts the contents of a numeric field into a string (the technical term for *bunch*) of characters. DTOS (for Date TO String) does the same thing for date fields.

To use these functions, get into the Expression Builder (as described in this section) and start creating your expression in the INDEX ON box. When you're ready to put in the numeric or date field, type STR (for numeric fields) or DTOS (for date fields) and then the field name in parentheses. When you're finished, the expression should look something like these examples:

```
STR(cust_no) + Company
item_id + DTOS(sale_date)
```

# *Choosing and Using Indexes*

So you have lots of indexes out there waiting to make your life easier. Now the trick is telling FoxPro which one you want to use. Here's how:

1. **With the table open, get into Setup mode by selecting Database⇨ Setup or Window⇨View⇨Setup.**

   As you've no doubt seen before, the Setup dialog appears.

2. **Click the name of the index you want to use, and then click Set Order to put it in charge.**

   By default, FoxPro only shows you the indexes in the table's compound structural index file. To include other compound or single index files, click Add, select the index file from the Open Index File list, and then click Open. All those indexes are now in the list along with the compound structural entries. Figure 11-5 shows indexes from the Customer table's compound structural file and an independent compound index file called Cust3. The Customer number index (from the structural file) is highlighted and ready for the next step.

**Figure 11-5:**
All the
indexes
currently
open are
listed in the
box.

Indexes

| | |
| --- | --- |
| Add... | ↑Customer:State_zip |
| | **↑Customer:Cust_no** |
| Modify... | ↑Customer:Company |
| | ↓Customer:Zip_code |
| Set Order | ↑Cust3:City |
| | ↑Cust3:State |
| Remove | |

Index Description
Index Expression:  cust_no
Index Filter:

3. **Click Set Order to use the index.**

   A little key appears next to the index name, as in Figure 11-6. That means the index is active.

   To stop using the index and see the records in their physical order, highlight the index that's in use and click No Order. The key promptly disappears and the table is returned to its previous state of sundry disorganization.

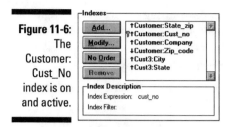

**Figure 11-6:**
The
Customer:
Cust_No
index is on
and active.

4. **Click OK to close the Setup dialog box.**

Now when you view the table in Browse or Change mode, all the records appear in order by the index you selected.

# Changing and Deleting Indexes

Time changes all things, even indexes. The little piece of digitalia that changed your life yesterday is today's unsightly piece of clutter on an otherwise pristine disk drive. Compared with building them in the first place, modifying or erasing indexes is a piece of cake:

1. **Open the table, and then start Setup mode by selecting Database⇨Setup or Window⇨View⇨Setup.**

   You've been through this before. After you succeed, the Setup dialog box appears.

2. **To change or delete an index, find it in the Indexes list and either click its name and then click Modify, or double-click the name.**

   The beloved Index dialog box pops back into your life. The index you chose is highlighted and ready for surgery. Even if you're planning on modifying or doing in several indexes, just pick one to start with. After you're in the Index dialog box, all the indexes in the current file are at your mercy.

   Depending on what you want to do, you may skip a step or two in the following list. Don't worry; it's supposed to work that way.

3. **To get rid of an index entirely, click Remove From List.**

   The index name vanishes. It's not gone yet, but it's well on the way. When you click OK to leave the Index dialog box, FoxPro gives you one last chance to change your mind and reprieve the condemned index (but you find that out a few steps from now).

**4. To change an index from ascending to descending or vice versa, highlight the index in the Index Key box, and then click either the Ascending or Descending radio button.**

You can set or clear the Unique check box the same way.

**5. To change a multiple field index, click its name in the Index Key list, and then click Index Key.**

Make your changes in the Expression Builder. To delete a field from the expression, highlight it by clicking and dragging across the field name in the INDEX ON box, and then press Del. Pick new fields from the Fields list. Don't forget to put a plus sign between each field name. Click OK when you're finished.

- If FoxPro complains about a `Missing operand`, look for an extra plus sign in the expression.

- If FoxPro says you have an `Error in expression`, you're probably mixing field types. Fields in a multiple field index *must* be the same type (character, numeric, and so on). If that's what you really wanted to do, see the "Really technical stuff about multiple field types in indexes" sidebar earlier in the chapter.

- If you hopelessly mangle the expression, click Cancel, and then answer Yes when FoxPro asks whether you really want to Discard changes to expression. Click Index Key to try again.

**6. To work on a different index, click its name in the list, and then do your damage.**

While you're here, you can add new indexes with the New Key button. See the earlier sections for help.

**7. When the dust settles and all the changes are finished, click OK in the Index dialog box and brace yourself for a gauntlet of annoying little questions.**

Depending on what you did, FoxPro for Windows puts you through the inquisitorial wringer with friendly little windows called *alert boxes*. Figures 11-7 and 11-8 show two common FoxPro alert boxes. The one in Figure 11-7 appears when you change an existing index; the one in Figure 11-8 comes around after you removed an index. If you choose No, the index remains in the file. Choosing Yes has the opposite, and rather obvious, effect.

**8. Click OK in the Setup dialog box to complete the sordid process.**

**Figure 11-7:**
The alert message giving you a chance to repeal the changes you made to an index.

**Figure 11-8:**
This is the 11th Hour Appeal message.

# Chapter 12

# The Relational Thing: Tables that Tango

*T*here's a lot to developing a relationship — things like finding the right match, making sure that you're compatible, learning about each other, discovering common interests, and figuring out what to do during the awkward pause between the dinner check hitting the table and someone (preferably not you) offering to pay it. Sure, some relationships are instant successes, but just as many are long, slow failures.

Dealing with relational tables feels much the same. It's often a cross between the tender affirmations of sweet infatuation and the lock-and-load realities of full-scale war. With enough planning, patience, and help from this chapter, your tables can live and work in simple, peaceful harmony.

## Creating Tables that Work Together

When you get right down to it, to build and use a relational database you only need to remember one rule: The tables involved must have at least *one* field in common. This field will link the two tables together — it's often referred to as the (ready?) *linking field*. If you want to link the Customer table with the Items table, they both need a customer number field; to link Items with Supplier requires a supplier number field. Precisely how you do it is up to you. The point is that these linking fields are the heart and soul of the whole relational thing.

✔ Linking fields must be identical in type (character, date, or whatever) and size (number of whatevers that fit in the field). Don't try to bend this rule — it will come back and haunt you.

✔ Tables don't just "start relating" on their own. Plan your tables on paper before building them in FoxPro. Design the links to accomplish your goals.

✔ Look for obvious linking fields, like customer number, stock keeping unit, phone number, or just about any unique identification number. If you can't find one, make one up and add it to your tables.

✔ Usually, the linking field is *unique* in one table but nothing special in the other. In the Customer table, customer number is really important, but in the Invoices table, invoice number is king and customer number is just along for the ride.

✔ There is no shame in sticking to flat-file tables and *never* using relational databases. Often, there is wisdom in that approach. If someone tries to tell you differently, whack them with this book (in the spirit of understanding and peaceful coexistence, of course).

## Meeting the relations: The Ones and Manys

There comes a time in every budding relationship when it's time to *meet the relations*. The electronic (and equally awkward) version of "dinner with the folks" happens when you decide what kind of relationship your tables need with each other. Luckily, this isn't an essay question — it's multiple choice. Here are your four options:

*One-to-One* relationships are the simplest: One record in this table matches one (and only one) record in that table. If a company assigns a car to each of its sales reps, that's a one-to-one relationship: Each person has just one car and each car has just one owner. Although this is the simplest relational model, you don't see it too often in real life.

*One-to-Many* relationships win the "most likely to star in a real-world situation" prize. In this model, one record in this table matches many records in another. Back in the fictitious company, each sales rep calls on a number of customers, but each customer only has one sales rep. This is a classic one-to-many relationship: One rep links to many customers.

*Many-to-One* relationships are the opposite of one-to-many (takes your breath away, doesn't it?). Reversing the preceding example, many customers have the same sales rep. Thus, it's a many-to-one relationship. Why isn't it a one-to-one, since each customer has only one rep? If each customer had one rep and that rep had *no other customers*, it would be a one-to-one relationship. That's not the case, so it's a many-to-one model.

*Many-to-Many* relationships are messy and troublesome. The basic idea is simple enough: Each record in this table relates to many records in another, and each record in the other table corresponds with many records here. Trotting out the sales reps one last time, each rep sells a group of products from the company's line and each product is sold by many different reps. To make sense of this morass, you need a table in the middle with one-to-many relationships to the other two. This is too deep even for a technical icon, so I'll just say this: If you think you're dealing with this situation, seek out a local wizard and get some wizard-level advice.

# Indexes and Relational Links

Behind the flitz and glitz (and sometimes Schlitz) of dealing with relational databases, there's an unsung workhorse: the index. Indexes make table relationships work. Without the right indexes, FoxPro for Windows won't even link the tables.

So what's the key to the index and relational thing? Hang on tight — here it comes: The field you're linking *with* must be indexed in the table you're linking *to*. Right. Any questions?

This is *not* a software manual. There's no reason you should be subjected to sentences like the one in the preceding paragraph in a friendly, helpful, and considerate book like this — it's simply inexcusable behavior. Unfortunately, the sentence in question is factually correct and cannot be simply tossed out on its ear. Such are the dilemmas of computer books and computer book authors.

When you're relating two tables, you're really relating one table *to* another — a *parent* to a *child*, to use the lingo — by some field that's common to both. The parent's indexes don't affect the link, but the child's indexes do. The child table *must* be indexed on the field you're using for the link. If it isn't, FoxPro for Windows won't let you link the two.

- ✔ If you're using a single index file, make sure that the index is open.

- ✔ Always open the indexes when you open the tables! Forgetting this step leads to out-of-date indexes, bad tempers on your part, and general feelings of ill will toward FoxPro (although it's not really FoxPro's fault).

- ✔ Make sure that the index is up to date. An old index yields bad results, because it overlooks new records and perhaps remembers records that are now deleted.

- ✔ All the preceding items are great reasons to use a structural compound index. Since this kind of index opens when the table opens, it's always up to date, always available, and never a pain in the patooty. If you simply *must* use some other kind index file, the responsibility to keep it current rests on your shoulders.

- ✔ In case you're using *some other kind of index file* and find yourself with an index that doesn't work right, there's an easy fix. Open your table and the index file in question (or was that the questionable index file?). From the main menu, select <u>D</u>atabase⇨Reinde<u>x</u>. FoxPro rebuilds all the open index files from scratch, making sure they're all correct. What a deal.

✔ If FoxPro can't find any indexes at all in the child table, it attempts to link the two tables by record number. This is nearly futile, unless you have a really novel situation. Please, just for my sake if nothing else, don't try to link tables without an index file, okay?

✔ See Chapter 10 for help and information on all this index stuff.

# Linking Tables with the View Dialog Box

The first step toward the inherent coolness of relational tables is creating the link between the tables. There are several different ways to do this, but I think it's easiest through the venerable View dialog box.

This assumes that the child table is *already* indexed. If it isn't, the process won't work. So there.

These steps work for simple relationships or big, complex arrangements worthy of a scandalous talk show. Building a complicated relationship is nothing more than building a series of single relationships — everything is done one step at a time.

And now, the relationship mystery unraveled:

1. **Open the View dialog box by selecting <u>W</u>indow⇨<u>V</u>iew.**

   If you're not familiar with the View dialog box, refer to "Viewing for Fun and Profit" in Chapter 7.

2. **If the parent table isn't listed under Work Areas, highlight a work area by clicking it, and then click <u>O</u>pen and choose the table.**

   This is personal preference, but I like to put the parent table in the first work area and the child (or children, depending on the family) in the others.

   For a quick refresher on opening a table, see Chapter 1.

3. **Repeat the same process for the child table.**

4. **Click the parent table name in the Work Areas list, and then click <u>R</u>elations.**

   The parent table somewhat mystically appears on the right side of the dialog box, as shown in Figure 12-1. The little line coming down from it makes more sense in a minute.

5. **Click the child table name in the Work Areas list. Set the child's index order, if necessary.**

   The results of this step go one of two different ways, depending on whether the child database is in order by an index yet — not if an index *exists,* but rather whether the index is active and ordering the data *right now.*

- If there's no order set for the child table yet (the most likely case), the Set Index Order dialog box appears. It lists all the indexes for the current table. Click the one for the linking field, and then click OK.

  - If you already specified an active index, be very, *very* sure you chose the one for the linking field. Then continue with the next step.

**Figure 12-1:**
The
Customer
table is
ready to
relate in the
View dialog
box.

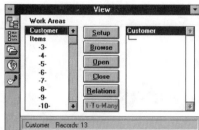

6. **The Expression Builder appears. If all is well and good with the relationship, the linking field's name appears in the** SET RELATION: <expr> **box. Click OK to make the Expression Builder go away. Otherwise, double-click the linking field's name in the Fields box and then click OK.**

   If the linking field's name is identical in both the parent and child tables, FoxPro automatically offers that field in the Expression Builder. If the names are different, it's up to you to choose the parent's correct linking field.

   If things aren't working (despite your best efforts), the child table may be in order by the wrong index. Press Esc, highlight the child table in the Work Areas list, and then click Setup. In the Indexes box, make sure that the right index is in use (it has a picture of a key next to it). If it's the wrong one, click the correct index and click Set Order. Click OK to get back to the View dialog box. Finally, go back to Step 4 and try again.

7. **The relationship is displayed for all to see on the right side of the View dialog box, just as in Figure 12-2.**

   The box visually shows the relationship of parent to child (Customer and Items, respectively, in the example). The diagram expands if you add more tables to the relationship.

   Now that the relationship exists, you can Browse the records, search the tables, or do just about anything your heart wishes, comfortable in the knowledge that these two tables have a good, strong relationship.

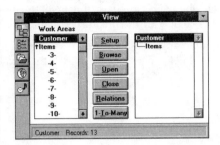

**Figure 12-2:**
The finished relationship between Customer and Items. Customer is the parent; Items is the child.

# Views Make Linked Life Easy

There's a lot of artful maneuvering involved in playing matchmaker to a couple of shy, young tables. Luckily, after you do it once, FoxPro for Windows can remember the link and restore it at a moment's notice. FoxPro does this with View files (also known as Views, since there must be at least two names for everything to maintain the appropriate degree of confusion).

A View is a really complete record of how things are set in the View dialog box. A View remembers what tables are open (even those wallflowers not involved in any relationships), which workspace each table is in, and all the relationships you built. It writes all these settings into a file with a .VUE extension (the infamous View file).

✔ If you're doing a particularly complex project requiring lots of open tables, use a View file to save the workspace you've created. Instead of wasting your valuable time reopening all those files (and rebuilding the relationships, too), make FoxPro for Windows do it. Who's in charge here, anyway, you or the software? Wait — don't answer that.

✔ View files save your *entire* workspace — not just related files. When you open a View, it completely resets the FoxPro workspace, closing files and undoing relationships. The View is truly a snapshot in time: Everything is recorded, everything is restored.

## Creating a View

Despite its power and flexibility, creating a View is pretty easy:

1. **Set up your workspace the way you want it.**

   Open whatever tables you want and build the relationships between them.

   Although FoxPro for Windows records relationships in a View file (and relationships are what this chapter is about), you can use a View file just to remember which tables were open in what work areas. It's a great shortcut.

2. **Select Window⇨View to bring up the View dialog box.**

   If the View dialog box is already on-screen, click it to make it the current window.

3. **Select File⇨Save As to bring up the Save As dialog box.**

   If the Save As option is grayed on the menu, make sure that the View dialog box is the *current* window — just having it on-screen somewhere isn't enough.

4. **Type a name for your View in the Save View As box, make sure that you're in the right directory, and then click Save to create the file.**

   If the Save As dialog box is pointing to the wrong directory, do the point and click dance to switch into the correct one. See Chapter 1 for a full briefing.

## Using a View

Using the View file is even easier than making it:

1. **Select File⇨Open to see the Open dialog box.**

2. **Click in the down arrow next to the List Files of Type box to drop down the selection list. Scroll through the list to the View item and click it.**

   If you're a keyboard maven, Tab to the box and type **V** for View. It can be upper- or lowercase — FoxPro catches on both ways.

3. **FoxPro lists the available views in the list area on the left of the Open dialog box. Click the one you want to use, and then click Open.**

   As always, if the file you want isn't listed, check the directory settings and make sure that you're looking in the right place.

4. **All the tables and relationships are restored.**

   Continue about your business like nothing magical happened.

## *Browsing Linked Tables*

Browsing takes on an interesting twist when two tables are officially "related." The Browse window for the parent shows all the records, but the child's window only lists the records for the current parent record. Figure 12-3 is a good example: Although there are many records in the Items table, only the three items that Thomas Fant has in the auction are displayed in the Items Browse window. Moving between Customer records with the up- or down-arrow keys automatically changes the Items list — the link takes care of that.

✔ Don't panic when your child table only shows *some* of its records. The others aren't gone — they just don't match the current parent record, so FoxPro doesn't display them.

✔ The quickest way to end the relationship (apart from standing your partner up on dates too many times) is to close either the parent or the child table from the View dialog box.

**Figure 12-3:**
The Items table displays only the three records that match the current Customer record. Moving to a different customer record shows the new matching records in Items.

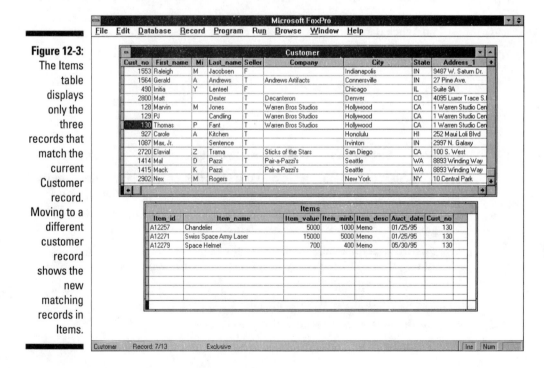

# Sorting Linked Tables

All this linking and relating adds a new dimension to the sorting process. In fact, it adds quite a bit of power. Instead of sorting just one table, now you can process the whole relational team, treating all the fields as parts of one big table.

This new capacity is hiding inside the From Table drop-down list. Figure 12-4 shows this little guy strutting his stuff, letting you switch from table to table in search of the fields you need. He's available in the Sort, Field Picker, and Expression Builder dialog boxes and works the same way everywhere.

- ✔ In the Sort dialog box, use From Table to switch from table to table, selecting the fields to sort by.

- ✔ In the Field Picker dialog box, From Table lets you include fields from each related table in the new sorted one.

- ✔ In the Expression Builder, your filtering expressions can include any field from any table in the relation.

- ✔ Overall, the sorting process itself hasn't changed at all. See Chapter 10 for everything you ever hoped to know about it.

- ✔ If this seems too neat for words, check out queries in Chapters 15 through 18 — they're *really* great.

**Figure 12-4:**
The From Table drop-down list lets you pick fields from any file that's relationally involved.

| | | | | Sort | | | |
|---|---|---|---|---|---|---|---|
| **All Fields:** | | | | | | **Sort Order:** | |
| cust_no | N | 6 | 0 | | Move | | |
| last_name | C | 20 | | | | | |
| first_name | C | 15 | | | Remove | | |
| mi | C | 4 | | | Field Options | | |
| company | C | 25 | | | ● Ascending | | |
| address_1 | C | 30 | | | ○ Descending | | |
| address_2 | C | 30 | | | ☐ Ignore Case | | |
| city | C | 20 | | | | | |

From Table: Customer / Customer / Items / Schedule

Input: ☐ Scope... ☐ For... ☐ While...

Output: Save As... ☐ Fields...

OK    Cancel

# Part III
# Vays to Make ze Data Talk

YES, MASTER?

# In this part...

**S**ometimes, pulling answers out of a table makes you feel like you're in the midst of "Little Caesar Meets Tron": the wild chases around the hard drive trying to find the table, the frustration at apprehending the wrong information, all leading to the final confrontation with Mr. Big Table ("C'mon, youse guys. I know you're in dere, so come out in ZIP code ordah and nobody'll git duhleted!"). Oooh — I get goosebumps just thinking about it.

If this sounds like an average day with your data, this Part is definitely for you. It has almost everything you want to know about getting answers from your tables. Part III covers looking for records, querying tables, and just about everything in between.

# Chapter 13

# Seek, and Ye Shall Find; Locate, and Ye Shall Continue

*I* lose things a lot. I'm not sure whether it's me or I just have sneaky stuff, but things like to hide from me. Unfortunately, this behavior carries over into my databases, which leads me to believe it's some kind of supernatural effect surrounding my house and office.

Hauntings aside, this database stuff is great for storing things in nice, neat columns, but when you forget where something is, you can't just start poking around under the laundry or in the kids' room looking for it. It's *in there* now — and finding it requires a new set of tools. Put down the pick and shovel from last week's Search for the Checkbook and dive into FoxPro for Windows' search commands: Seek, Locate, and Find.

## Different Commands, Different Situations

Different needs require different solutions. FoxPro for Windows tries to be all things to all data, so it offers three different searching commands. Each has its good points, but they have limitations as well. The choice is yours, as always, to use whatever works best in your current state of affairs.

Seek, Locate, and Find aren't your only options. In Chapter 15, you get into relational query-by-example (RQBE), which is really cool (RC), very fast (VF), and pretty easy to use (WHEW).

## Seek for fast results

The first (and fastest) of the searches is Seek. This only works on indexed fields, so you can't go picking through any old field. Since memo fields can't be indexed, you can't use Seek on them. Any other field is fair game, though, provided it has a valid, open index attached to it.

Since Seek works with indexes, it's fast — really fast. Seek especially shines when you're searching a big table. By using the index, it goes directly to its target without window shopping through the other thousand or so records.

One thing to watch out for: Seek finds only the *first* match; it's up to you to look further if there is more than one matching entry. FoxPro doesn't have a "Seek again" command; a judiciously applied Find is about as close as you can get.

## Locate for the slow and steady approach

Another option is Locate. Playing the tortoise to Seek's hare, Locate's motto is "Try Harder." Locate is more flexible than Seek ever dreamed of being. It works on *any* type of field, even memos. The price of this flexibility is speed. Locate can't hope to match Seek's lightning-fast results, because Locate finds things the old-fashioned way: It looks. It checks every entry in the field you specify — *every* one. After it finds a match, Locate stops and proudly shows off what it found. If that wasn't what you wanted, use Locate's sidekick Continue to keep looking.

Because Locate uses the one-at-a-time approach to data searching, it works best with small tables; with big tables, it takes its time. You are forewarned.

## Find for "It could be anywhere" searching

Finally, the most amazingly useful and basically neat way to search that FoxPro ever came up with: the Find option. It should be called the "Find From Here" option, because it starts looking from the current record and continues until it hits a match or the end of the table, whichever it comes to first.

## Why there are three different search commands

Why are there *three* search commands? Why *anything* about FoxPro for Windows? This is one of those unasked questions. It's like asking why you and I put up with ones and zeros on power switches. I'm sure there's a sound product development reason, but the person who knows is locked up in some Microsoft dungeon for being overly normal.

I have my own guess about the origins of FoxPro's three search commands, heretical though it is. I

think that some programmer-type came up with Locate first because he was too lazy to build a query to find what he was looking for. Next, he developed Seek because Locate was too slow for the humongous database he wanted to search. I can only attribute the Find command to some rational person's suggestion, because it's *way* too useful to draw lineage from a programmer.

There's a way around this "Find From Here" problem. Check out the Find step-by-step stuff later in this chapter to uncover it.

Trivial details aside, this command is just too easy to use: Tell it what you're looking for, and it finds it. No field names to think about, no Expression Builder to contend with, no quotes or logical operators to insert correctly. Find, and it shall be found — too easy.

Like the Seek command, it won't look in memo fields, but it *will* find things in the middle of records. For example, if you search for the word "Studio," Find considers "Warren Brothers Studios" a match, but Locate doesn't (because "Studio" isn't at the beginning of the entry).

# Seek: Searching an Indexed Field

Here's how to Seek out something in an indexed field:

To use Seek, your table must be indexed on the field you're searching.

1. **Open your table, put it on-screen in either Browse or Change mode, and turn on the index you want to Seek with.**

   Although the Browse or Change part is personal preference, the other things are required. Seek won't even be an option if your table isn't ordered with an index.

   For help using, creating, or pondering indexes, see Chapter 11.

2. **Select <u>R</u>ecord⇨<u>S</u>eek to open the Expression Builder.**

If Seek is grayed, your table doesn't have an active index yet. Go back one step, lose a turn, and give me all your money.

3. **In the Value to SEEK box, type the value you're looking for in the table.**

This is straight typing for a change — no double-clicks or anything like that. Simply type in the value you're Seeking, as in Figure 13-1. As long as you put quotes around words and numbers pretending to be words (like ZIP codes), this step is easy.

If you're unsure whether you should use quotes, FoxPro gives you a tip, provided you have some tech-weenie like me to explain it. Right after Value to SEEK, there's a little thing that says something like <expN> or <expC> (there are others, but these are the most common). If it's <expC>, FoxPro is saying "this expression is a Character type," so put your entry in quotes. If it says anything else, don't use quotes. If you get it wrong, FoxPro informs you and, after the beating, lets you rectify the error.

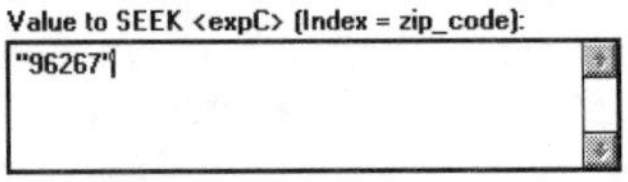

**Figure 13-1:**
You provide
the value to
find.

Value to SEEK <expC> (Index = zip_code):

"96267"

4. **Click OK. FoxPro for Windows moves the cell pointer to the first matching record, provided it found one.**

FoxPro doesn't exactly shout when it doesn't find a match. If the pointer is on the last record, that's a *big* clue. When this happens, look in the lower left corner of the FoxPro window. If the words No find appear way down there on the gray bar, FoxPro failed — there aren't any matches.

5. **If FoxPro found a record, but it's not the one you want, use the arrow keys to find the object of your search.**

Seek only finds the first occurrence of your entry. If you have more than one match in the table, Seek doesn't particularly care about the others — it found a match and is happy. Because the table is in order by that field, use the arrow keys to browse through the other matching entries to find the one you want.

# Locate: Hunting in Any Field (Even Memos)

The secrets of Locate and Continue begin here:

1. **Before doing anything important (like turning on the computer or starting FoxPro for Windows), ask yourself what you're trying to find and write down your answer on a sheet of paper.**

   Perhaps I'm exaggerating a little, but not much. Don't take this step lightly, especially if this is your first time around the block with Locate. By thinking through your search before doing it, the whole process is smoother. After a while, you *can* skip this step, because you'll do it automatically.

2. **Open your table and set it for Browse or Change mode viewing.**

   Locate doesn't require any participation from an index, so you don't have to worry about setting the order — get it open, and you pass the test.

3. **Select Record⇨Locate to pop up the Locate dialog box.**

   The three buttons on the box, Scope, For, and While, control the Locate command. The one you're primarily interested in is For.

   - Scope lets you limit the records FoxPro looks at during the search. You can set it to include everything (the default choice), all records from the current one to the end, just the next so-many, or only certain record numbers. Unless you're feeling particularly adventuresome, don't mess around with this setting.

   - While is for people who care far too much about FoxPro. Normal people (even people like me who keep their normalcy in a box next to the desk) shouldn't ever use or even need this. If you think you do, ask a FoxPro Wizard to do some magic for your problem.

4. **Click For to open the Expression Builder.**

   Gird yourself up for a brief skirmish with your buddy and mine, the Expression Builder. Don't be overwhelmed by the myriad controls, buttons, and whirligigs. Keep breathing steadily and concentrate on two areas: the Fields box and the Locate Record For box.

5. **In the Fields box, scroll through the list until the field you want comes into view. Double-click it before it escapes.**

The field name appears in the Locate Record For box. The name may look funny, but that's not your fault.

FoxPro for Windows displays the field names in "dot notation," which is a techie way to say "filename then field name." Since there's a period in the middle, they call it "dot notation." I'm as astounded as you.

6. **After the field name in the Fields box is a blinking vertical cursor. That's the place to type the logical operator your expression needs.**

*Logical operator* is the technical term for the equals sign and other comparison symbols like that. Most of the time, all you need is the equals sign. "Greater than" (>) and "less than" (<) are always popular, along with that old favorite "not equal to" (<>).

For a lot more than you may want to know about things such as logical operators, sign up for Mr. Boole's Amazing School of Logic in Chapter 30.

7. **Finally, type what you're looking for or comparing to. Remember to put it in quotes if it's a word or a number masquerading as a word (like ZIP codes).**

Figure 13-2 unveils a completed expression, ready to take the table by storm.

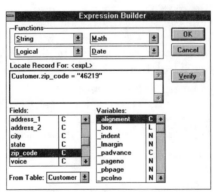

**Figure 13-2:** The expression caught in a moment of reflection. Quite emotional, isn't it?

8. **Click OK to exit the Expression Builder, and then click Locate to begin the search.**

If FoxPro for Windows yelps `Boolean expression required`, look at your entry from Step 7. If it's encased in quotes, remove them. If it's naked, clothe the poor thing in some inexpensive quotation marks. Try the OK button again when you're finished.

9. **FoxPro moves to the first matching record. If that's not the one you wanted, select Record⇨Continue or press Ctrl+K to Locate the next match.**

When FoxPro runs out of matches, it highlights the last record and sighs this tiny little message into the bottom left corner of the window: `End of Locate scope`. That means it's done.

# Find: Ferreting out Anything Almost Anywhere

Using Find is almost too easy to have its own section, but it does add pages to the book.

Find won't look in memo fields, so don't expect it to. Also, remember that it starts at the current record and quits at the end of the file, unless you override this behavior with the Wrap Around option described in the following paragraphs.

1. **Open the table and view it in either Browse or Change mode.**

Remember that Find starts wherever you currently are in the table, so move the cursor back to the top if you want to search the whole table.

2. **Select Edit⇨Find or press Ctrl+F to open the Find dialog box.**

3. **Type what you're looking for in the Look For box.**

Figure 13-3 shows a search in the making. Geez, you don't even have to worry about quotes — Find doesn't care. Is this a great command or what?

| | |
|---|---|
| **Figure 13-3:** The flexible Find dialog box. | **Find**<br><br>Look For: `wood`    [ Find ]<br><br>[ Replace All ]<br>⌐Options<br>☒ Ignore Case  ☐ Match Whole Word  [ Cancel ]<br>☐ Wrap Around |

4. **Set any of the options you're interested in using by clicking in the appropriate checkbox.**

   Find comes with three options that are truly useful. They are Ignore Case, Match Whole Word, and Wrap Around.

   - Ignore Case is already turned on. This is usually a good thing, but sometimes you need to be case sensitive. When you do, click this option off.

   - Match Whole Word is pretty cool when you need it. It's normally off, which lets you look for "wood" and find things like "Hollywood", "Woodstock", and "Wood is good food." Turning it on limits FoxPro to entries that contain your example *as a unique word.* Searching for "wood" with this setting turned on finds "wood lot", "teak wood", and "Wood is still good food."

   - Wrap Around makes the Find command complete. Turning this on makes Find look through the whole table, beginning wherever you are right now, then going back to the top and searching down to the starting point. What a deal. I recommend turning this on every time, just to make sure that you find what you're looking for.

5. **Click Find to start your search.**

   FoxPro highlights the first match it comes across.

6. **If that's not the one you're looking for, select Edit⇨Find Again or press Ctrl+G to keep looking.**

   Find beeps at you when it's out of ideas and doesn't want to play any more.

# Chapter 14

# Filtering Out the Goo

. . . . . . . . . . . . . . . . . . . . . . . . . . . . . . . . . . . . . . . . . . . . . . . . .

. . . . . . . . . . . . . . . . . . . . . . . . . . . . . . . . . . . . . . . . . . . . . . . . .

Have you ever noticed how many kinds of filters there are in one day of life? Water filters, furnace filters, oil filters, gas filters, menthol filters, reverse osmosis filters (they sound so incredibly cool) — the list goes on and on. It makes you wonder why everything is so dirty to begin with.

This chapter adds one more to the growing filter list: the data filter. Data, like just about everything else in the world, gets murky sometimes. Data filters clarify your tables and help you see trends, discover anomalies, and generally strain out the goo.

## What Filters Do

When you get right down to it, filters are pretty straightforward things: They "filter out" records you don't want to see. The records aren't gone, they're just stuffed out of sight for a while. If you remember how you "cleaned" your room as a child (or reacted to random parental visits during college), the whole filter thing becomes clear in no time.

Filters are quick to build and give you very flexible ways to cruise your stuff. They're available when you're viewing and indexing tables, and let you, well, limit what you view or index. I especially like them when I'm poking around through my files, playing mental "what-if" games. Darn it, they're just kind of fun.

Like all fun and useful things, filters have their drawbacks. The biggest one is that FoxPro for Windows doesn't remind you when a filter is active; it just assumes that since you set it up, you know it's there. Silly program — of *course* you forget about these things (at least I do).

It gets really frustrating when you're viewing a table with a filter and suddenly decide to enter a new record. If your record doesn't "pass" the filter, it suddenly vanishes — poof! Talk about a disconcerting experience.

When you first receive your copy of FoxPro for Windows, take a minute to sit down with the box and talk to it about your work habits. Be sure to take the cellophane off, though; otherwise, it can't hear you. It's an experimental approach, but perhaps this simple gesture will foster better human-software relations and make your time working together a little better. It also gives people around the office something interesting to talk about.

# *Building the Filter*

Assembling a filter isn't too big a deal. Here's how:

1. **Make sure that your table is open for use.**

   This is important, because otherwise you won't get far. In fact, you probably won't get anywhere at all.

2. **Select Database⇨Setup. The Setup dialog box pops up.**

3. **At the bottom left side of the box, click the Filter Data button. The Expression Builder appears.**

   If the table already *has* a filter, it appears in the box next to the button. Odds are, though, that the box is empty right now.

   If, perchance, there *is* a filter in that box, then the filter also appears in the SET FILTER Expression box of the Expression Builder. Smile at it, wave to it, and then press Del to be done with it.

4. **Like all your other forays into expression building, begin by double-clicking a field in the Fields box.**

   If FoxPro for Windows heard you, the field name pops into the SET FILTER Expression box. If it doesn't, try double-clicking once more — and do it louder.

5. **Type an equals, greater than, or other sign after the field name to continue the expression.**

You can use about any sign (techie term: *operator*) from Mr. Boole's Amazing School of Logic in Chapter 30 in your expression. Zodiac signs do not work except in California, Oregon, and areas designated by the World Center for Such Things as "zones of general mysticality."

6. **Type the example you're comparing with the field. Put quotes around words or ZIP codes.**

Most of the time, you're dealing with character or numeric fields, but occasionally a logical field volunteers for a filter. This kind of field has only two possible values (true or false) and requires some special treatment. Figure 14-1 shows a finished expression for a Logical field. The .T. part is FoxPro's way of saying "true." If you immediately guessed that .F. means "false," you get today's cleverness prize.

See the sidebar for a cool idea about magical, self-updating filters that might change your whole life. Really, they might.

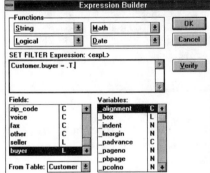

**Figure 14-1:**
A logical
expression
to display
the buyers.

7. **With the expression complete, click OK and return to the Setup dialog box. Your new filter is in residence next to the Filter Data button.**

If the friendly "Boolean expression required" box pops up, double-check your expression. Your expression probably has a quote problem (they're there and shouldn't be, or vice versa).

## Filtering for past-due dollars

Here's a really neat but vaguely technical trick for tracking things by date. The scenario: You're following the company's receivables and need to find out which bills are more than 30 days old. The person leaving the position painfully explains how he manually creates a new filter *each day* to see the appropriate aging records. You smile gracefully, pick up the last box of his stuff, and show him the door, all the time wishing him well in his new position with the Greater Pennsatoola Buggy Whip Council.

Trash all that manual labor — make the filter *automatically* figure out what records to display. Say your table is called Billing and the field you're interested in is Due_Date. Here's the magical filter to change your life:

```
Billing.due_date > DATE()-30
```

The cool part is Date(). This is a *function* (a special FoxPro code word) that knows today's date. Well, it doesn't really know — it cheats and asks your computer. Anyway, by putting this function into your expression, FoxPro always looks 30 days back from whatever today is. If you want to look 45 days into the past, just change the **-30** to **-45**.

So, where do you make this magic? Where all good magic is made: in the Expression Builder. Select the field just like you normally do, but then type the **> DATE( )-30** part after it. Don't forget the parentheses; otherwise, FoxPro has a conniption. One more thing: There's no space between the parentheses, even if it looks funny without one. If you want to make magic every day, save your filter as a View file (the "Saving It with a View" section tells you how).

---

8. **Click OK again to close Setup. To see your filter in action, view your table in Browse or Change mode.**

   Only records that pass the filter's test appear in the View. It's almost too cool.

   If the filter isn't working correctly, consider the records that shouldn't show up but stubbornly appear. Is there something obvious about them, like they're from the same date or have another value in common? Usually, problems stem from a filter set for "greater than" when you meant "greater than or equal to," or from some other "logic" problem. If you can't discern any under-the-weather logic, call in the FoxPro Geniuses and feed them well.

# *Saving It with a View*

Now that you invested all that time creating a filter, here's some good news: As soon as you close the table, FoxPro's going to forget that the filter ever existed. Rats.

Fortunately, FoxPro for Windows has an easy, although not obvious, way to save your work. Through clever manipulation of the View dialog box and the File⇨Save As command, you can create a View file. This file is like an operational picture of FoxPro: It remembers which files are open, what workspace each file is in, any relationships between the files, and (the reason I bring this up at all) the current filter for each file. When you open the View file later, FoxPro for Windows restores all the settings just like they were. This is a serious time saver.

Creating and using View files isn't difficult at all. Look at the "Views Make Linked Life Easy" section of Chapter 12 for all the details. You won't be sorry.

# Filters and Indexes

Filters add a new dimension to an index's natural power, giving an index the capability not only to organize but also to control the data you see. Talk about a flexible tool — a filtered index is really a pretty cool thing.

Filtered indexes have 70% less tar than regular indexes.

An index filter is just like a regular table filter. Here's the lowdown on creating one:

1. **I know you're getting tired of me saying this, but make sure that your table is open for use.**

2. **Select Database⇨Setup to open the Setup dialog box.**

3. **In the Indexes box, click the index that's getting a new filter, and then click Modify. The Index dialog box appears. If you're creating a new index, click Add, and then click New when the Open dialog box pops up.**

    You can double-click the index name and go directly to the Index dialog box without using the Modify button — it's a shortcut.

4. **If this is a new index, select the index key, tag name, and all those other fun index things. If you're modifying an existing index, go on to the next step.**

    Refer to Chapter 11 for all that detailed build-a-successful-index-in-your-spare-time stuff.

5. **Click the Index Filter button. The Expression Builder appears.**

    If there's currently a filter on this index, it's in the not-quite-big-enough box next to the Index Filter button. It makes another appearance in the Expression Builder's FOR Clause box. To get rid of it, press Del after the Expression Builder pops up.

**6. Create your filter expression.**

This process is just like creating a regular table filter. For the blow-by-blow process, see Steps 4-7 in the "Building the Filter" section earlier in this chapter.

**7. Click OK to escape the Expression Builder's clutches. Your new filter appears next to the Index ̲Filter button.**

If it does, that's a good sign. If not, something went wrong. Try creating your filter again. Make sure that you click OK and not Cancel to leave the Expression Builder. You may *feel* like canceling it, but this isn't the time or place for vindictive outbursts.

**8. Click OK again to save your work. If FoxPro asks whether it's okay to overwrite the old index, click ̲Yes.**

You only see this if you're modifying an existing index. Those of you with bouncing baby indexes can skip this step entirely — you have enough on your hands (and it looks gooey — eeew!).

**9. One more OK button to freedom — click OK in the Setup dialog box, and you're finished.**

Congratulations — your index is hereby filtered.

# Chapter 15

# RQBE 101: Queries for People with Work to Do

*W*elcome to the Big Kahuna of FoxPro for Windows searching. It doesn't get bigger than this; it doesn't get faster than this. And some people don't ever get this. That's why I dedicated four chapters to the art and power of the FoxPro query. You, I promise, won't be one of the lost souls for whom querying is forever locked in a misty shroud.

This chapter gives you the overview and gets you started. Chapter 16 helps you fiddle with the knobs and buttons as you get into some truly cool topics. Chapter 17 takes off FoxPro's socks and teaches it some counting. Chapter 18 tells you how to use the neato new Query Winzards.

## *What's a Query?*

*Query* is the puffed-up computerese term for "question." When you query a table, you're asking a question about the data in that table. Queries are very powerful tools, giving you a fast and flexible way to examine your data. You can even tell a query to create a report or new table for its output (but more on that later).

FoxPro for Windows queries have a formal name: Relational Query-by-Example. Worse yet, they have a formal acronym worthy of such a name: RQBE. FoxPro uses "query" and "RQBE" interchangeably, so don't get too hung up on one or the other. I like to call them queries, so that's the term you find in this book.

Queries make their biggest impact with large tables and complicated questions. Because you can save a query and use it repeatedly, they're great for on-going analysis or regular processing tasks. I feel like I'm gushing about them, but they're really *that* cool.

# When a Query Is Better than Locate, Find, or Seek

As you've no doubt found out by now, queries aren't the only search-the-data game in town. Other tools, like Locate, Find, and Seek (filters, too, for that matter), want to put in their two cents as well. I'm not out to sell you on one over another — I want you to have the right tool for the right job at the right time.

Locate, Find, and Seek work well when you're looking for something in one or two records. Find is particularly flexible, because you don't need to tell it anything except what you're looking for. Locate lets you peek inside memo fields, something the others don't do at all. Seek is great for big, indexed tables because it's so fast.

If you need more information, Chapter 13 has the lowdown on Locate, Seek, and Find.

All three share one drawback, though: You can't look at a *group* of records; you can only see things one at a time. That's where queries come into play.

Queries have a communal approach to searching. Instead of seeing the *current* match, a query shows you *all* the matches at once. Look at them all, compare them all, analyze them all — and do it all in one step. Queries help you find trends and similarities, because you see a group instead of a record, the forest instead of the trees.

# Building a Basic Query

Here's how to build your basic FoxPro for Windows query:

**1. Write down your goal for the query — what you want it to show you.**

Time for the "clean sheet of paper" routine again. It may seem embarrassing or silly, but this step makes a lot of difference. Thinking through your goal makes creating the query that much easier. I'm serious — I do this step myself.

**2. Open the table you want to query and make sure that it's active.**

If the table's already open, that's fine. Otherwise, open the little thing by selecting File⇨Open, or use the Open button in the View dialog box (select Window⇨View).

To make sure that it's active, open the View dialog box and click the table's name in the Work Areas box. The table name is now highlighted — it's the active table. You can close the View dialog box if you want, but there's no rush. You don't have to open the table in a Browse or Change window, either. Just making it the active table is enough.

**3. Select File⇨New⇨Query and click the New button. A fresh, clean, and untitled RQBE dialog box pops into place.**

Figure 15-1 shows a plain RQBE dialog box, ready for the adventure of its life (boy, does it have a dull life if this is adventure).

Don't be bullied into techno-timidity by the controls and contraptions — they're painlessly covered in Chapter 16. Ignore them, and they won't bother you.

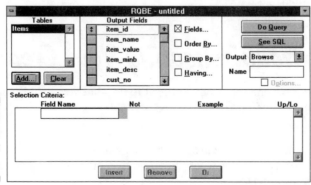

**Figure 15-1:**
A ready and able query dialog box.

4. **Click in the box under Field Name, and a drop-down list of (amazingly enough) field names appears. Click the field for the interrogation and the list rolls back up.**

   • Use the scroll bar to move down the list if there are more fields than window space. If you click the wrong one, click the name, and the list pops back into place. Then try, try again.

   • The Not button and the box next to it are explained in Chapter 16.

5. **After you select a field, two boxes and two buttons appear on the line. Of these new arrivals, you're interested in the Example box. Click there (or move into it with the Tab key) and type what you're looking for.**

   Unlike the Expression Builder, you don't have to worry about quotation marks or the like here. Type the text, number, or date you're looking for, and leave the quoting to someone else.

   If you're querying with a Logical field, type **.T.** for true and **.F.** for false, just like you did with the Expression Builder. It's nice to know that some things never change.

6. **To make FoxPro for Windows ignore case during the query, click the Up/Lo button.**

   As you probably guessed, Up/Lo has no effect if you're not querying a Character type field.

7. **Click Do Query to reap your data harvest.**

   Your query is off and running — hopefully. Continue to the next section if everything works but not the way you anticipated.

   If FoxPro gives you an Operator/Operand Type Mismatch error, look at your example. Make sure that it's *really* the kind of data that's in the field you selected. If you clicked the wrong field by accident, click it again and pick another.

# Testing and Troubleshooting Your Creation

Creating a query is one thing, but getting it to do what you want is sometimes another. Despite your best efforts, things sometimes go wrong. Such is the way of life.

If FoxPro for Windows gives you a specific error (like Invalid Date), so much the better. At least you know what the program is upset about. Look into it and give its repair your best shot.

## If you liked the RQBE, you'll love the SQL

When you create a query with the RQBE dialog box, FoxPro for Windows converts all the pointing, clicking, and typing into a special database language called *Structured Query Language,* or SQL. Like many modern acronyms, it has a pronunciation, just like a real word: sequel.

Believe it or not, people spend money and time learning to do nothing but write queries in SQL.

All you have to do is fill out an on-screen form, and FoxPro for Windows does the dirty work. Why doesn't everybody do it the easy way? In the immortal words of whoever writes T-shirt sayings: "It's a programmer thing. You wouldn't understand." Here's to hoping you and I never do.

But what if FoxPro didn't seem perturbed about the query, but gives you an answer that makes no sense? Take another look at the query you created. Better yet, ask someone else at your own experience level to look at it and tell you what the query is supposed to do. Having another pair of eyes check things out works miracles.

If the query passes inspection and still gives flaky results, try building a new query from scratch — perhaps you're dealing with what we in the business call a "spurious anomaly" (or, in the vernacular, a "flaky problem"). If not even a complete rebuild changes the query's performance, it's time for some serious help. Haul out that package of peanut butter Easter eggs (or the home-baked double fudge brownies) and call in the guru.

# *Saving It when You're Finished*

So, the gauntlet is behind you and the query works. Great! Save that puppy before it's too late:

1. **Click anywhere on the RQBE dialog box to make it the current window, and then select File⇨Save As to open the Save As dialog box.**

   You must use a mouse for this maneuver. Pressing Alt+F for the File menu unexpectedly gets you into the RQBE Select Fields dialog box (which isn't quite what you had in mind).

2. **In the Save Document As box, type a name for the query file.**

   Query files have the same naming rules as everything else: up to eight characters. Letters, numbers, and underscores are okay; spaces definitely are *not* to be included.

3. **If necessary, change the directory or disk drive, or both.**

4. **Click Save to create the query file.**

   FoxPro query files have a .QPR extension.

# Reusing It in the Future

The whole point of saving the query is that you can use it again. Here's how:

1. **Select File⇨Open. The Open dialog box appears.**

   You don't even need to open the file (or files) you're querying — FoxPro for Windows sets up everything it needs when you open the query file.

2. **Click in the List Files of Type box to drop down the list. Scroll through it to Query and then click it. The list rolls back up like a window shade.**

3. **From the large box on the left side of the dialog box, click the name of your query, and then click Open.**

   If it's not listed, check the disk drive and path settings — it always pays to look in the right place.

4. **The disk drive light flickers for a moment, and then your query appears front and center, ready to run again.**

# Making Changes without Losing the Original

After working with queries for a while, you may have one that *almost* works for a new project, but needs some minor tweaks to be perfect. You don't want to lose the original though, because it's still near and dear to your job. Ah, dilemmas, sweet dilemmas.

---

# A shameless plea for documentation

I know you can't see me right now, but I'm down on my hands and knees, pleading with big mournful eyes and tightly clasped hands: "Please, oh please, write some notes about your queries. The world will be a better place if you do."

I'm not talking about extravagant gothic missives — merely a few words about what you're doing and why you're doing it. FoxPro for Windows even gives you a really easy way to do it. When you're building the query, select RQBE⇨Comments, click in the Comment box, and start typing. Type and type and type your

heart out. The more explanation, the merrier the person who reads it — that's my motto. When you're finished, click OK. When you save the query, your comments are recorded for posterity as well.

So please, pretty please with sugar and strawberries and whipped cream with a big juicy cherry on top — please use FoxPro's comments option to explain your queries. Someday in the future, those who follow after you (or, perhaps, you yourself) will be grateful.

---

This one has an easy answer: Work on a copy of the original query, giving the copy a different name. Open the query as you normally do, but turn right around and select File⇨Save As. The Save As dialog box appears. The query's current name appears in the Save Document As box, but when you start typing, the new name replaces it. When the name is complete, click Save. Now you have a fresh copy of the query, ready for fine-tuning. Tune it 'til you drop, safe in the knowledge that your original is untouched.

Remember to save the changes to the new query when you're finished.

## Chapter 16

# RQBE 205: The Stuff that Makes Queries Cool

*T*his chapter is the black sunglasses and '57 Chevy convertible for your query — it's the stuff that turns it from a mere query into BQOC (big query on computer). This stuff is *really* cool. Slip on those shades, tilt the ergonomic chair all the way back, and put on some jazz. Be cool and get into what queries can do.

The cool stuff in this chapter emanates from the query dialog box. If you're new to queries, flip back a chapter and read up on them before attempting to get truly cool.

## Picking and Choosing Some Fields

You don't always want *every* field in response to your query. Most of the time, you need a few particular fields, but that's all. To accommodate this requirement, FoxPro for Windows provides the Fields option in the query dialog box. It lets you choose just the fields you're interested in and leave the others behind.

1. **Click the Fields checkbox or select RQBE⇨Fields to see the RQBE Select Fields dialog box.**

   The Fields box is already checked (has an X in it), but that's okay — click it anyway. After the RQBE Select Fields dialog box pops up, you won't care how you got there.

- If you're using the keyboard equivalents, press Alt+F instead of trying to get into the RQBE menu with Alt+Q. The RQBE dialog box mistakenly thinks that Alt+Q means "run the query," not "let me into the RQBE menu, darn it."

- When it first appears, the Select Fields dialog box looks kind of funny: All the field names in the Table Fields box are grayed, as are most of the buttons. Geez, doesn't anything work in this box?

- The Selected Output box lists all the table's fields. That's because FoxPro for Windows assumes that you want every single field in your output.

2. **The easiest, quickest, and cleanest way to begin is by clicking Remove All to empty out the Selected Output box.**

   One quick click, and all the fields jump back to the Table Fields box. What could be easier?

   - Just because it's easy doesn't mean it's best for everyone. If you only want to remove a few fields from the output list, skip ahead to Step 4. Completely rebuilding the list when you want to make some small changes is like tearing down the house so you can put in new carpet. I tried that and it turned out to be a really bad idea.

   - Notice that the All button is alive now and Remove All is dormant. All is the opposite of Remove All, but you probably figured that out on your own.

3. **To include a field in your query's output, click its name, and then click Move. The field name appears in the Selected Output box; its corresponding entry in Table Fields withers and turns gray.**

   Double-clicking the field name moves it to Selected Output in one step.

   If you want the fields to come out of the query in a particular order, just pick them in that order from the Table Fields box. Another way to accomplish the same end is in the next section under "Changing the field order." Both techniques do the same thing; they just approach it differently.

4. **If you accidentally move the wrong field, click the errant field in the Select Output box and then click Remove.**

   The field leaps back into the Table Fields box with the innocent exuberance of a swan-diving lemming.

5. **To change the field order by hand (in case Step 3's suggestion about selecting the fields in order doesn't work for you), click and hold down the mouse button on the gray button next to the field name in the Selected Output box.**

   The mouse pointer becomes a two-headed arrow to reinforce that you're on the right track. With the mouse button down, drag the field to its new position. Release the mouse button when the field is in place.

6. **If you don't want duplicate records in your answer, click the No Dupli-cates checkbox.**

   Turning on this option only prevents *exact* duplicates — if two records are *mostly* alike, both still appear. They have to be clones before No Duplicates prevents one from showing.

7. **When you've exhausted the options and want to leave, click OK to return to your query.**

   You're ready to finish building the query and give it a go.

# Putting Your Answers in Order

There's nothing in this world worse than a disorderly query response: fields here and there, records all jumbled — what a mess. FoxPro for Windows likes such things less than you do, so it gives you two ways to get your answers under control: by changing the order of the fields in your output and by sorting the records. The following sections explain each option.

## Changing the field order

Just because your table has its fields in a certain order doesn't mean they're stuck that way forever. Put them in any order you want with some skillful clicking and dragging in the Output Fields box. Here's what to do:

1. **Decide in what order you want the fields in your query's output.**

   This is a good paper and pencil step, although just pausing to think about it will do for a start.

2. **Find the field you want to move in the Output Fields box of the query window. Click and hold down the mouse button on the blank gray button to the left of the field name.**

   Your mouse pointer changes into a double-headed arrow.

   The left part of Figure 16-1 shows the item description field, item_desc, ready for relocation. Notice that it has a gray dotted border, but item_id, which isn't doing anything but sitting there, is nicely highlighted.

   The field name won't necessarily be highlighted when you click the gray button. It's moving, so it gets a dotted gray border but nothing fancier than that.

3. **Move the field to its new location. When you're there, let up on the mouse button. The field drops gingerly into place.**

   The item_desc field comes in for a three-point landing in the right portion of Figure 16-1. Remember to wait until the mouse comes to a full and complete halt before letting up on the mouse button. Thanks, and have a great day with FoxPro!

   If you put it in the wrong place, pick it back up and move it again.

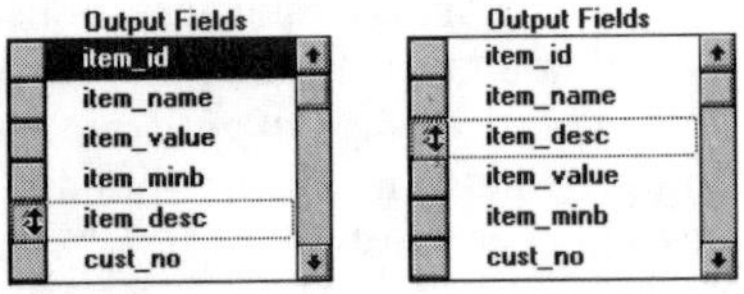

**Figure 16-1:**
In part (a), the item_desc field is ready to go. In part (b), item_desc has arrived at its new home.

## Changing the record order

It's really a pain when you work hard for an answer, but the records come out in some seemingly random order that only FoxPro comprehends. You don't have to stand for it — sort those records with the Order By option. The steps are right here:

1. **Think about how you want your query output sorted. Decide which fields are required and remember their names.**

   Most of the time, you can sort with one field. If more than one record has the same value in that field (multiple customers in the same ZIP code, for example), pick a second field to break ties.

   If you're getting in the pencil-and-paper habit (which is good), write down the field to sort with. Keep it handy for Step 3.

2. **Click the Order By checkbox. The RQBE Order By dialog box appears.**

3. **In the Selected Output box, double-click the field name you decided on in Step 1. The field name leaps into the Ordering Criteria box.**

   If you're using two or more fields, repeat this step for each one.

   If you double-click the wrong field, double-click its name under Ordering Criteria, and it does a double-twist reverse leap back to Selected Output. It isn't necessary to clap, although appreciative nodding is always a good idea.

4. **Click OK when you're finished. The RQBE Order By dialog box returns from whence it came.**

# Doing the "Not" Thing

Each query line includes — at no extra charge — a small gray button under the heading "Not." Clicking this button turns your query around 180 degrees and makes it mean the opposite of what it says. If a query looks for all customers in South Dakota, clicking Not makes it find all customers who *aren't* in South Dakota. Truly amazing.

Using Not is too easy: Click the button, and a check mark appears. That means Not is turned on. Click it again to turn it off. Click it repeatedly for a disco strobe effect (this works best with the room lights dim).

# Comparisons for the Detail Oriented

By default, FoxPro for Windows uses "Like" to compare the table's fields with your example. Most of the time, it's a good idea to leave it that way.

There are times when you need a different comparison, though, so here's the scoop on some of your other choices:

Exactly Like     The field has to *exactly* match the example — no variations allowed.

More Than        The field must be bigger than the example.

Less Than        The field must be smaller than the example.

To simulate a "more than or equal to" condition, choose Less Than and click the Not button. Click More Than and the Not button to create a "less than or equal to" comparison.

# Output Any Way You Like It

Working with a query is like ordering from room service at a fine hotel. All you do is ask, and someone delivers your order right to your door, just the way you want it, complete with a flower. Ah, good service is a grand thing.

You can get that kind of service from your query, too. Normally, a query's answers come up in a Browse window, but if you ask nicely, the query can put them in a table, report, or graph instead. Ring for service by picking an option from the Output box on the right side of the query window:

1. **Click the down arrow next to the Output box. The list steward drops down a list of today's options from the query cellar.**

   Red wine goes with beef; white with chicken or fish. The rules for rosé are nebulous, so avoid it on dates.

2. **Click your selection.**

   ✔ Browse is the default. It's good for most purposes.

   ✔ Report/Label sends the answers directly into a report. See Chapter 20 for more about this.

   ✔ Table/DBF creates a table for your answers. If you choose this, FoxPro for Windows presents you with a Save As dialog box. Type a name for the table in the Table/DBF box. Change directories or disk drives if necessary. Click OK when you're finished.

   ✔ Graph makes pretty pictures from your answers. Chapter 22 gives you the details.

   ✔ Pay no attention to the Cursor option. It has deep technical significance that's beyond the comprehension of our mortal minds. Leave it to the techno-weenie acolytes of the Secret Order of Myopia.

# Chapter 17

# RQBE 310: Teaching Queries to Count

- - - - - - - - - - - - - - - - - - - - - - - - - - - - - - - - - - - - - - - - - - - - - - - -

## In This Chapter

▶ Summaries for every season

▶ Creating one big summary

▶ Summarizing with a group

- - - - - - - - - - - - - - - - - - - - - - - - - - - - - - - - - - - - - - - - - - - - - - - -

*O*ne of my favorite comedy routines ponders how things would be different today if humans had 8 fingers instead of 10. People would count by 8s, use a metric system based on 8s, and laugh at math teachers as they tried to explain base 10. *Count by 10s? How ridiculous! Another octoliter of coffee, anyone?*

Physical revisionism aside, most computers these days can count and cipher. It's something they're even good at. They never become bored, rarely lose their place, and (I think) even *enjoy* the whole thing. Sick, isn't it? As long as they're happy, let them do their thing — that's what I always say.

FoxPro for Windows does cool counting things with special query fields called *summaries.* This chapter explains the whats and where-to-fors of the process for you. Be careful, though — you may start to enjoy it. And that's really sick.

## Summaries for Every Season

For everything, there is a summary; and for every summary, a season. Okay, I'm feeling a little philosophical, but summaries are really neat tools. Your computer counts, adds, or averages thousands of records in less time than it takes you to get far enough along to lose your place respectably. If you're interested in simplifying your life, this is useful stuff.

FoxPro has five different query summaries. The first two meet most people's needs, but the others certainly have their moments:

| | |
|---|---|
| SUM | Totals numbers in a field |
| AVG | Averages numbers in a field |
| COUNT | Counts the number of entries |
| MIN | Finds the smallest entry |
| MAX | Finds the largest entry |

AVG and SUM only work with numbers — you cannot SUM a bunch of ZIP codes or AVG some addresses. No summary function works with memo fields — what a surprise.

## *Creating One Big Summary*

Much of the time, you want a summary of all the values in a particular field. This is the easiest one to make. Here's how it's done:

1. **Create a new, blank query for your table.**

   If you need a reminder, check out "Building a Basic Query" in Chapter 15.

2. **Click the Fields checkbox. The cleverly named RQBE Select Fields dialog box appears.**

3. **Click the Remove All button to clear everything from the Selected Output box.**

   This kind of summary wants to be alone. The group summaries later in the chapter work and play well with others.

4. **Click the down arrow in the Functions box. The functions list drops down.**

5. **Click the summary function that tickles your fancy (usually SUM or AVG). When you do, the list of available fields appears.**

   Some of the fields may be grayed like those in Figure 17-1. That's okay — it's even good. FoxPro only lets you pick a field that works with the summary you selected. Everything that won't work is grayed so that you can't choose it by accident.

6. **Click the field to summarize it. When you do, the wimpy lists disappear (thank goodness), and the muscular young summary calculation flexes for you in the Functions/Expressions box.**

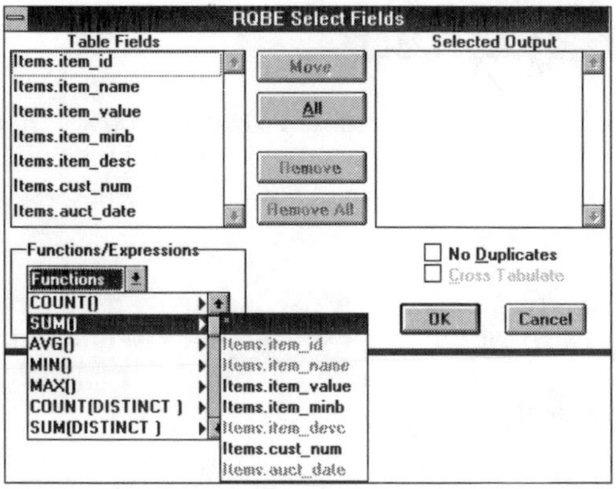

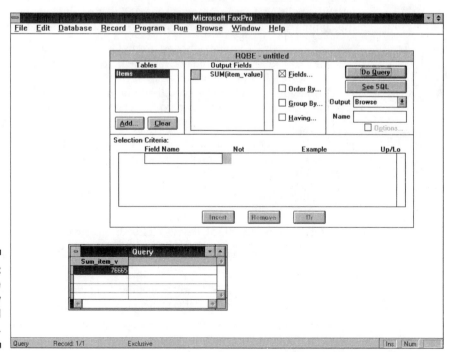

**Figure 17-1:** Because the SUM function only works with numbers, all the non-number fields are grayed.

7. **You're almost finished. Click Move to install your summary in the Selected Output box. Click OK to get back to the query dialog box.**

The summary is ready to run, so make any other adjustments and click Do Query to make the whole thing happen. Figure 17-2 shows the finished query dialog box and a window with the results. FoxPro isn't particularly creative, so it named the answer field after the summary that created it. Unfortunately, it ran out of letters a little too soon.

**Figure 17-2:** Here's the summary query and the answer.

# Summarizing with a Group

Knowing the total number of products rusting in the warehouse *is* helpful, but sometimes more information is necessary. Perhaps it would be nice to see the quantities by product type or supplier — then you'd know what's selling, what isn't, and possibly whom to blame for the mess.

This is called a *group summary*. You set it up just like an overall summary, but include a *group field* so FoxPro for Windows knows what to summarize on. FoxPro calculates a summary for each unique value in the group field. Pretty slick, eh? Here's the play-by-play:

1. **Create a new query, click the Fields checkbox, and then click Remove All.**

   These are the same steps that kick off "Creating One Big Summary." If you want them in more detail (although not *much* more), refer to the preceding section.

2. **In the Table Fields box, click the field you want to group by, and then click Move to propel it over to Selected Output.**

   You need something to tell you which summary value belongs to which group; otherwise, you have a list of numbers with no meaning (and the last thing you want to do is add something meaningless to the world — that's what the politicians are supposed to do). The group field appears next to the summary in your output and gives it the much-needed identification.

   Nothing says you can have only one group field. If there are more fields you want to include, by all means, include them. To do that, just repeat this step for each group field you want in the query output. The results you get defy simple explanation — you'd end up more confused than I am. Try grouping with one field, and then go back to the same query and use two.

3. **Create your summary function by clicking the down arrow in the Functions box, clicking a function, and clicking the field to summarize. A final click on the Move button puts your summary in the Selected Output box.**

   Nothing new here, either. You're creating a normal summary, same as before. No magic yet.

4. **Click OK to close the RQBE Select Fields dialog box.**

5. **Click the Group By checkbox. The RQBE Group By dialog box pops proudly into place.**

   Finally — the magic begins! Watch carefully, because the whole trick is pretty short and you'll miss it if you aren't paying attention.

TIP

If you like this trick and want to see more, I'm available for weddings and bar mitzvahs.

6. **Find the name of the group field (the same one you used in Step 2) and click it. Click Move to put it in the Group By Fields box.**

   Figure 17-3 has a group based on the customer number field in the Items table. In the query dialog box, customer number and the item value summary are the only output fields. In the query's Output Fields box, you see the results of Steps 2-4; customer number and the item value summary are ready for output.

7. **Click OK to close the RQBE Group By dialog box. Click Do Query to try out your creation.**

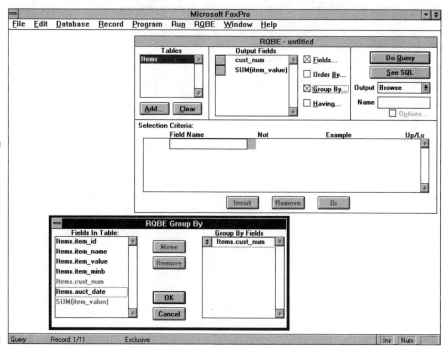

**Figure 17-3:**
With a wave of my mouse (and a click on the Move button), the customer number field jumps into the Group By Fields box.

## Multiple questions require multiple summaries

Sometimes, you want to know the total number of rusty things *and* their total dollar value (or things like that). There's nothing that says you're stuck with just a single question when you create a summary. Actually, you can include as many summaries as you want.

To create more than one summary, just repeat the steps you used to make the first one. FoxPro isn't too picky about what goes in a query's output. In fact, you could make a query that *only* developed summaries. Why you'd do it is a different question, but that's not important right now. The important thing to remember is that if you *need* multiple summaries from the same query, FoxPro for Windows can give them to you. So there.

# Chapter 18

# RQBE 550: Queries at the Wave of a Wand

· · · · · · · · · · · · · · · · · · · · · · · · · · · · · · · · · · · · · · · · · · ·

## In This Chapter

▶ FoxPro's answer to the automatic breadmaker

▶ Building queries with the SQL Query Wizard

▶ Using your Wizard-built query in the real world

▶ SQL's mysterious sister: the Updatable Query Wizard

· · · · · · · · · · · · · · · · · · · · · · · · · · · · · · · · · · · · · · · · · · ·

$S$omewhere inside Microsoft last year, an overworked software engineer whispered to a coworker. "I don't care *what* they say — making queries is hard," he said. "Heretic!" yelled the other. "Eddie's spreading truthful observations about perceived ease-of-use problems with FoxPro's RQBE subsystem. And I heard him, too." Naturally, common visitors aren't allowed back into the engineering pens, so the conversation can't really be documented.

However, you can deduce that other people noticed how frustrating it was to build queries. In its latest incarnation, FoxPro includes two automated Wizards that do the work *for* you. This chapter focuses most of its attention on one of them, the SQL Query Wizard, because that's the most generally useful one.

# FoxPro's Answer to the Automatic Breadmaker

The SQL Query Wizard builds queries the way an automatic breadmaker bakes bread: They both make your job easier, but neither gives results as good as when you did things the hard way. "It's the taste of elbow grease," my grandmother used to say. What a pleasant culinary thought.

Getting out of the kitchen and back to the magical software, the SQL Query Wizard leads you through the basics (and some of the advanced-ics) of building a query. It handles multiple tables, record grouping, and even summary expressions (whoa!). The Wizard creates a standard query file, which you can change with the RQBE tools. The Catalog Manager lets you *modify* queries with the Wizard as well (provided you built them there in the first place).

✔ The Wizard is mainly a query-building tool. It can handle some maintenance work, but that's really not its forte.

✔ After you change a Wizard-built query with the RQBE tool, the Wizard disowns the query and won't edit it any more. The Wizard is very touchy about things like that.

✔ You may be wondering (and rightfully so) precisely what a *summary expression* is. A summary expression lets your query count things in a table. Summaries come in all shapes and sizes, but the most common ones find the biggest, smallest, or total of something. For the whole story, see Chapter 17, "RQBE 310: Teaching Queries to Count."

✔ For more about queries and the old-fashioned RQBE tools in general, see Chapters 15, 16, and 17. Information about the Catalog Manager is lounging in Chapter 24.

✔ The SQL Query Wizard isn't alone in the world — the Updatable Query Wizard lives in the same menu. It's rather scandalous, but life seems to be going that way these days. To find out more about this sordid arrangement, skip ahead to "SQL's Mysterious Sister: The Updatable Query Wizard," later in this chapter.

# Building Queries with the SQL Query Wizard

Time to get on with things. Here's how to use the SQL Query Wizard to make the query your tables always yearned for. Don't fret about the number of steps — it's one of those things that's quicker to do than to explain.

1. **Figure out what your query is supposed to do.**

   Write down — or at least *think* about — your goals for this informational venture. It often helps to know where you're going, or so my wife tells me whenever we set out on a trip.

   • Determine which table (or tables) is required and note where to find it (them).

- Consider how you want your information arranged. Does it need to be in a particular order? Should like items be grouped together? Do you want the records sorted in a particular way? Will Gina marry Morgan despite the fact that she's engaged to Noriyuki Yamashita, the coma-stricken sumo wrestler who may or may not survive the next round of plot complications? Who writes stuff like this?

- You can open the tables for your query if you want to, but it's not required. The Wizard has a special button for that very task.

2. **Start the SQL Query Wizard by selecting Run⇨Wizard⇨Query. Make sure that the SQL Query Wizard is highlighted in the Select a Wizard list, and then click Next.**

3. **If your table is already open, choose it for the query by double-clicking its name in the Available Tables list. If the table isn't on the list, click Open Table and hassle with the Open dialog box to get it there. When you're finally finished, click Next.**

Figure 18-1 shows two tables selected for the query. In the example, Customer is the parent table, so it was selected first. Items is the child, thus it's after Customer in the list.

- To make a query with two (or more) linked tables, choose the parent table first, and then choose the child (or children). When all the tables are chosen, click Finish (or Finish).

- If you're linking tables (no more parenthetical remarks, I promise), make sure that you know which fields link the tables. If you don't know, find out fast, because that's FoxPro's next question when you click Finish.

- For help on linking tables, see Chapter 19.

- The Open Table button brings up a standard FoxPro open-a-file-from-the-disk-drive dialog box. If those are still giving you trouble, refer to Chapter 1 for some help.

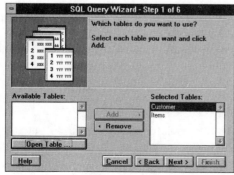

**Figure 18-1:** When you're querying linked tables, it's parent first, then child.

4. **For you linked-table folks in the audience, the Query Wizard wants to know which field links your tables together. Select the field from both the Parent Table and Child Table pull-down lists. Click Add to cement the link, and then click Next to continue.**

If there's a field with the same name and type in both tables, FoxPro assumes that's the linking field and suggests it when the dialog box appears, just as in Figure 18-2.

Skip this step if you're only querying one table.

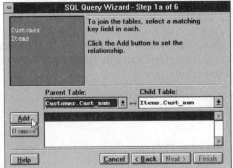

**Figure 18-2:**
FoxPro
guessed the
right linking
field, so it's
Add'n time.

5. **Time to choose fields for the query's output. Scroll through the Available Fields list and double-click the ones to include. When you're all clicked out, summon up enough energy for one more click — right on the Next button.**

The fields end up in the order you choose them, so use that to your advantage. Pick them in whatever tortured sequence you deem necessary, and rest assured that they'll always come out that way in the output.

This is where you create a summary expression, if you want one. Click the Expression button to start the process. When the Enter an Expression dialog box appears, click the down arrow in the Math box and scroll down the list until you find the summary you want. Click it. FoxPro types it into the Expression box. Next, click the down arrow in the Fields box and, in the same way, pick the field to summarize. Click OK to include the summary in your query.

For a summary of summary how-tos, summarily see Chapter 17.

- Double-click a field in the Selected Fields list to remove it.

- Add All includes all the Available Fields in your output. Remove All hauls out *all* the Selected Fields so that you can start choosing from scratch.

6. **If you want your output grouped by state, ZIP code, customer number, or some other way, choose that field in this dialog box. Click Next to stroll on through the Wizard.**

If you're using a summary expression, you should choose a grouping field. If you don't, FoxPro only gives you *one* summary for everything. If that's what you want, great — but if it's not, choose that grouping field now.

7. **Click Next again.**

This dialog box is a borderline techno-weenie thing. The less time you spend here, the lower your risk of contracting *nerdiosis*. Hurry — while you still have your normalcy.

8. **The Wizard can sort everything in the query's output, provided you tell it what to sort with. Choose a field in this dialog box, and then click Next.**

In Figure 18-3, the Wizard is set to sort the query's output records by customer number. Other common choices are state, ZIP code, or fields like *dollars spent with our company.*

If you want the records sorted from largest to smallest, click the Descending radio button.

**Figure 18-3:**
Choosing
customer
number as
the sort field
was the only
logical thing
I could think
of, so that's
what I did.

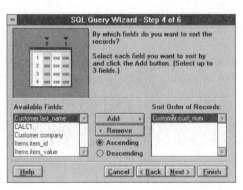

9. **Because you often want to look only at a given group of records (those within a certain state or ZIP code, for example), the Query Wizard lets you limit the records included in the output. You don't *have* to do this, but it's an option.**

Choose the appropriate field (state, ZIP code, or whatever) from the Fields pull-down list, choose a logical operator from the next list, and then type whatever limit you're looking for in the Value box. Click Add to store the whole nasty affair, and then click Next to run away as fast as possible.

- To skip the whole sordid thing and include all the records in your table, leave everything alone and click Next.

- This is *definitely* something that's easier to look at, so Figure 18-4 shows an expression that *only* accepts records for customers living in California. Why California? There must be a reason — let me get back to you on that.

- To test the limit you built, click Preview. FoxPro runs the query and shows off what it found. If this looks *nothing* like what you expected, press Esc, click Remove to kill the limit, and try again.

- You don't have to remember which values to put in quotes — the Wizard takes care of that on its own.

- For help, assistance, and witty conversation about setting up limiting conditions, see Chapter 16.

- I chose California because I have friends there, that's why. I knew I'd remember.

**Figure 18-4:**
The Wizard
put quotes
around CA
for me by
itself.
Wasn't that
nice?

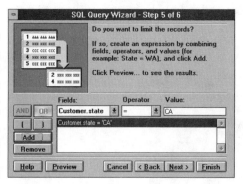

10. **Take a deep breath — you're almost there! Choose a Save option and click Finish. Type a name for the query in the next dialog box, and click Save to complete your quest.**

It's a good idea to click Preview once more before saving the query for posterity. Check the Preview output window carefully — make sure that FoxPro understood everything you said about the query. When you're satisfied, press Esc, make your Save choice, and click Finish.

- If you're tired, worn out, and just want to be done with this whole thing, choose Save Query for Later Use.

- To see your results in Browse mode, choose Save and Run Query.

- For the Grand Presentation of Results, choose Save and Create an AutoReport.
- The SQL Query Wizard saves your hard work and effort in a .QPR file.

# Using Your Wizard-Built Query in the Real World

Now that you've created the monster, what do you do with it? After all, Dracula had London; Frankenstein had a countryside packed with pleasant villages and panicky villagers; you're stuck with a hard drive full of FoxPro tables and a growing population of query files.

There are several options open, depending on what you want to do. You can run the query, open it with the RQBE tools for intense surgery, or modify it with the Query Wizard. The choices aren't endless, but they're better than finding Frankenstein balanced atop your PC one morning.

To run the query and see your answers, select Run⇨Query from the main menu. Double-click the query in the Open dialog box. In a moment or two, FoxPro runs the query and creates a temporary answer table. To see the answers on-screen, select Window⇨View, and look for a work area named Query. When you find it hiding in there, click it, and then click Browse.

If you're *really* feeling surgical, select File⇨Open and choose Query from the pull-down list under List Files of Type. Double-click your query to strap it onto the operating table. Feel free to make changes to your heart's content, but remember that after you save your work, you can't use the Query Wizard to make other changes. Just something to keep in mind.

You can organize, run, and modify queries through the Catalog Manager. See Chapter 24 for the scoop on those options.

# SQL's Mysterious Sister: The Updatable Query Wizard

The Updatable Query Wizard is a *really* new feature of FoxPro for Windows. The old FoxPro had queries, but nothing like this.

The new Wizard runs, works, and acts a lot like its sibling, but with an impor-tant difference: If you change the data in the Updatable Query Wizard's output, FoxPro writes your changes *back to the original tables.* You're editing, for goodness' sake!

The output from normal queries stands on its own — it's not linked to the original at all. You could hack away at all the records in the output table, delete those that displeased you, and rest easy in the knowledge that all the original information was safe and sound in the original tables.

Although it's a powerful feature, I recommend steering clear of it until you're very comfortable with the regular SQL Query Wizard and with building queries by hand with the RQBE tools. This Wizard builds a direct link to your precious data, so go slow and get your favorite guru to help the first time or three.

# Chapter 19

# The Relational Thing:
# Now It's Getting Serious

*E*very relationship gets to what I call the *warning bell* moment. That's the single, unique point in time when someone suddenly thinks, "Gosh, this is getting serious." My own moment hit when I found out that my fiancée purchased the silk for her wedding dress the same day I proposed. Not a problem, you might think, except that I proposed in the evening and she was shopping at noon. *Red Alert! Red Alert!*

Using two tables together qualifies as a "gosh, this is getting serious" moment. It's not difficult (as you find out in this chapter), but it can be scary. If fear wells up inside you, remember these words as you press on: Fear not, jump in, and brush after every meal.

## Adding Another Table to Your Query

There are few things lonelier than a single table in a query. I can't think of what they might be, but that's beside the point. The point is that *you* can fix your table's problem by adding another table to the query. Paired tables are happy tables, so here's how to play Yenta the Query Matchmaker with your data:

**1. Start a new query for your table, regardless of how morose it is.**

At this point, only the table you're starting with needs to be open and active. FoxPro for Windows automatically worries about opening any unopened tables in a later step. After all this time, it's nice to see FoxPro standing up and taking responsibility for something.

2. **In the Query dialog box, click the Add button. To show its appreciation, FoxPro for Windows displays the Open dialog box.**

   The Add button is on the left side of the dialog box in the Tables section. After you find it, stop looking and click before you lose it again.

3. **Scroll through the table list under the reassuring Select a Table: heading until you find the table you're looking for.**

   You can select a different disk drive or directory. Just don't click yourself into electronic oblivion — it's not safe this time of year.

4. **Double-click the table name. The jovial Open dialog box is quickly replaced by the overwrought RQBE Join Condition dialog box.**

5. **If FoxPro for Windows finds a field with the same name in each table, it suggests using that field to connect the tables. If it finds no matches, all the boxes are blank and it's up to you to find the linking fields.**

   Figure 19-1 shows FoxPro all excited because it found an identically named field in each table. It sure doesn't take much to get software all worked up. Being a helpful program, it suggests using the field it found to link the tables. In this case, it's a good suggestion. Don't expect the same level of performance all the time — sometimes it picks a clinker. If the boxes turned up blank, click in the down arrow of the far-right and far-left boxes and pick the linking fields from the drop-down lists.

   - FoxPro's suggestion may or may not be the best way (or even a *possible* way) of linking the tables, but it's usually a place to start. You can change it by clicking in the down arrow and choosing a new field from the list.

   - This is the reason consistent field names are a Good Thing. If you use *cust_num* in one table, use *cust_num* in all of them. FoxPro can't tell that *cust_no* is the same as *cust_num* — it's not that bright (quite an editorial comment, isn't it?). Uniform field names save your time and sanity.

   - The middle box (the one with "Like" in it) contains the logical operator for the link. My advice: Leave it alone. Contact a FoxPro guru if you suddenly experience a burning desire to dink with it.

   - Remember that FoxPro for Windows is case sensitive, so if that might cause you problems, turn on the Ignore Upper/Lower Case checkbox by clicking it.

6. **Click OK to declare the link a "done deal." The query dialog box takes center stage again, but with additions much like those in Figure 19-2.**

**Figure 19-1:**
FoxPro
found the
same field in
both tables.

Both table names are ensconced in the Tables box, and there's a new line in the Selection Criteria box.

- The new line links the tables together. If you change it, you're changing how the link works. I recommend leaving well enough alone.

- If you get this far and suddenly realize you linked the *wrong* table, it's no big deal. Click the erroneous table name in the Tables box, click the Clear button, and then click Yes when FoxPro nervously worries that you've lost your marbles and are headed off on some wild deleting rampage.

- Running your query right now yields some surprising results — none of the fields in the table you just linked bothered to show up in the output. Geez, dress the table up, introduce it around, and it's still uncooperative. If your patience is holding, check out the next section for an easy fix; otherwise, go for a nice long walk and reflect on what life was like before computers drove everyone nuts.

**Figure 19-2:**
The
sideways
double-
headed
arrow
signifies that
this line links
the query's
tables
together.

RQBE - untitled

| Tables | Output Fields | |
|--------|---------------|--|
| Items | item_id | ☒ Fields... |
| Customer | item_name | ☐ Order By... |
| | item_value | |
| | item_minb | ☐ Group By... |
| | item_desc | ☐ Having... |
| | cust_num | |

Do Query
See SQL
Output Browse
Name
☐ Options...

Add... Clear

Selection Criteria:

| | Field Name | Not | Example | Up/Lo |
|--|-----------|-----|---------|-------|
| ↔ | Customer.cust_num | Like | Items.cust_num | |

Insert   Remove   Or

## Fields of a feather link together

Linking two tables is hard enough. Trying to link them together when you're not sure which field to use is *insanity*. That's why it's a good idea (no, a *great* idea) to always name the linking fields identically in your tables.

If one table calls it Cust_No, by golly, any other should too. It's not that I'm against creativity —

heck, some of my closest friends are creative — but rather that I'm for sanity (particularly yours and mine). If the fields have the *exact same name,* FoxPro can find them on its own. It's one less thing you have to think about.

Isn't that worth a little a little standardization?

# Including Fields from Both Tables

Linking the tables together is great, but if you want to see any results from the new table, you're not finished yet. FoxPro for Windows doesn't automatically include any of the new table's fields in the query's output — you have to specifically tell it yourself. Isn't that just like a program?

Luckily (and amazingly), you already know how to do this. You know how, that is, if you read through the "Picking and Choosing Some Fields" section of Chapter 16. Those steps still work perfectly, despite the fact that you're choosing fields from two tables instead of just one.

Most of the time, you want to see everything — all the fields in both tables — so here's how to do that. If you want to be picky and include some of these and some of those, refer to Chapter 16.

1. **From the RQBE Query window, click the Fields checkbox. The RQBE Select Fields dialog box pops up.**

2. **Click the All button.**

   This moves all the fields from the new table into the Selected Output box in one quick step. See, I *told* you it would be easy.

3. **Click OK to save the changes and get back to your query.**

   Now when you run the query, all the fields from both tables show up in your output.

   This is the appropriate time for a big celebratory cheer. Stand up, clear your throat, and bellow loudly a few times. For maximum effect on your career, do this in a crowded office.

# *Summarizing These with Those*

It's pretty amazing, but multiple table summaries work just like single table summaries. They have the same concerns, the same steps, and the same results. This level of consistency is obviously a mistake. Don't worry — I'm sure someone will fix this problem in the next version of the software.

Until then, summarizing fields in different tables really is a snap. Use exactly the same procedure you discovered in Chapter 17's "Summarizing with a Group" section.

- The only difference is that now you see fields from *both* tables instead of only one (and that's not much of a difference).

- Figure 19-3 shows a two-table summary in the making. It includes regular fields from both the Items and Customer tables, plus a summary of the item value field. Not much different from the old single-table summary, is it?

**Figure 19-3:** The more things change, the more they stay the same.

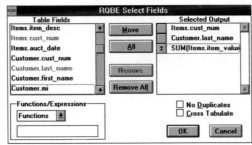

# Part IV

# Presentation Skills for Introverted Databases

The 5th Wave                    By Rich Tennant

All through High School he wouldn't talk to anyone - hardly said a word. Now he's graduating from an Ivy League college with an advanced degree in communications.

# In this part...

*I*f you think speaking in front of a group is bad, just try putting a bunch of raw data up there on the podium. The mind boggles at the mix of blank stares, uncomprehending glances, and excuses to be anywhere else that immediately pour forth from the audience. It's not a pretty sight.

That's precisely why FoxPro for Windows has a whole slew of tools to make your data presentable. And this Part covers them all. Want slick reports with a lot of fonts? No problem. The boss can't read and likes pictures? You're covered. Have a bulk mailing in your future? It's in the bag. You're gonna love this stuff.

# Chapter 20

# Creating Reports the Old-Fashioned Way

*B*uilding reports the way our fore-users did gives FoxPro a certain nostalgic quality. It builds appreciation for the trials they endured to give you the Windows-based life you live today. It kinda brings a tear to my eye (sniff).

This chapter explores FoxPro's reporting features from the perspective of FoxPro for Windows 2.5. The steps in this chapter are completely applicable to the new 2.6 version, but the following chapter (the one about the Report Wizard) is a little *more* applicable. Now that there are Wizards to help, why make magic on your own? I'll tell you why: because, well, it's good for you. Yes, that's it — it's good for you. It gives you the proper underpinnings and a thorough comprehension of what's happening. Yes. Quite so.

It's just so much hot air. I included this for the people who either don't have the new version or really *do* want to do it manually.

Reports in FoxPro are flexible, powerful tools for seeing your data, either on-screen or on paper. This chapter gets you going in the right direction — it even explains using reports with queries to create an all-powerful weapon of cosmic proportion (or at least capable of solving some hairy problems at work).

# *Building a Quick Report*

For once, something in FoxPro for Windows is aptly named — quick reports really *are* quick. And they're easy, so you can make loads of them in no time. Here comes one now. {*Zoom!*} Wow, was that fast or what? Before the rest >*zing!*< of them show up /*zip!*\, here's how to build [*whing!*] one yourself:

1. **Because reports are based on tables, open a table and make it active.**

   It's easiest to do this from the View dialog box. It's available by selecting Window⇨View.

   If you're getting a total brain-blank on this step, check out the "Viewing for Fun and Profit" section in Chapter 7.

2. **Select Database⇨Report from the FoxPro menus. As tangible evidence of your success, the Report dialog box appears.**

   Figure 20-1 captures the moment just before the dialog box bursts onto the scene, complete with the View dialog box looking on from the rear. The Items table is highlighted under Work Areas in the View dialog box, so that's the table this report is based on.

   • There's nothing to this stuff once you know how it's done.

   • The same can be said of skydiving, brain surgery, and piloting the space shuttle.

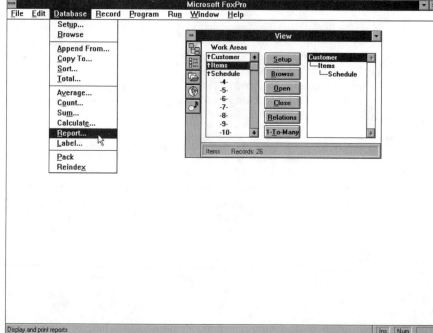

**Figure 20-1:**
On-screen life just before the Report dialog box arrives.

3. **Click the Quick Report button to specify the kind of quick report you want. The Quick Report dialog box pops into place, ready to serve up your choices.**

   Bold, almost brash in its exuberance, it stands tall in Figure 20-2 (at least as tall as a short dialog box can).

**Figure 20-2:**
Your friend and helper, the Quick Report dialog box.

4. **The dialog box is dominated by two (relatively) huge buttons that control field layout. The one on the left, for a Browse mode-style report, is "depressed." Click the other one if you want a Change mode-style report.**

   • The left button builds the report to show your records in a table layout, the way Browse mode looks. This is the best choice most of the time (plus, it's FoxPro's default setting).

   • The right button displays your table as complete records with the fields for each record listed vertically, as in Change mode. This layout is particularly good for tables with a lot of fields, because it's a sure bet that all the fields are going to fit on the page. It takes more paper, though, so don't use it for a large table unless you have a good reason.

5. **If you want to limit the fields included in the report, click the Fields check box to bring out the Field Picker. Make your selections and click OK when you're finished.**

   This is the same Field Picker you've used before, so go to it.

   • Double-click the fields in the All Fields box and watch them hop, skip, and pole vault over to the Selected Fields box.

   • If you click the wrong one, click it under Selected Fields, and then click Remove. To trash everything and start over, click Remove All.

6. **Click OK to close up the Quick Report dialog box and send it packing. Click OK once more to close the Report dialog box.**

   Ignore the other dialog box options. They're fine.

7. **No sooner is the Report dialog box gone than it's replaced by Save As, which would like to know what you intend to call this marvelous report you just spent all that time creating. Type a clever name, select a clever drive and directory (if cleverly necessary), and click Save (or press Enter).**

   - Don't be too clever, or you won't be able to find your report in the future.

   - I often use the first three or four letters of the table name as part of the report name so that I can remember which report belongs to which table.

   - You may get a message worrying that a report with that name already exists. If this is news to you, click No and type in a different name. If you intended all along to trash some old, innocent report file and endow its name on a young usurper, click Yes.

   - It isn't very nice, you know, to trash old, innocent report files just to give their names to young usurpers. It's not very nice at all.

   - FoxPro saves the report in a file with an .FRX extension. If your report contains a memo field, FoxPro also makes a .FRT file to go along with the .FRX file as part of its never-ending quest to fill up all your disk space.

8. **Your report appears on-screen in a cool preview. Click through it with Next, Previous, Zoom In/Out, and Page. When you're finished, click OK to leave.**

   Sometimes, all you *need* is an on-screen display. Even if you're planning to print, it's always a good idea to look through your report on-screen beforehand. It's your one last chance to make sure that everything is okay before killing another tree in the name of the paperless office.

   When your report's ready for the printer, check out the next section.

# Running It Again

Wouldn't it be a pain if you had to do all that every time you wanted a report? You bet it would. I'm sure some programmer considered doing it that way, too.

Programmers should be fed and not heard.

FoxPro for Windows has a quick way to preview or print any report. It's right there on the menu, hiding under the Run option. Here, let me shine the flashlight in there so you can see it:

1. **Select Run⇨Report from the menu. The Open dialog box pops up.**

2. **Click the report you want to run, and then click the Run button. The Run Report dialog box takes its place on-screen.**

   It's not much, but I'll take it instead of asparagus any day. Figure 20-3 shows what there is to see (which, as I established before, isn't much). Note how the Run Report dialog box isn't obnoxious, doesn't have a lot of confusing choices, and helpfully shows the name of the report file you selected.

**Figure 20-3:**
The Run
Report
dialog box.

3. **To print the report, click the To Print radio button. To preview it on-screen, click Preview.**

   This shouldn't surprise anyone (except possibly one of my old college roommates, since he spent most of his time in a state of speed-induced anxiety — anything moving faster than moss startled him), but you cannot print and preview at the same time.

**4. Click Run when you have made your lone choice.**

If you decide this is all a terrible mistake and you really meant to run *to the grocery store,* click Cancel and head out.

Pick up a head of lettuce for me, okay?

# Making Changes

Goodness knows, you're thorough and a good planner, but sometimes things just don't work correctly the first time. That's why FoxPro for Windows lets you change your reports without requiring any kind of monetary offerings to Microsoft or other forms of penance.

To make changes, pretend you're creating a new report and follow along:

**1. Go through Steps 1 and 2 in the "Building a Quick Report" section.**

See, I said you'd pretend to create a new report. But did you believe me? Nooooooooo.

**2. When the Report dialog box appears, click the Form button in the Input section. An Open dialog box, um, opens.**

**3. In that self-same Open dialog box, double-click the name of the report you want to modify. The Open dialog box goes away, leaving you at the Report dialog box from whence you came.**

Figure 20-4 shows the minor change you effected with all that clicking and pointing. The report you're modifying is in the fox — uh, sorry, *box* — next to the Form button.

If you want to set up some criteria for your report, here's the place to act. See the "Filtered Reports Don't Need Queries" section later in the chapter for the details.

**Figure 20-4:**
FoxPro captured not just the report name, but the entire DOS path leading to it as well.

| Report |
|---|
| Input |
| Form...    c:\foxprow\fpwd\itemlist.frx     OK |
| ☒ Restore Environment    Quick Report...     Cancel    More >> |
| Output Location |
| ☐ To Printer |
| ☒ Page Preview |
| ☐ Console On |

**4. Click the Quick Report button and make any changes you desire.**

You can change the field layout or fields included in the report. Heck, live large and change them both.

**5. When you're finished, click OK to close the Quick Report dialog box. Click OK again to make the Report dialog box go away as well.**

**6. FoxPro gets all alarmed because you're about to trash the old report (the one you didn't like and wanted to change). Click Yes to calm its fears and let it know you're still in charge.**

Just so you know precisely what FoxPro looks like when it's in a panic mode, see Figure 20-5. Notice that the mouse pointer is proactively solving the problem.

**7. With its fears allayed, FoxPro gets back to work and displays your new, improved report.**

**Figure 20-5:**
FoxPro for
Windows
desperately
pleads for
guidance.

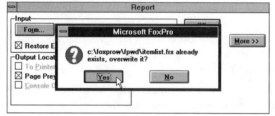

# Using Reports with Queries

So far, FoxPro reports are a solo act. They take material straight from the table and present it in a generally pleasing manner. Not a bad act, if I do say so myself. But you should see 'em in a duo with queries. Now *that's* impressive.

Given the proper instruction, pep talk, and display of force, queries and reports work well together. The query does the legwork of figuring out what records pass the test; the report does its presentation thing. And the crowd goes wild. The best part is that you do it all right from the query through the Output and Options settings. Here's how:

**1. Create a query for your favorite table.**

Just a basic query will do; it doesn't need to be anything fancy. Reports are notoriously easy to get along with, so there's no need to put out the fancy china.

2. **On the right side of the Query dialog box, click the down arrow next to the Output box. A list of choices drops down. Click Report/Label.**

    There's no real positive feedback from this, except that the Name box (the one right under the Output box) completely vanishes and the Options checkbox becomes active. If these are good signs, so be it.

3. **Options is available, so click it. The RQBE Display Options dialog box appears.**

    You were just waiting for it, weren't you? You know the FoxPro motto: "Where there's an option, there's a dialog box."

4. **Click the Report radio button. Several options immediately become available.**

5. **Click the Quick Report checkbox. A somewhat friendly face, the RQBE Quick Report dialog box, pops up.**

6. **Choose the record layout you want (Browse-like or Change-like) and change the name in the Save As box.**

    FoxPro provides your new report with the temporary name *query*. This just won't do — won't do at all. Double-click right on the word *query* and type a proper name to replace it. *Query* of all things. Hmpf. What's the world coming to these days?

7. **By now, your RQBE Display Options dialog box looks much like the one in Figure 20-6, except that the names are different. Ignore the other options for now (and the remainder of the year). Your work here is finished — click OK to retire the dialog box.**

8. **Finish filling everything out and click Do Query. Your data appears in the new report like clockwork.**

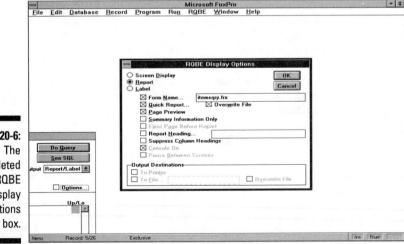

**Figure 20-6:** The completed RQBE Display Options dialog box.

# *Filtered Reports Don't Need Queries*

Reports have a streak of self-sufficiency in them — they'd just as soon work *with* a query as work *without* one. The cool thing is that they actually can.

Secreted away under the More button in the Report dialog box are the tools to give your reports freedom — yes, freedom! — from the imperialist queries that condemn the working classes to perpetual electronic slavery. (ahem) Sorry, I got a little worked up there. Let me try that again without the rhetoric.

When you click the More button in the Report dialog box, lots of confusing options appear. The useful side of the chaos is the new bottom third of the dialog box — it's nothing but a huge Criteria section, just like the one the Locate command uses. By putting a condition in the For area, your report can independently limit the records it includes.

Unfortunately, settings in the Criteria section *are not* saved when you leave the Report dialog box. They're meant to resolve temporary problems, not to be a permanent part of your report's life. Alas, the freedom thing is a farce.

Since the first few steps are repeated several times in earlier sections of the chapter, they're kinda bare-bones. If you're wavering on anything, check out "Building a Quick Report" and "Making Changes" for detailed information.

1. **Open your freedom-loving table and make it active.**

   I recommend using the View dialog box. Select Window⊏>View, and you're there.

2. **Select Database⊏>Report from the FoxPro menus. The Report dialog box, such as it is, appears on-screen.**

3. **Click the Form button in the Input section. The Open dialog box does its thing — it opens.**

4. **Click the More button to expand the dialog box with your other options.**

5. **In the Criteria box, click the For button. The Expression Builder comes to life. Create the expression you need to limit what's included in the report, and then click OK when it's complete.**

   See the information about the Locate command in Chapter 13 for help doing the whole Criteria thing. It explains all the options and safely walks you through your friend and mine, the Expression Builder. It's good stuff.

6. **Carry on with the other "Making Changes" steps (if you have other changes to make).**

   Now your report has its freedom. Figure 20-7 displays the Report dialog box with the finished expression in place.

7. **Click OK when you're finished with the Report dialog box. Your report comes up on-screen, displaying only the records that pass your criteria.**

**Figure 20-7:**
This report
needs no
help to
include only
records that
have an
item_value
greater than
$5000.

TECHNICAL STUFF

# Dangerous information about printing from the Report dialog box

Shhh — this is top-secret stuff. If you want to, you can print *directly* from the Report dialog box without having to run the report and do the preview or print selection. To do this, click the Page Preview checkbox off, and then click the To Printer checkbox on. That's it; the report is on its way. I've gotta go — I think I heard something move behind the bookshelf over there.

## The 5th Wave                    By Rich Tennant

"FOR US, IT WAS TOTAL INTEGRATION OR NOTHING. FOR INSTANCE-AT THIS TERMINAL ALONE I CAN GET DEPARTMENTAL DATA, PRINTER AND STORAGE RESOURCES, ESPN, HOME SHOPPING NETWORK *AND* THE MOVIE CHANNEL."

# Chapter 21

# Reports, Labels, and Junk Mail at the Wave of a Wand

. . . . . . . . . . . . . . . . . . . . . . . . . . . . . . . . .

**In This Chapter**
▶The three Report Wizards
▶The Label Wizard
▶The Junk Mail Wizard

. . . . . . . . . . . . . . . . . . . . . . . . . . . . . . . . .

*W*hen I was a kid, I loved watching Rocky and Bullwinkle. I always liked the part when Bullwinkle grabbed a top hat and yelled, "Hey, Rocky — watch me pull a rabbit outta my hat!" You never knew exactly what he'd get, but you could be sure it would be anything *but* a rabbit.

The new version of FoxPro for Windows has its own hat tricks. This chapter works through the magical Report Wizards and helps you pull the right report out of your hat. The Report, Label, and Junk Mail Wizards do the pulling, but it's up to you to tell them what they're pulling for.

This chapter only applies to FoxPro 2.6, the current version of the program. If you don't have this version yet and need to do lots of mailing labels or reports, I heartily recommend buying a copy of version 2.6 right now. You really *need* the upgrade — your whole FoxPro life will be simpler.

## The Three Report Wizards

It wasn't enough to merely revolutionize the way you make reports. No, Microsoft went beyond simple electronic insurrection into full-scale software anarchy by including not one, not two, but *three* different report Wizards in FoxPro 2.6.

Each one puts a little different twist on reporting, so there's an easy way to build almost any report you can think of. The basic Report Wizard (drum roll, please!) does simple reports. The Multi-Column Report Wizard formats your records into one, two, or three columns of information. The Group/Total Report Wizard (ta da!) lets you group your data up to three different ways, and includes subtotals and grand totals at no extra charge. Seems like they ought to throw in a Ginsu knife too, doesn't it?

The following sections walk through a session with each Wizard. The Wizards generally work alike, so it's easy to shuffle between them.

✔ Despite the fact that the Wizard is doing the legwork for your new report, you *still* need to think through the design. A 597-page report is great, provided it actually says something. Decide on the report's goal and layout before doing the Wizard thing.

✔ If you want to make a report with data from related tables, you need to establish the relationships *before* starting your Wizard. Magic only works with what's already there, so make sure that you're not missing any all-important relationships before turning the Wizard loose.

✔ To get the best overall performance, bellow "Presto! Changeo! FoxPro!" at the top of your voice every time you're ready to use a Wizard. Although the Wizards appear to work *without* your yelling the magic words, it's much safer to use them.

✔ You can start the Query Wizards directly from the Catalog Manager, if that's more your cup of interface tea. Check out Chapter 24 for everything you want (and perhaps some things you didn't want) to know about the Catalog Manager and it's amazing powers.

✔ One of the best things about Wizards is that you can back up through your steps and make changes. This isn't a lockstep thing — you're always free to change your mind.

## *Report Wizard*

This is your basic, fresh-out-of-magic-school Wizard. It's not fancy, but it does a good job with the simple report thing.

1. **While yelling the magic words, select Run⇨Wizard⇨Report from the main FoxPro for Windows menu. The Report Wizards dialog box pops onto the scene.**

   If the table you want to work with is already open on the workspace, that's fine, but it's not required.

**2. In the Select a Wizard box, double-click Report Wizard.**

You may have to wait a moment for the call to go through. The Wizards are very busy. Sometimes it takes a moment for them to disengage from whatever vitally important work they're doing and get to the phone.

**3. Time to tell the Wizard which table to report on. Do so and click Next to continue.**

If you already have tables open, the Wizard displays them in the Select a Table box. Otherwise, you must click Open to get your table ready to go. When the name of the table you're interested in appears in the Select a Table box, click it, and then click Next.

If you start the Report Wizard from the Catalog Manager and already have an active table, FoxPro skips this step.

**4. FoxPro offers you three report styles, so you can look calm, sophisticated, or totally cool, depending on your particular needs at the time. Examine the options and click the Executive, Ledger, or Presentation radio button. With that choice behind you, click Next.**

When you change formats, the magnifying glass graphic changes and displays a sample of your selection.

If you're not sure what to choose, use Executive. Ledger shines with lots of figures (because everything appears in lined columns). Presentation is okay, but a little busy for my taste.

**5. It's time to choose the fields for the report. Make your selections, and then click Next.**

If you want all the fields, simply click Add All and you're there. To pick and choose, scroll through the Available Fields list, and double-click each field that strikes your fancy. When you're finished, click Next to advance onward.

Figure 21-1 shows a few fields chosen for a customer phone list. As you've no doubt discovered by now, this is not brain surgery.

✔ The fields appear on the report in the order you select them from the Available Fields list, so if you have a particular order in mind, choose them that way.

✔ If you pick the wrong field, double-click it in the Selected Fields list. It immediately goes (poof!) away, just the way it should in a magic act of this quality.

✔ If you become completely frustrated and want to start the whole field-selection process over again, click Remove All. That trashes the whole Selected Fields list in one easy step.

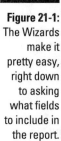

Figure 21-1:
The Wizards
make it
pretty easy,
right down
to asking
what fields
to include in
the report.

6. **With the fields chosen, the Wizard wants to know how to arrange them on the page. Make your choice, and then click Next.**

The Horizontal method looks like a table in Browse mode; Vertical resembles Change mode's layout. Click the appropriate radio button, and then click Next.

- If a window pops up, warning you that the Wizard can't make all the fields fit in the layout you chose, you can either use fewer fields (click Adjust Fields), change the layout (click Adjust Layout), or just blow off the warning (click Ignore) and suffer the consequences.

- Out of pure curiosity, what *are* the consequences of clicking Ignore? Your report is trimmed unceremoniously at the edge of the page wherever the Wizard runs out of space. It's the electronic version of a bad haircut — you get the idea.

7. **If you want to sort the report in a particular order, define it in this dialog box, and then click Next to continue.**

Choose the order direction by clicking the Ascending or Descending radio button, and then double-click the field name in the Available Fields box. Your selection immediately appears in the Sort Order of Records box. As before, click Next when you're ready to continue.

Figure 21-2 shows the selections for my customer phone list.

When you set the order direction (Ascending or Descending), you're setting it *for the whole report.* You can't have it sort in one direction for the first field and another for the second. FoxPro is capable of doing it, but the Wizard can't quite comprehend the process. Isn't it nice to know that computers *still* have limitations?

**Figure 21-2:**
Even though
it's sorting
by last and
first name, I
can only
choose one
direction for
both sorts.

8. **At the top of this last dialog box, type a title for the report. When you're finished, click Preview to see how everything looks. If it passes muster, click OK to get out of the preview.**

9. **Choose between saving and printing the report or just saving it by clicking the appropriate radio button. Click Finish, and FoxPro requests a filename for the new report. It offers the table name, but you can be creative and call it anything you want. Click Save or press Enter when your file-naming creativity is spent.**

## Multi-Column Report Wizard

For the most part, the Multi-Column Wizard works step-for-step like the plain vanilla Report Wizard. But, just when you're wondering if you accidentally clicked the wrong Wizard, there's an extra question about the number of columns you want in the report. It's a good question to ask, especially since that's the whole reason to use the Multi-Column Report Wizard.

Use the same steps given in the preceding section, but double-click the Multi-Column Report Wizard instead of the normal Report Wizard in Step 2. The columns question comes up between Steps 4 and 5, and looks significantly like Figure 21-3.

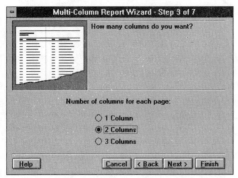

**Figure 21-3:**
You can
squeeze
your data
into two or
three
columns and
look oh-so-
professional.

After choosing the style (Executive, Ledger, or Presentation), FoxPro asks how many columns you want on the page. You can choose one, two, or three. Two columns should meet most of your needs. There's no point in using one column — that creates a normal report. Click the radio button for your choice, and then click Next to plow onward.

## Group/Total Report Wizard

This Wizard (or the Big Wizuna, as I like to call it) has some really useful tricks. In particular, it can *group* your records by up to three different fields. No, I don't expect you to immediately bubble over with joy, but I think you'll be perking in a minute.

So what's a group and why do you care? *Grouping* lets you see the trees *and* the forest in your data. It means arranging the report according to the value of a field. FoxPro creates subtotals for each group, plus a grand total for the whole report. If you create an annual sales report, the grouping feature lets you see sales by customer number, product type, or time of the month. It automatically figures subtotals by group (if you want them) and puts a grand total at the end of the report. All automatic; all done by the Wizard. Are you bubbling yet?

There's more: You can build groups using up to *three* different fields. Turning back to the sales example for a moment, you could organize the report by ZIP code, then by number of purchases in the last 12 months, and *then* by total sales dollars. Talk about juicy information — whoa!

You can also tell FoxPro to split groups by looking at the *whole* field or just the first one, two, or three characters in it. Yes, this is a techie-type feature, but I mention it in case there are any techie-wannabes out there. (This *is* an equal access book, you know.) Get some guidance from a FoxPro guru if you want to mess with this feature.

Is the Big Wizuna all-powerful? Nope, not by a long shot. First, it can't make anybody fall in love with you. Second, you're limited to a maximum of three groups. Third, regardless of how many groups you use, you can only choose one sort direction *for the whole report*. The whole thing is sorted ascending or descending — no mixing and matching is allowed.

Lastly, the Big Wizuna doesn't like related tables. Well, I suppose it *likes* them (socially speaking), but it doesn't like dealing with them. If you base the Wizard's report on a table that's in a relationship, the Wizard won't let you create groups — in fact, it skips over the group steps entirely. It *will* create a summary for any numeric fields in the report, but it simply ignores the whole group thing. Personally, I'd call this a "problem," but software developers usually refer to things like it as a "design feature." I guess it's the same either way. If this presents a major problem for you, talk to a human FoxPro wizard and see if he or she can help.

1. **Select Run⇨Wizard⇨Report from the main menu to list the Report Wizards. Double-click the Group/Total Report Wizard (or click once and then click Next) to get the show on the road.**

   As with the other Report Wizards, you don't need to have any tables open when you start, because the Wizard lets you open things later.

2. **Choose the table for the report. This dialog box lists all the tables that are currently available. If the one you want isn't there, click Open to include it on the list. When you've chosen the table, click Next to continue your quest for the ultimate report.**

   • If you started right from the Catalog Manager and are currently using a table there, FoxPro blissfully ignores this step and continues to the next one automatically.

   • This Wizard doesn't work quite the way you expect if you use related tables. Just something *else* to keep in mind.

3. **Decide on the style for your report. Your choices are Executive (an all-around good option), Ledger (best for lots of numbers), and Presentation (a final, ho-hum alternative). Click the radio button of your favorite, and then click Next.**

4. **You can't have a report without data, so pick the fields in this dialog box. To include them all, click the Add All button. To be selective, scroll through the Available Fields list, click your choice, and then click Add. When you're finished, click Next to continue.**

   See Step 5 in the Report Wizard section for all the details about adding and deleting fields.

5. **Here's where this Wizard's magic begins. You can group your report by up to three fields. Choose the fields in the order you want things grouped (the first field is the main group; the second groups data within the first; thus and so with the third). Double-click the field in the Available Fields list to move it into the Group Levels list.**

If you're using a set of related tables, FoxPro skips this step and the next one. The fox is fast, but if you jump ahead to Step 8, you can catch it.

Figure 21-4 shows a setup with two groups. All records are organized by ZIP code first. Any records with identical ZIP codes are sorted by last name.

- You are limited to three group fields. You can have fewer, but not more (just like candy at the holidays).

- If you move the wrong field, double-click it in the Group Levels list to move it back again (or click it and then click Remove).

- I'm getting hungry. Are you?

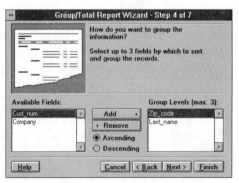

**Figure 21-4:**
This report
uses two
groups to
organize its
data.

6. **Before leaving the dialog box, make your sort direction choice by clicking either Ascending or Descending. Continue to the next step by clicking Next.**

If you're not sure which direction you want to sort, leave it set to Ascending.

7. **The magic continues as you tell FoxPro to group by whole or partial field values. The default is Entire Field — and that's what I recommend you use. Leave everything alone and click Next unless you have expert help at hand to guide you.**

If you simply *must* try this on your own, here's a couple of tips. For alphabetical reports, use First Character. ZIP-code-based reports work well with either Entire Field or First 3 Characters. Choose the options from the pull-down list by clicking on the down arrow, and then the option you want.

8. **Take a deep breath — you're almost finished. If your report has a numeric field in it, the Wizard can create subtotals for each group and a grand total at the end. Click Next to finish the job.**

   By default, it offers to do both the subtotal and grand total. If that sounds good to you (and it probably does), just click Next and get on with things.

   - FoxPro skips this step if there aren't any numeric fields in the report.

   - If you're using related tables, only the totals option is available. Because the Wizard can't group fields in related tables, there's nothing to subtotal.

9. **Type a meaningful title for the report and click Preview to see what you (and FoxPro) have wrought.**

   If you like what you see, either save and print your masterwork, or just save it by clicking the appropriate radio button. Click Finish when you're, well, finished.

10. **The Save As dialog box pops into action so that you can name your work. Click Save to complete the job and make the dialog box go away.**

# The Label Wizard

The Label Wizard is an absolute gift. If you ever tried to make labels in FoxPro for Windows 2.5, you know what I mean. If you haven't, don't try. Use the Label Wizard instead and save your nerves for another day.

It's a powerful and relatively intuitive tool. Come to think of it, I don't think I've seen an easier label maker in any database program. And I've seen *lots* of database programs — far more than common sense recommends.

The only prerequisite for the Label Wizard is knowing the size of your labels and how many are across on a page. If you know the manufacturer's model number for your labels, remember it, too.

1. **To kick off the show, select Run⇨Wizard⇨Label from the main FoxPro menu. The Label Wizard appears, resplendent in its glory.**

Here's the quick tour of the Label Wizard window: In the upper corner, FoxPro displays a model of the label you're building; Available Fields lists the stuff for the label; Selected Fields shows what's appearing on-label; the punctuation and new line keys fill in the extra space between the field lists.

2. **Pick the table destined for printed-label immortality. Click Next after you choose the lucky winner.**

   If the table you want isn't listed, click Open and pull it up from the disk drive.

3. **Break out the notes about the labels you're using — FoxPro has some questions. Choose the entry that most closely resembles your labels. If you know the manufacturer's number for your labels, use that to find the right one. Click Next to continue.**

   The sizes are given as height by width, so an Avery 5161 is 1" high by 4" wide. If you're using metric labels, click the Metric radio button to see your label options.

4. **Now you're ready to design the label. Table 21-1 steps through almost everything you do to build a layout. When you're finished, click Next.**

| Table 21-1 | Designing Labels |
|---|---|
| *What you want to do* | *How to do it* |
| Place a field | Double-click the field name in the Available Fields box. |
| Put two fields on a line | Place the first field, click Space (the on-screen button, not the spacebar on the keyboard), and then place the second field. |
| Add a new line to the label | Click the bent arrow button under Space. If you want a blank line between two existing lines of the label, click the line *above* where the new line goes, and then click the bent arrow button. |
| Put in City, State, and ZIP | Double-click the city field, click the comma button, and then click Space. Place the state field, and then click Space twice. Place the ZIP code field. |
| Remove a field | Click the left arrow button (it looks like a "less-than" sign). This removes the last field you placed. If you want one further back than that, keep clicking. Not a particularly *handy* feature, is it? |
| Clear a whole line | Click the left arrow button until the line fills with little dots (that means it's empty). |

Figure 21-5 shows the dialog box awaiting your artful touch. Thanks to the miracles of modern technology and book-a-vision, Figure 21-6 displays a finished mailing label. See — that didn't take long to make, now did it?

- If two big right-pointing arrows appear with your model label (like Figure 21-6), it means the Label Wizard thinks one of your lines is too wide for the label. There's an easy fix: ignore the arrows and finish your label. When you're finished, preview your labels. Scroll through a lot of them — make sure you see the longer ones. Did any text run off the right side of the label? If so, either get bigger labels or change the layout to fix the problem. If not, you're fine and the Wizard was all worried for nothing.

- See the sidebar "Why the Label Wizard gets confused" for a brief commentary on the Wizard's peculiar actions.

**Figure 21-5:**
A blank label window is a simple thing, sort-of.

**Figure 21-6:**
The fields are in place, but all is not well with the label.

5. **In this next-to-final dialog box, you can tell the Wizard to sort the labels by up to three fields in the master table. Double-click the fields for the sort, and then click Next to be done with the matter.**

   Although the Wizard lets you choose up to three fields, most of the time you only need one: ZIP code.

6. **Click Preview to see your work on-screen. When you're thoroughly amazed, either save or save and print your work by clicking the radio button of your choice. Click Finish to call it quits for the day.**

   FoxPro automatically squeezes out all the extra blanks in your data, so the fields look right on the label. If there's a blank line in the middle, it moves the rest of the lines up without messing up the other labels. It's almost too cool for words. I'm speechless. (I guess it *was* too cool for words).

7. **The Save As dialog box appears so that you can name and save your label. Click Save when you're finished.**

# The Junk Mail Wizard

Okay, it's not really called the Junk Mail Wizard, but that's what it is. The Mail Merge Wizard (its real name) doesn't actually do a mail merge; it just helps convert your tables into a format that most word processing programs (like Microsoft Word or WordPerfect) can understand.

## Why the Label Wizard gets confused

Sometimes, the Label Wizard panics. (Luckily, it isn't a big piece of software, so you're dealing with a relatively small bout of digital agitation.) It worries that all of your text won't fit on the label.

The Wizard shows its concern by displaying two big, right-pointing arrows in the model label. Yes, *that's* what those arrows mean. The Wizard compared the number of characters it can fit on the label with the number of characters you want to put there. If the total field size is wider than the label, the Wizard goes into hysterics.

Luckily, this is not a big deal. You see, the Wizard only knows how wide the *field* is, not the width of the field's actual *data*. For example, a City field might be 25 characters wide, but the largest city name in the table only has 18 letters. The Wizard allows space for the whole field (all 25 characters) without actually looking at the data to find out whether it needs that much. In this case, it only needs 18 spaces, but does *it* know that? *No!* (Poof!) One panic-stricken Wizard, screaming hither and yon that the labels look like heck. The Wizard is *guessing*, and sometimes it guesses *wrong*.

That's why you should ignore the Wizard's warnings and check out the labels for yourself. If they're okay, the label layout is fine, despite what the Wizard says. Otherwise, pat the Wizard on the head and fix your label layout. Either way, *you* be the final judge and let the Wizard sit and stew.

If you care (and I hope you don't need to), the Mail Merge Wizard converts FoxPro's .DBF files into comma-quote or tab-quote delimited text files, or WordPerfect binary data files. Comma-quote is a fancy way to say that there are commas between each field and that character fields have quotes around them. The tab-quote format uses tabs to separate the fields instead of commas. And nobody knows what WordPerfect's up to in its little corner of the digital world, but that's old news.

1. **From the main FoxPro menu (where all good things start), select Run⇨Wizard⇨Mail Merge. If your Wizard fees are paid up, the Mail Merge Wizard pops to attention.**

2. **From the Select a Table list, choose the file you want exported to the word processor. Click Next when you're finished.**

   As usual with these Wizards, if you want a file that's not in the list, click the Open button to, well, open it.

3. **From the list of common, everyday word processors, click the radio button of the one you're using. Click Next to press onward.**

   If you're not sure what program you're using, choose Word for DOS, just as in Figure 21-7.

   The Word for DOS entry makes a comma-quote delimited file; the Other option makes a tab-quote delimited file. Most word processors can read either of these formats.

   Although the Wizard is supposed to do some extra tricks with Microsoft Word for Windows versions 2.*x* and 6, I *don't* recommend trying it — I couldn't ever get it to work correctly. Use the Word for DOS option to export the data, and then quit FoxPro and do your junk mail thing in Word itself.

   The mail-merge process in both versions of Word for Windows is reasonably user-friendly, so why add another layer of electronic complexity? Besides, I'm not completely convinced that Microsoft has all the bugs — sorry, *undocumented features* — worked out of the process yet. Call me a heretic, but that's my observation.

4. **That's it — you're finished (with this part, at least). Click Finish to bring up the Save As dialog box so that you can name the newly translated file. FoxPro offers the completely intuitive name *mmrgdata.txt*, which you may want to change. Click Save when you're finished.**

5. **Quit FoxPro (select File⇨Exit) and start your word processing program. Go through whatever mail-merge dance it requires, and then celebrate when your junk mail hits the printer.**

**Figure 21-7:**
Use the
Word for
DOS option
with the
Mail Merge
Wizard.

# Chapter 22

# Mystical, Magical, Metaphysical Graphs

• • • • • • • • • • • • • • • • • • • • • • • • • • • • • • • • • • • • • • • • • • • • • • •

### In This Chapter

▶ Picking the right graph

▶ Creating a graph from a query

▶ Saving your pretty pictures

▶ Seeing and not printing them later

• • • • • • • • • • • • • • • • • • • • • • • • • • • • • • • • • • • • • • • • • • • • • • •

*W*ho decided that a picture is worth 1000 words? Where's the research, the statistics? Is it worth *exactly* 1000 words, or is that rounded? Do you get the *same* words you did in the '50s, or does a picture only rate 1000 little dinky words these days? Hey — graphing minds want to know this stuff.

Graphing minds also want to know when to use a graph, which graph to pick, and how in the world you do all this in FoxPro. This chapter knows all, sees all, and tells all, and even does it with some graphs. Graphing minds *love* stuff like this.

## Picking the Right Graph

Graphs tell great stories. Pick a story, any story, and FoxPro probably has a graph that can handle it. Graphs show how things change, how they compare to each other, and how they look *then* versus *now*. FoxPro's Graph Wizard does bar, pie, line, area, and 3-D charts of all shapes and descriptions. It's a whole army of visuals at your beck and call.

So, which one do you use? Good question. The answer, you'll be pleased to know, is a firm, forceful, solid "It depends."

✔ What kind of data is it? If it's stock prices, your choice is easy. If it's monthly sales for the last few years, a line or bar graph sounds good — perhaps even a pie would do the trick.

✔ What are you trying to show? Figure out what your data says (perhaps by looking at it through various graphs) and pick a graph that's suited for the message.

✔ Who is your audience? Are they "numbers" people who want detail? Then a graph may *not* be the best answer. Are they visually-oriented sales types? They *love* graphs.

Is there exactly *one* way to present a given set of figures? No, most certainly not! Using different graphs lets the figures tell different stories. Consider Figure 22-1. Here's a mild-mannered chart if ever there was one. At a glance, you see how things look for different products in different markets. (Note that, to enhance your confusion, FoxPro is particular about its terms. Charts with sideways bars are Bar charts; old-fashioned ones with vertical bars are now Column charts. Why'd they bother?) Take the same data, stuff it into a different chart, and you get Figure 22-2 — the teller of a different tale. Do the same thing again, and Figure 22-3 appears (but does it tell you anything?).

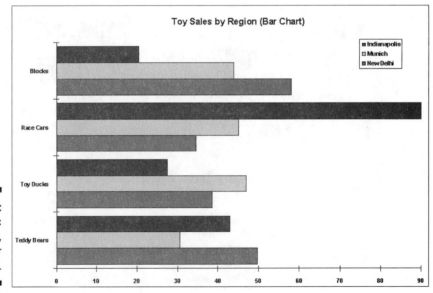

**Figure 22-1:**
The classic Bar chart, doing its bar thing.

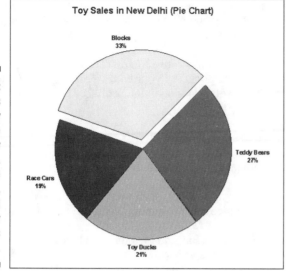

**Figure 22-2:**
Pie charts
are probably
used more
than any
other.
They're
easy, quick,
and
everybody
understands
them.

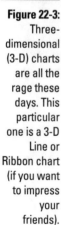

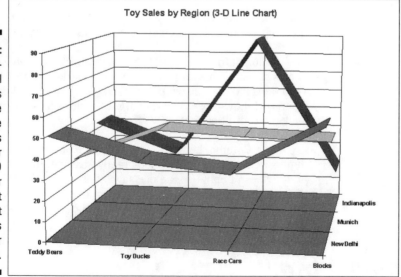

**Figure 22-3:**
Three-
dimensional
(3-D) charts
are all the
rage these
days. This
particular
one is a 3-D
Line or
Ribbon chart
(if you want
to impress
your
friends).

While all that's swirling in your head, take a gander at this roster of graphs from FoxPro's Graph Wizard. It's not an exhaustive list, either — there's still more it can do. Amazing, isn't it?

For the rest of the information, look in the *Microsoft Graph User's Guide*. It's hidden away in the cardboard pocket of your FoxPro box. As contradictory as this sounds, it's actually a pretty good manual, probably because it's not from the FoxPro group. (Did I say that?)

Area
: Best used to show how two sets of data change in proportion over time. Weak for displaying how fast things change. They're cool to look at, though, which covers a multitude of sins.

Bar
: Great for displaying a lot of figures over time or drawing compari sons. Bars are nice because almost everyone knows how to read one.

Column
: Related to both the Bar and Pie charts. It takes some practice to use correctly, but is very powerful after you've mastered it. Columns are easier to read than create.

Line
: Marvelous for trends or anything else that happens over time. They're lines — what more can you say?

Pie
: Good for seeing what makes up a set of data — *one* set. It doesn't do comparisons. Like Bar charts, Pies are easy to read and interpret.

High-Low-Close
: The darling of the stock and investment markets. High-low-close charts show a value range with an extra marker for the final price. Variations include the simple High-Low and the complicated Open-High-Low-Close. These charts often look like a convention of stick men with beer bellies.

3-D
: Area, Bar, Column, Line, and Pie charts are all available in three-dimensional versions. They look really neat, but the extra graphic punch doesn't enhance the message at all. Use them if you're trying to hide something, because everyone remembers how great the graphs look, but usually not a thing about what they say.

# Creating a Graph from a Query

In FoxPro, you don't just sit down and think "Today, I shall create a graph." No, the correct phrase is "Today, I shall build a query and then graph the results," because that's what you do. Here's how:

1. **Pick a table and build a query.**

   The query stuff is covered in gory detail back in Part III. I like you too much to review it again here.

- Only include the fields necessary for your graph in the query's Output Fields section (controlled by the Fields checkbox). If you leave other fields in there, the Graph Wizard gets confused and you end up plotting customer numbers on a bar chart or something like that. It's not a pretty sight.

- You can't build a graph from the Query Wizard. Sorry, but that's life in the FoxPro lane (at least in this version). You *can* use the Wizard to create the query, but to do the graph, you have to modify the query using the old-fashioned, manual approach in Chapter 15.

2. **In the Output box (on the right of the query window), click the down arrow to pull down a list of options. Choose Graph.**

   Don't worry about the Name box below Output. If a name appears in there, fine; if it's blank, no big deal.

3. **Click Do Query. The Graph Wizard makes her first appearance, resplendent in colors impossible to reproduce in Figure 22-4.**

   Applaud now. Wizards *love* stuff like that.

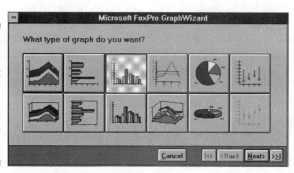

**Figure 22-4:** Click the graph that suits your fancy (or, better yet, suits your data).

4. **Choose your graph from the 12 on display. Click your choice, and then click Next.**

   The Wizard usually suggests your basic bar — excuse me, column — chart as a starting point. Remember, you can always go back and change your mind, so this is a *set in Jell-O* kind of decision.

5. **The Wizard considers the Output Fields from your query and decides where they go. It's usually right, so click Next to continue through the screen.**

   If you get weird results in your graph, look at what you included in the Output Fields section of the query. If there's extra junk that's just along for the ride, take it out. The Graph Wizard is picky about such things and can't deal with extra fields.

6. **Type the title for your graph. Click <u>N</u>ext to build the little bugger.**

   Creating the graph may take your computer a moment or two (or 13 or 14, depending on its speed). Don't panic if it doesn't appear right away. When it *does* pop into existence, it's small and illegible in the preview window, but it's yours nonetheless.

7. **Now that the graph is finished, you have three main options: <u>Z</u>oom, <u>P</u>rint, and <u>S</u>ave As.**

   • <u>Z</u>oom makes the graph larger so that you can actually see it. To get *out* of zoom mode, double-click the upper left corner of the graph's window. You quickly return to the Graph Wizard.

   • <u>P</u>rint sends a copy to your printer. Remember that the on-screen colors only print if you have a *color* printer. Nothing magical happens to the ol' black-and-white laser printer just because you're making graphs. FoxPro substitutes dot and hatch patterns for the colors, depending on the printer you have.

   • <u>S</u>ave As stores the details and the graph itself in a table so that you can do things with it in the future. See the following section for the lowdown.

   • If you want to change the style, color, size, or just about anything else about the graph, click <u>Z</u>oom and then double-click anywhere on the graph itself. That starts Microsoft Graph, which lets you edit and generally muck about in your creation. Refer to its manual (in the cardboard insert inside the FoxPro for Windows box) for all the details.

   • If you click the Graph Wizard's OK button without saving your work, *it's gone.* FoxPro dumps you back at your query without any further questions. If that happens to you, I recommend some frustrated pounding on the desk, perhaps a hurled paper clip or two, and a brisk walk outside in the rain to properly deal with your feelings. When you come back, start rebuilding the graph. Have fun.

8. **When the graph is printed, saved, or otherwise dealt with, click OK to return to the query. Close and save the query if you want to use it again.**

# Saving Your Pretty Pictures

There's nothing to saving your graphs in FoxPro. It's almost too easy. When you face that last screen in the Graph Wizard, click the <u>S</u>ave As button. In the forthcoming Save As dialog box, choose a table to store the graph in and click Save. (Poof!) It's saved.

✔ The graph is saved in a *table?* Hey, that's what I said the first time someone told me (in fact, I think I used the same inflection that you did just now). Yes, in addition to some trivial details that nobody really cares about, FoxPro stores *the graph itself* in a field of this incredible table. It's techno-magic that uses a general field and a Windows feature called *Object Linking and Embedding* (or OLE, for "hooray" in Spanish).

If you're dying to learn more about OLE, get some help immediately. There are many government programs and private therapists that help people work through problems just like this. If they can't help you, get a copy of IDG's *Windows For Dummies.*

✔ In case your creativity is having an off day, FoxPro offers to save your graph with the clever name QryGraph.DBF. Feel free to change it.

✔ You can save more than one graph in the same table. When FoxPro wants to know what table to use, enter the name of a table that already has a graph or two in it. After you click Save, FoxPro discovers what you're up to and displays the dialog box in Figure 22-5. Click the Append button, and FoxPro makes a new record in the table for your current graph. A last-minute twitch onto the Overwrite button sends all your previously saved graphs out to the digital dumpster quicker than you can say, "Rats!" (and that's pretty quick). The moral of the story: Click carefully — your tables depend on it.

**Figure 22-5:**
Click
Append to
expand your
graph
collection.

# Seeing and (Not) Printing Them Later

Finding the graphs again is almost as easy as saving them in the first place. Use any of FoxPro's innumerable ways of opening a table to pull your "graph" table up from the disk drive. View it in Browse mode (that's personal preference, not FoxPro law). It *should* look something like Figure 22-6, but perhaps with fewer graphs in it.

Pay no attention to anything in the table except for the Olegraph field — the last one on the right. To see a graph, double-click the Gen entry in that field. Your graph pops up from nowhere, just like mine in the figure. It's beautiful to look at, all pretty and colorful there on-screen, isn't it?

Print it? You don't want to just look at it on-screen? Oh. Well, you can put it in a report and print it that way. No, I'm sorry, but you can't just print it. I think this may be another *undocumented design feature,* but you can't directly print a graph from its saved form. You can recreate it through the query and then print directly from the Graph Wizard, but that's it. Makes you just want to spit, doesn't it?

**Figure 22-6:** It doesn't look much like itself in the table, but the graph pulls itself together after you double-click the Olegraph field.

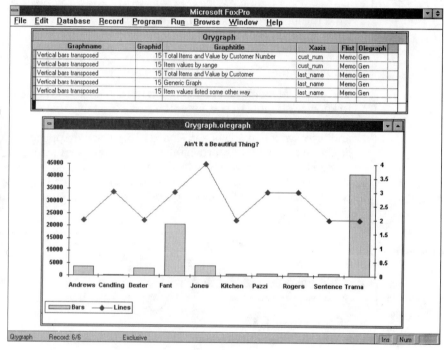

# Chapter 23

# The Relational Thing:
# Now They All Want to Talk

*In This Chapter*

▶ Making reports from two tables

▶ Making labels from two tables

▶ Graphs with two tables

**A**s soon as one table gets to be in a report or a mailing label or a graph, the floodgates open and everybody wants to play. It's like the "chain-reaction pottying" behavior among toddlers (or at least my toddlers). One toddler says, "I need to potty." Immediately, every other toddler nearby chimes in with the same statement, whether it's true or not. It gives me shivers just thinking about it.

FoxPro for Windows helps you handle the "I want to be in a report/label/graph, too" crisis with its flexible Wizards and other tools. This chapter explores the hoops, hollers, and how-tos of letting all your tables play the presentation game.

## Making Reports from Two Tables

If you're sold on using relational tables (which is fine with me), it follows that you have to use more than one table to make a report. After all, the whole point of related tables is to store some of your data in one place and the rest somewhere else, so that means it's not *together* anywhere.

FoxPro makes it reasonably easy — at least as easy as you can expect a more advanced step to be. This section contains all the steps you need to build two-table reports the manual way (for FoxPro 2.5) and the magical way (using FoxPro 2.6's Report Wizard).

Go forth and enjoy. (No, I'm *not* being sarcastic.)

## Kids — don't try this at home

One brief thought before you gallop too far into this chapter: Make sure you're ready for the ride.

Combining tables with a query and feeding the results into a report with FoxPro 2.5 just isn't very easy. This chapter puts padding on the process, but it's still a bumpy ride. You need to understand how to link tables together, build a query, and create a report. If you do these in your sleep, you probably have a strange-looking bedroom. If you're very comfortable with such things (table linking,

not strange-looking bedrooms), plow ahead toward your goal. Otherwise, skip back to Chapter 12 for linking tables, Chapters 15-19 for queries, and Chapter 20 for reports.

If you have the newest version of FoxPro, just skip ahead to "Waving the Wizard Wand" — you're all taken care of. It's still good to understand all this stuff (particularly about linking tables in Chapter 12), but the Wizard handles all the dirty work.

## *Doing it the old-fashioned way*

If you don't have the latest, greatest version of FoxPro, or if you just like the challenge of wresting things from your computer, here's how to use fields from two tables in a single report.

This can only be done with a query and report working together. The query links the tables and provides the fields for the report; the report makes everything pretty.

If you wouldn't know a query if it walked up and did unspeakable things to you, check out the RQBE chapters in Part III.

1. **Open the first table.**

   You can use the View window (<u>W</u>indow➪<u>V</u>iew) or any other method that suits your mood. If there are other tables open as well, make the one for your report active by clicking it in the Work areas list of the View window.

2. **Select Ru<u>n</u>➪<u>N</u>ew Query from the menu.**

   A blank query window pops up from nowhere and awaits your command.

3. **Click <u>A</u>dd and select the other table for your report. Click Open to finish the job.**

   The computer will think for a moment, and then the Join Condition dialog box appears. That's FoxPro's way of telling you everything is going along just fine, thank you.

   If the table you want isn't listed, you need to change directories or disk drives. If you don't like what you're doing, you need to change jobs.

4. **In the Join Condition dialog box, choose the fields to link the tables together. Click OK when you're finished.**

   If FoxPro finds a field with exactly the same name in both tables, it auto-matically suggests that field as a link. For your viewing pleasure, Figure 23-1 shows a completed Join Condition dialog box. When you click OK, Join Condition goes away, leaving you back at the RQBE dialog box.

**Figure 23-1:**
The linking
field
between
Customer
and Items is
cust_num.

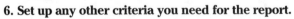

| RQBE Join Condition |
|---|
| Items.cust_num ▼  ☐ Not   Like   ▼   Customer.cust_num ▼ |
| ☐ Ignore Upper/Lower Case        OK        Cancel |

5. **Click the F̲ields checkbox to open the Select Fields dialog box (now appearing in Figure 23-2). Choose the particular fields for your report, and then click OK to return to the query window when you're finished.**

   The Selected Output box already lists all the fields from the first table. A good first step is clicking Remove Al̲l to clear the Selected Output box completely.

   Choose your fields from the Table Fields box by double-clicking the field names. All the fields from both tables are listed. If you pick the wrong one by accident, double-click it in the Selected Output box and watch it run away.

   Pick the fields in the order you want them to print on your report. The fields in Figure 23-2 will appear on the report in the same order you see them in the Selected Output box: starting with Customer.cust_num and ending with Items.item_value.

6. **Set up any other criteria you need for the report.**

   You may not need any criteria; you may need a lot. If you don't know what you need, refer to Chapters 15 through 18, in Part III.

7. **Because the whole point of this exercise is to create a report, click the down arrow of the Output box. Choose Report/Label from the list. Click in the Options box to define the report.**

8. **You want a report, so click the R̲eport radio button.**

   This activates several other parts of the dialog box. Luckily, there are only a couple that you're interested in.

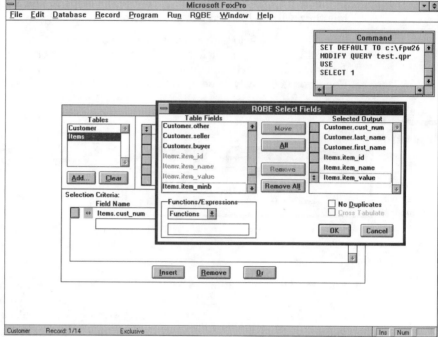

**Figure 23-2:**
This query
includes
some fields
from both
the
Customer
and Items
tables.
Notice how
FoxPro
cleverly
distinguishes
them.

If you want the report to print out instead of appear charmingly on-screen, click off Page Preview, and then click To Printer in the stuffily named Output Destinations box at the bottom of the screen.

9. **Click Quick Report to quickly bring up the Quick Report dialog box. Click OK to just as quickly send it away.**

10. **Click OK once more to close the Display Options dialog box.**

11. **That's it for the settings. Click Do Query to check your work.**

If you get a message telling you that the report file already exists, click Yes to overwrite it. FoxPro is creating a temporary report file, so you don't lose anything important when you overwrite it.

12. **Be sure to save your query if you want to use this report again. Select File⇨Save and type a name for your query.**

## Waving the Wizard Wand

The three Report Wizards make this multiple table report stuff too easy. It's love at first click. All you need to do is open the tables you want for the reports and establish the links between them, and then run the Wizard like you always do. That's it. See, it's easy.

If your mind is saying "dyauhhhh" over the whole link-the-tables thing, refer to Chapter 12 for a quick refresher.

After the links are in place, run the Report Wizards by selecting Run⇨Wizard⇨Report from the main FoxPro menu. Choose your preferred Report Wizard from the list.

When the Wizard asks what table to use in the report, choose the parent table. Proceed through the process until you get to the part about choosing fields for the report. Scroll through the Available Fields list, and — hey, check it out! — the fields from both the parent table and the linked child are in the list. Pick the fields you want and finish the process just like you did for a single-table report.

# Making Labels from Two Tables

I have some bad news: There's no easy way to make labels from two tables, with or without the Label Wizard. Well, that settles that.

If you're dead set on doing this and you have the newest version of FoxPro, there is a way, but I only recommend it if you're feeling really confident or if your frustration level is low and you want to raise it a notch or two. First, create a query that links the two tables together. Set the query's output to Table/DBF. In the Fields area, include the fields you want on the finished label. Run the query and create the new table. Then run the Label Wizard and have it use your new, query-produced table. It's a roundabout solution, but it gets the job done.

If the preceding paragraph made you think "why bother with all this?" I don't blame you one bit. See whether your local FoxPro guru can either help or do it for you.

# Graphs with Two Tables

Creating a graph from two tables is almost exactly like making a two-table report. The only differences are that you're creating a *graph* this time (no big surprise there) and you need to be very careful when picking fields.

For the most part, you use the steps from "Doing it the old-fashioned way," earlier in the chapter. There are only two changes:

✔ When you choose fields in Step 5, include only the fields you absolutely, positively, *must* have for the graph. If you toss in some extra fields, the Graph Wizard is liable to start muttering incoherently and walking into walls. This is not a good thing.

✔ In Step 7, select Graph as the Output instead of Report/Label.

✔ Skip Steps 9 and 10, because they aren't even options now.

Okay, so there were *three* changes. It's still about the same thing. Anyway, when you're finished, run the query and massage the Graph Wizard to create your colorful, informative masterpiece.

See Chapters 15 through 18 in Part III if you're drawing a blank about multiple-table queries. Likewise, see Chapter 22 for help with creating graphs in general.

# Part V
# Things that Didn't Quite Fit Elsewhere

"I STARTED DESIGNING DATABASE SOFTWARE SYSTEMS AFTER SEEING HOW EASY IT
WAS TO DESIGN OFFICE FURNITURE."

# In this part...

Some things never quite fit in. That's why your job description has that cryptic line at the end — you know, the one that says something like "other duties as assigned." That way, if they need a nest of Arkansas Kiss O' Death spiders removed from the ceiling *right now,* you're available. After all, it's in your job description.

This Part is home to all the things that didn't quite fit elsewhere. It's the "topics that need some attention but defy rational organization" section. There are tales of Wizards, secret buttons, and things that make you go "hmmm" in the night. Sounds like a cheap romantic mystery, doesn't it? Gosh, maybe I got the manuscripts mixed up and it *is* a cheap romantic mystery. Um . . . I need to read this real quick — I'll get back with you later.

# Chapter 24

# What's a Catalog and Why Manage it?

*I*t's easy to understand why catalogs are a relatively new invention. Why bother having a scribe illuminate a beautiful catalog? He could be illuminating a beautiful *manuscript* instead and making some *real* money. Nope, this catalog phenomenon needed technology to really catch on.

In the new version of FoxPro, the technology machine burped again and catalogs entered the Realm of the Fox. Catalogs offer a lot of bang on a short learning curve, so I give them three and a half fox heads out of five. They would have done better, but I couldn't dance to them.

## What Catalog Manager Does

Put simply, the Catalog Manager is a tool that manages catalog files (don't hit me yet — keep reading and see if you still want to hit me in a few sentences). This begs the question, "So what's a catalog file?" It's a great way to keep all of your tables, queries, screens, reports, mailing labels, and FoxApp programs organized. I mean *really* organized. You know, organized so that you can *find* things in the time it used to take to explain why it was taking so long to find things. *That's* the kind of organization I'm talking about.

Catalog files are flexible, too. You can have multiple catalog files; make one for each project you're working on. That way, when you're working on Invoices, for example, all the relevant tables, reports, queries and such are right there at hand. You don't have to fiddle around trying to remember which one is which or where you left them. Properly applied, Catalog files are a big time saver.

And Catalog files don't take up much valuable disk space, so you won't even know they're there. It doesn't matter whether you use the same table or screen on two or three projects — just include them in all the relevant catalogs. Everything can appear in more than one Catalog file, so add things in wherever you need them.

There's more to catalogs than merely providing clean, safe, and orderly housing for your stuff, though. The Catalog Manager itself is an electronic, full-service storage, maintenance, and construction facility. You can make new tables, change existing screens, delete old queries, or any combination in between. Of course, it's completely graphical, dotted here and there with cute little buttons, menus, and lists — exactly the kind of visual experience you expect from a good Windows application.

✔ Did I mention that the Catalog Manager is only available in FoxPro 2.6? Well, at least you know now.

✔ If you're migrating from dBASE, the Catalog Manager wants to be your *special* friend. See Appendix B for more information about how it helps make you comfy-cozy in your new software home.

# A Look at the Screen

Because the Catalog Manager is a graphical animal, this discussion desperately needs a visual component. Figure 24-1 is particularly well suited for this grueling *Tour de Interfacé*, since it does, in fact, depict the Catalog Manager.

The screen has five distinct parts.

| | |
|---|---|
| Menu bar | The File, Edit, View, Data, Tools, Window, and Help menus that sit across the top of the screen. The only ones you'll likely ever use are File and Data. May the others rest in peace. |
| Permanent picture buttons | These four buttons (one on the upper left, three on the upper right) are permanent fixtures in the Catalog Manager dialog box. Apart from being cute and decorative, they do important things like browse tables and |

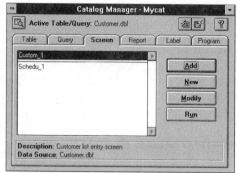

**Figure 24-1:**
The Catalog
Manager, in
lavish
graphical
glory, now
appearing
under the
menu bar.

queries, create reports and screens, and run FoxPro's Help system (the electronic equivalent of a cement life raft — it's better than nothing, but it doesn't go far).

**File tabs**   These six tabs switch you among the various file storage areas. They're marked Table, Query, Screen, Report, Label, and Program.

**Action buttons**   This set of four buttons (arranged vertically on the right side of the dialog box) does stuff. The top three buttons, Add, New, and Modify, are the same for every file tab. The last one can't quite make up its mind and vacillates between Use, Run, and Print, depending on the tab.

**List and description areas**   Although they take up most of the dialog box, they're the least complicated. The main list area is huge and white — you can't miss it. The Description area runs across the whole bottom of the dialog box and is bounded by a cool looking, chiseled box.

Why is there a bar between the two filenames in the big list area? That's the Catalog Manager's clever way to show you files that are related to the current table or query. Whatever is *above* the bar is a relative of the current table or query. In the figure, the Customer table is active. The screen Custom_1 is based on the Customer table, so the Catalog Manager put it at the top of the list so it's easy to find.

# Minding Your Stuff

So much for the travel brochure overview. Here's how to do the things that 9 out of 10 people surveyed said they'd do if they had something like Catalog Manager to do them with, provided they needed to do things with FoxPro at all. The tenth person fainted dead away during the interview, but recovered nicely.

## Getting into Catalog Manager

When you first start FoxPro for Windows, it displays the screen shown in Figure 24-2. Click the Proceed to the Catalog Manager button, and you will, in fact, proceed to the Catalog Manager. *This* is truth in advertising.

- ✔ If you become deeply involved with the Catalog Manager and want to see it every time you run FoxPro, click the Don't Display This Introductory Screen Again checkbox, and then click the Catalog Manager button. The introductory screen goes away, never to be seen again.

- ✔ The very first time you use Catalog Manager, it asks you to name the default catalog. Pick a name you like, because this is the beginning of a long and hard-to-escape relationship.

From Command Mode (the way that *everybody* used FoxPro in the old version), start the Catalog Manager by selecting File➪Catalog Manager from the main menu.

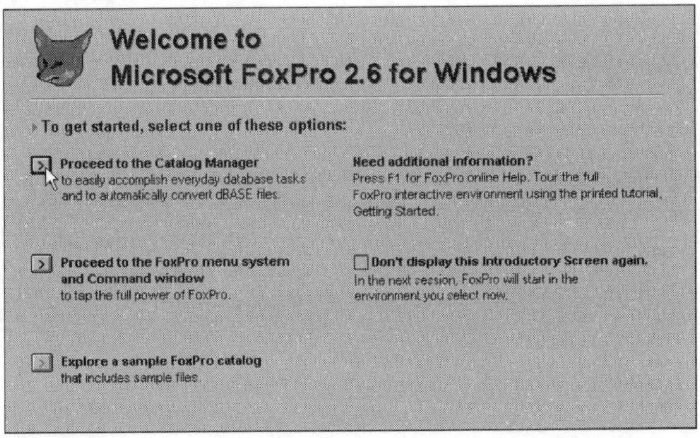

**Figure 24-2:**
FoxPro's
new way to
say, "Hello,
and
welcome
to the
program."

> ## Welcome to
> ## Microsoft FoxPro 2.6 for Windows
>
> ▸ To get started, select one of these options:
>
> ☒ **Proceed to the Catalog Manager**       **Need additional information?**
> to easily accomplish everyday database tasks    Press F1 for FoxPro online Help. Tour the full
> and to automatically convert dBASE files.     FoxPro interactive environment using the printed tutorial,
>     Getting Started.
>
> ☒ **Proceed to the FoxPro menu system**     ☐ **Don't display this Introductory Screen again.**
> **and Command window**     In the next session, FoxPro will start in the
> to tap the full power of FoxPro.     environment you select now.
>
> ☒ **Explore a sample FoxPro catalog**
> that includes sample files.

# Choosing the active table or query

1. **Click the Table or Query tab.**

   Which one you choose depends solely on whether you want a table or a query, but you knew that already.

2. **Click the particular file you want in the big list area, and then click Use.**

   FoxPro displays the active file's name at the top of the Catalog Manager dialog box.

   The file's description (if there is one) appears along the bottom of the dialog box.

# Browsing a table or query

1. **Make sure that the table or query you want to browse is active.**

   If you need help, the whole make-it-active thing is explained in the preceding series of steps.

   If you want to browse a file that's not the active one, just double-click its name in the list area. It becomes the active file and pops up in a browse window, all in one easy step.

2. **Click the permanent picture button (remember those?) in the upper left corner of the Catalog Manager. The one you want looks like a table being scrutinized by a magnifying glass. Look at the picture of it next to this paragraph.**

   If you're using a query, FoxPro runs the query and displays the results in a Browse window. Tables just come up in Browse mode.

3. **When you've finished looking at the window, press Esc, and the window flees the screen immediately.**

   I never have figured out why everything in FoxPro is so afraid of the Esc key. It doesn't seem particularly mean or overbearing to me.

# Adding things to the Catalog

1. **Click the appropriate tab for the file you're adding.**

   I tried very hard to come up with a clever turn on *birds of a feather flock together*, but it's just not happening right now. Sorry.

2. **Click Add.**

3. **Double-click the lucky file in the Open dialog box.**

   If the file you want isn't there, frantically change directories (and possibly disk drives) until you find it. Give it a sound scolding for not being where you thought it would be and remind it of all the nasty people in the world who prey on good little data files.

   Success — the filename appears in the list area.

   Files can appear in more than one catalog — there's nothing wrong with that.

## Deleting (and really deleting) stuff

1. **Click the appropriate file tab.**

   I know this step is getting boring and redundant, but it really does start almost every one of these procedures. Please remain calm and continue buying IDG books.

2. **Click the item you want to delete from the catalog.**

3. **Select File⇨Remove File from the menu.**

   The Remove File dialog box springs into action, displaying a really sick level of enthusiasm for its job.

4. **To merely remove the file from the catalog, click Remove. To *completely delete it* from the disk, click the Delete File from Disk checkbox, and then click Remove.**

   ✔ If you turn on Delete File from Disk, FoxPro permanently erases the file from the disk *and* removes it from the catalog. Don't click this checkbox unless you're *sure* you want to delete the file for good.

   ✔ When you remove a file from the catalog, you lose the file's description. If you put the file back into the catalog in the future, you have to reenter the description. No, I don't like it either. If file descriptions are new to you, see the following section to find out about more about this marvelous new documentation tool.

## Entering descriptions

1. **Click the file that needs some documentation.**

   A few good words of documentation never hurt anyone.

**2. From the menu, select File⇨File Description.**

The File Description dialog box appears, ready to serve you and your table.

**3. There's only one place to type, so fill the big text box with as much useful stuff about the file as you can think of.**

Type the most important part of the description on the first line. This line appears in the Description area at the bottom of the Catalog Manager dialog box, so it's visible every time you click the file.

**4. When your description is a thing of beauty (or at least information), click OK.**

The dialog box goes away, and your description is safely stored wherever it is that FoxPro stores such things.

## Modifying your stuff

**1. Click the file (table, query, report, or whatever) so that it's highlighted.**

**2. Click the Modify button.**

Depending on what you choose, the Catalog Manager may ask whether you want to modify the *whatever* (that's the technical term) with a Wizard or FoxPro's Official Appropriate Complicated Power Tool. When it's an option, I recommend using the Wizard.

## Getting an AutoReport or AutoScreen

**1. Decide which table or query you want to use and make it active.**

**2. Click the AutoReport or AutoScreen button, or select Tools⇨AutoReport or Tools⇨AutoScreen.**

- AutoReport rings up the the Report Wizard and orders a default report (without onions). It's a plain report, but easy to get.

- AutoScreen uses the Screen Wizard to make a nothing-fancy kind of screen for your file. It uses the Wizard's default settings.

- If you have a burning desire to make the AutoWhateverItIs look or work better, you can modify them with the Wizards. Follow the steps in the preceding "Modifying Your Stuff" section.

The Catalog Manager automatically stores the report under the (you guessed it) appropriate tab.

## Using an index

1. **Choose the table you want to use and make it active.**

   Indexes only work with tables.

2. **Select Data⇨Order Table from the Catalog Manager menu.**

   The Order Table dialog box appears. It's also appearing as Figure 24-3.

3. **Scroll through the list of Available Tags/Indexes and double-click the one you want.**

   Only the structural index file is automatically available in the Catalog Manager. If you want to use a different index file with your table, you have to specifically add it to the Catalog Manager's index list. See the following section, "Adding an Index to the Catalog File," for all the details.

   Your table is now in order by that index.

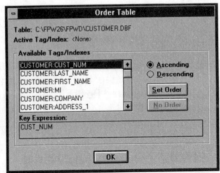

**Figure 24-3:**
Pick your index, doh-si-doh. Click Set Order, away you go!

## Adding an index to the Catalog file

1. **Make the relevant table active.**

   Holding a hot iron near its header usually makes the table as active as you want. In fact, it may take some time to calm it back down after the procedure. For the best results, use a steam iron set on "roast."

2. **From the Catalog Manager menu, select Data⇨Add/Modify Indexes.**

   The Add/Modify Indexes dialog box appears. (Do you ever wonder where they get the names for these dialog boxes?)

3. **Click Add to see the list of available index files.**

A standard Open dialog box comes up and shakes your face. You can choose either a compound index file (.CDX for you technically inclined readers) or a single index file (.IDX for the same group).

4. **Scroll through the list and double-click the index you want.**

FoxPro lists *all* the index files in the current directory. Just because something's on the list doesn't mean it has *anything* to do with the active table. Only choose an index that's for the *current, active table*.

5. **The Open dialog box disappears. Your newly added index appears with the others in the Add/Modify Indexes dialog box. Click OK to make the dialog box get out of your face.**

## Changing an index file

1. **Choose the table in question and make it active.**

2. **Select Data⇨Add/Modify Indexes from those marvelous menus.**

The Add/Modify Indexes dialog box runs up and snaps to attention.

3. **If you have more than one index file for this table, click the index you're modifying, and then click (appropriately enough) Modify.**

The Change Index dialog box appears.

4. **You have several options at this point, including adding, changing, or removing an index.**

   • To add a new index using a single field, choose the field in the Available Fields list, and then click Add at the top of the dialog box.

   • To add a multifield index, click the Add button inside the Expression area. In the Create Expression dialog box that appears, type a name for the index in the Tag Name box. Click the Expression button to start the fearsome Expression Builder and breathe life into your handiwork. When you're finished, click OK to create the index.

   • If you have a multifield index that needs some maintenance work, click it in the Index Keys list, and then click Edit (it's in the Expression area).

   • For a detailed explanation of the intricate, boggling, and occasionally rewarding process of making multiple-table indexes, see the "Indexing on Multiple Fields" section in Chapter 11.

   • Removing an index is quick and easy. Click the condemned index in the Index Keys list, and then click Remove. It's toast.

5. **When all the adding, changing, and removing is done, click OK to make things as permanent as they ever get with computers.**

If you suddenly decide you didn't mean to do these terrible things to such an innocent index file, click Cancel instead. That tells FoxPro to throw out all the changes and leave the index file as it was.

6. **Click OK once more to close the Add/Modify Indexes dialog box and return to the regularly scheduled Catalog Manager session, already in progress.**

## Making a new index file

1. **Choose the table that needs the new index and click Use.**

Take heart — that's the last time in this chapter for this particular instruction. It's worked hard (and I'm as sick of it as you are).

2. **Select Data⇨Add/Modify Indexes from the menu bar.**

A menu bar is nothing like a piano bar. For example, I doubt that anyone will ever sing, "Give us a choice, you're the menu bar; give us a choice tonight."

3. **Click New in the Add/Modify Indexes dialog box.**

You can *only* create compound index files (so-called .CDX files) with the Catalog Manager.

If you want one of the old-fashioned single-index files (with an .IDX extension), refer to Chapter 11.

4. **Start building indexes with a frenzy.**

- To add a new index based a single field, click the field in the Available Fields list, and then click Add at the top of the dialog box. The field appears in the Index Keys box.

- Don't panic because the field name is suddenly gray in the Available Fields list. That means there's already an index using that field.

- If a multifield index is your goal, click the *other* Add button — the one inside the Expression area. When the Create Expression dialog box poofs into being, type a name for the index in the Tag Name box. Grit your teeth and click the Expression button to start the Expression Builder. Build your expression (for what else is one to do with an Expression Builder?). When you're finished, click OK to create the new super-index.

5. **Click OK to finish the process. When the Save As dialog box appears, type a name for the new index file and click Save.**

The dialog box vanishes. In a moment, the newly created index file appears in the Add/Modify Indexes dialog box. Whew.

The Catalog Manager won't let you save your new index with the same name as an old one. It pretends that it's going to do it, but chickens out at the last minute. Instead, it complains that there's already an index file with that name, so you need to pick a different one for your new index, thank you very much.

6. **Click OK once more to close the Add/Modify Indexes dialog box.**

## *Making a new catalog file*

1. **Select File⇨New Catalog from the menu.**

Isn't this stuff intuitive?

2. **In the Save As dialog box, type a name for the catalog, and then click Save.**

The new, blank, empty Catalog file appears, ready to do your bidding.

## *Opening a different Catalog file*

1. **Select File⇨Open from the Catalog Manager menu bar.**

2. **Double-click the Catalog file you want.**

As always, you can participate in the ritualistic Searching of Directories and Flipping between Drives if you need to (or if it's nearing the vernal equinox and you want to get the ceremony out of the way).

The Catalog file hops up, glad that you recalled it from that dark, dismal disk drive.

## *Quitting the Catalog Manager*

There are two ways to do it, depending on where you want to end up. Select File⇨Command to return to the old-fashioned way of life you used to know in earlier versions of FoxPro. If you're ready to call it a day (or night, or darn-why'd-I-have-to-come-in-this-Saturday), select File⇨Quit to bid FoxPro a possibly fond farewell.

# Chapter 25

# Drawing Screens at the
# Wave of a Wand

*In This Chapter*

▶ Creating with the Screen Wizard

▶ What you see is what you ordered

▶ Changing your mind means rebuilding the screen

. . . . . . . . . . . . . . . . . . . . . . . . . . . . . . . . . .

*F*oxPro's not exactly flush with options for looking at your tables. "Would you like Browse or Change? Perhaps Browse mode would suit you — it's one of our biggest sellers. Then again, have you considered Change mode?" In a word, B-O-R-I-N-G.

Programmers and other gurus always had a way of out this trap with the Screen Builder. They could create custom screens that looked and acted however they wanted. Unfortunately for the normal FoxPro user, creating something useful with the Screen Builder was the software equivalent of scaling the north face of Mount Everest in shorts.

The new version of FoxPro fixes that problem. In fact, it goes so far as to make the process *fun*. (Heretical, isn't it?) Give the Screen Wizard a try the next time you're so sick of facing a plain vanilla Browse window that you're seriously thinking of sprucing it up with a nice stapler shoved right through the screen.

### A screen by any other name

Screens (particularly from the Screen Wizard) are great for hacking around in your table. Consider these attributes:

Beauty | They're a sight to behold. I'm talking about major league jealousy from your office buddies.

Functionality | All those buttons make adding, editing, and deleting a breeze.

Ease of Use | Everything you want to do is covered with an on-screen button.

Quick Browsing | Buttons move you hither and yon through your table with a single click.

If you have FoxPro 2.5, you don't have a Screen Wizard. {sigh} Have you considered upgrading?

## Creating with the Screen Wizard

The Screen Wizard makes building a custom screen *really* easy. In fact, it's one of the simplest Wizards in FoxPro. There are still a few pitfalls, though, so click carefully through the following steps.

1. **Pick a table that needs some help in the visual appeal department. Open it by selecting Window⇨View⇨Open or by going through the Catalog Manager.**

   To make a screen with fields from related tables, build the screen from the parent table. Later, when you're picking fields, all the fields from related tables are available.

   Like some of the other Wizards, the Screen Wizard isn't completely fond of related tables. If you need a screen that displays fields from several related tables, that's no problem, but there is a limitation: You can't use the new screen to add new records to a table that's in a relation. Even if your screen only shows fields from one table, if that table was related to another one *when you ran the Wizard*, the Wizard considers it a related table and disables the screen's Add Record button.

2. **Select Run⇨Wizard⇨Screen to summon forth your electro-magical help. The Wizard's first screen appears.**

3. **Choose the subject of the screen from Wizard's table list. Click Next for the next screen.**

    • If the table you want isn't listed, click the Open button to include it.

    • If you're thoroughly confused and don't know why on Earth you ever started the Screen Wizard when what you really wanted to do was go have a sandwich at a small deli near the office, click Cancel to make the bad old Wizard go away. After you're freed from his clutches, go have lunch.

4. **It's decision time — choose the fields the Wizard should include in your screen. To use everything the table has, click Add All. The result looks something like Figure 25-1. Click Next to sally forth.**

    To pick and choose only a few fields, scroll through the Available Fields list and double-click the lucky fields. If you get the wrong one by accident (or design), double-click it in the Selected Fields list.

    By the way, if you're using related tables, the Available Fields list includes the current table's fields *plus* all the fields from the related tables. You needn't do anything special to include them — the old double-click routine works very nicely.

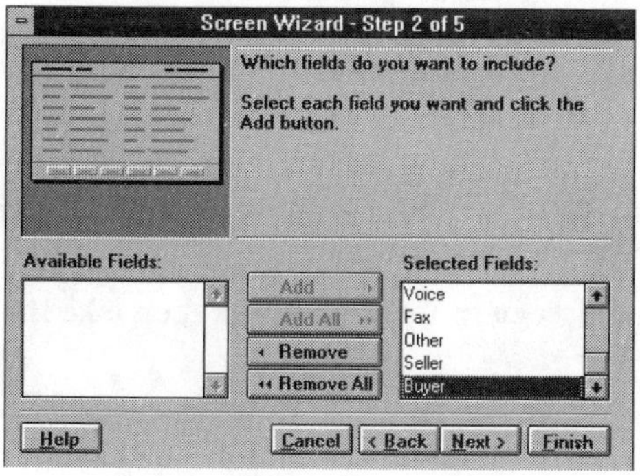

**Figure 25-1:** I wanted all the Customer records, so I clicked Add All.

5. **If you want the records sorted in any particular way, explain it to FoxPro in this dialog box. You can use up to three fields for the sort. Choose them just as you did in the last step. And, as you did before, click Next to keep going.**

    Figure 25-2 shows the Cust_num field selected to be in charge of the sorting. Lucky little guy.

    • If you want the records sorted from largest to smallest, click the Descending button before clicking Next.

• If you want to see the records by state, then ZIP code would be a good second field. Without a second sort field to break the ties, all the records within each state would be jumbled up in no particular order.

**Figure 25-2:**
Because
my
customers
have unique
customer
numbers, I
only need
one sort
field.

6. **This window enables you to choose the look for your new screen. Just click Next to accept the defaults.**

After you're comfortable with making screens, try experimenting with the different styles on the left side of the screen (my personal favorites are Shadowed and Embossed). As for the button type setting, unless you're seriously addicted to little picture buttons, leave them set to Text. The pictures alone just don't cut it.

7. **You're near the finish line — the checkered flag is in sight. Type a title for your screen in the space provided.**

8. **Click the Save and Run Screen radio button, and then take the flag with a quick click on Finish.**

Make sure that you click Save and Run Screen before clicking Finish. That tells FoxPro to save all your choices and to create a working screen. Otherwise, it saves your work but doesn't do anything about it.

9. **Type a file name for the screen (yes, even screens live in files on the disk) and click Save. Then sit back and watch FoxPro do its build-a-screen thing.**

When the pixel dust settles, your screen, in its immaculate glory, sits enthroned on the screen.

# What You See Is What You Ordered

The basic Wizard-created screen is split into four parts: title, data, navigation buttons, and editing buttons. Figure 25-3 helps you with the geography.

Title
This is the title you entered in the preceding Step 7. Looks good, doesn't it?

Data
It's your table's fields, shamelessly on display for the whole world to see.

Navigation buttons
These buttons give you an easy way to flip from record to record. They're reasonably self-explanatory, too — a pleasant change from the software world's normal performance.

Editing buttons
Rounding out your complete control over the table, the screen even buttons lets you add, change, delete, and print records at the click of a button. The Close button sends the screen itself packing.

Data

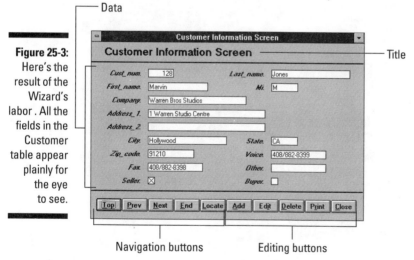

**Figure 25-3:** Here's the result of the Wizard's labor. All the fields in the Customer table appear plainly for the eye to see.

Title

Navigation buttons          Editing buttons

By the way, to open a screen after it's saved, select Run➪Screen. Choose the screen file from the list, changing directories if you're not where you should be. Click Run to make things happen.

# Changing Your Mind Means Rebuilding the Screen

When something is easy, there's often a *gotcha!* waiting in the shadows. The Screen Wizard has one, but given how easy it is to create a screen in the first place, the gotcha isn't very big. The gotcha in question is this: After it's created, it just ain't easy to make changes to your screens. In fact, it's a lot easier to rebuild them from scratch.

This isn't to say that you *can't* make editorial changes; I'm just saying that it's not for everybody. In fact, I'm not sure exactly who it *is* for, but when I find them, I'll let you know.

To replace a screen entirely, go back through the steps to build it, and then save it with exactly the same name as the original. FoxPro will fret that your proposed name is already attached to a file, but a simple click on the Overwrite button puts FoxPro back to work.

# Chapter 26

# Watching FoxApp Build
# a Program for You

. . . . . . . . . . . . . . . . . . . . . . . . . . . . . . . . . . . . . . . . . . . . .

## In This Chapter

▶ What's a FoxApp?

▶ Your contributions to the process

▶ Creating and running the application

▶ Applications with two linked tables

. . . . . . . . . . . . . . . . . . . . . . . . . . . . . . . . . . . . . . . . . . . . .

*R*obots are the stuff of both fiction and reality. Fiction says they emerge from spaceships and terrorize small towns, often carrying off beautiful heroines (to the infinite glee of the more average-looking town residents). Reality says robots weigh a lot and paint cars, disarm bombs, or do other glamorous things.

Did you wonder why the FoxPro box is so heavy? It's because there's a robot in there. It's called FoxApp (short for "FoxPro Application Generator"), and it will change the way you think about programming; that is, if you think about programming at all these days (which I hope you don't).

## What's a FoxApp?

As you may (or better yet, may not) know, FoxPro for Windows comes with a super-powerful programming language. Lots of people *love* FoxPro for its rich programming environment. Granted, that's not what excites you or me, but different people are tweaked by different things.

So, FoxPro has this swell programming language. But there's a problem: To use it, you have to *write programs*. And you know what happens next, don't you?

People start calling you a *programmer. Eeew* — I get shivers just thinking about it. So there you are, between a Fox and a hard place: all-powerful programming language on one side; one-way ticket to nerd-dom on the other. What's a normal person to do? Use FoxApp, that's what!

FoxApp is a program that writes programs. You tell it about your favorite table and screen, and then FoxApp gets out a pen and starts programming. When it's finished, you have a full-featured data entry and editing application, complete with custom menus. It may *sound* really technical, but you don't have to worry about that. Just remember that FoxApp does the hard parts *for* you.

If you absolutely, positively *must* learn to program, you can dissect FoxApp's work and see how the experts do it. Heck, you can even dissect FoxApp — it's just a program.

# Your Contributions to the Process

Despite the amazing (and perhaps disquieting) fact that FoxApp is a program that writes programs, take comfort in knowing that FoxApp can't do it alone. You're still in the loop — the computers haven't taken over yet. At least they hadn't by press time, but you know how fast these things can change.

So, if FoxApp does the hard parts, what's left for you? The easy part, that's what. All you have to do is show up with a ready-made table and a screen; FoxApp takes it from there.

## Why applications are different from (and perhaps better than) screens

If you have ever used the Screen Wizard, you know about the incredibly useful and good-looking screens it produces. So what does FoxApp do to top the Wizard? It does *menus*, that's what.

FoxApp starts with the Screen Wizard's marvelous work and builds an application with a whole set of custom menus. Instead of seeing the standard FoxPro menu bar, you see options that are specially customized for working with a table. Everything you need is there, but without the confusing noise of the full menu system. The application makes managing your table a breeze. You've *gotta* try this thing.

## A table

First, FoxApp needs a table. Without one, there's nothing to build an application for. Any table will do — there aren't any fancy requirements or limitations. You can even use more than one table if you want.

    ✔ Check out Chapter 6 for a quick refresher about tables in general. If linked tables are fogged in your memory, look in Chapter 12.

    ✔ If you want the application to use linked tables, you need some extra information. See the cleverly titled section "Applications with Two Linked Tables," later in the chapter, to find out more.

## A screen

The other main ingredient is a screen. I recommend using the new Screen Wizard to whip one up in no time. The screens look great, which is a lot more than I can say for the ones I made by hand with FoxPro's screen builder. Plus, the Wizard puts an incredibly useful set of control buttons at the bottom of the screen. You can't ask for much more than beauty and functionality. Well, you can *ask*, but you probably won't get anything.

    ✔ It helps if the screen has the same name as your table. That way, you only have to tell FoxApp the table name — it automatically assumes that the screen has that name, too.

    ✔ For the whole story on the Screen Wizard, flip back to Chapter 25.

# Creating and Running the Application

So much for the dramatic build-up — it's FoxApp time:

1. **Before starting FoxApp, create your table and screen.**

    • Although FoxApp gives you the opportunity to create either or both while building the application, it's like an opportunity to cover yourself in raw meat and swim laps in a piranha tank. Make your table first, and then build the screen. When the dust settles from those experiences, proceed to the next step.

    • See Chapter 6 for table building help. Chapter 25 introduces you to the Screen Wizard (a really fun person — er, program — to know).

- Make sure that the table has data in it before running FoxApp. Although it's not absolutely required, having at least one record is a really good idea.

2. **From the main FoxPro menu, select Run⇨Application. The Open dialog box appears.**

3. **Click New to start FoxApp. The FoxPro Application Generator (known to a favored few as FoxApp) dialog box stomps ominously onto the screen.**

Hang on tight — the ride's just beginning!

4. **Now for the ceremonial Opening of the Table. In the box labeled Step 1 — Create or Modify a Table — click From File.**

The Open dialog comes back for a (brief) repeat performance.

5. **Double-click the table you want.**

- As always, if the table's not listed, use the dialog box to gyrate through your available drives and directories until you either find it or forget what you're looking for and absentmindedly wander off to do something else.

- If you multiple-mash the mouse just right, the Open dialog box goes away (which is almost reward enough). But wait — it gets better! Look carefully at Figure 26-1. Not just one, but *both* blanks in the FoxApp dialog box are filled in. Can I have an "ooooooh" from the audience, please?

- The name of your chosen table is ensconced in the area marked Table Name. FoxApp guessed that the screen has the same name as the table and scribbled it under Screen Name. That's why I recommended that you name the screen just like the table — if you did, then FoxPro just finished the dialog box for you.

- If you *didn't* give your table and screen the same name, you have to enter it yourself. Just tab down to the Screen Name box and type in whatever peculiar moniker you chose or use the From File button in the Step 2 area.

If you want the application to use linked tables, now's the time to link. Look ahead to the section "Applications with Two Linked Tables" later in this chapter for the details.

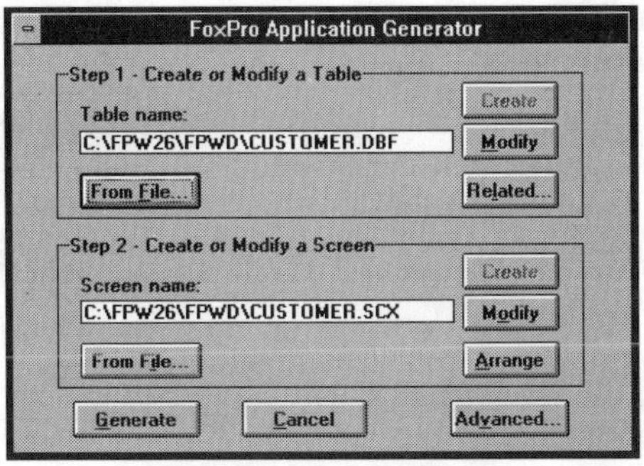

**Figure 26-1:**
FoxApp filled
in both the
table name
and the
screen
name.

6. **It's time to turn your attention to the area marked Screen Name. If FoxApp came up with the right name, go on to Step 7. Otherwise, click From File and choose the appropriate screen.**

   It's another Open dialog box — try to control yourself. All the same rules and peculiar traditions apply that always applied in these situations. So there.

7. **Click Generate. In the Save As dialog box that pops annoyingly onto the screen, type a name for the new application, and then click Save.**

   Bring on the dancing chickens! FoxApp leaps cavernous disks, tames wild tables, and explores strange and exotic memory addresses as it builds your application. Granted, it's not high drama, but it is kinda fun to watch.

8. **When the process is complete, the exciting message portrayed in Figure 26-2 appears on-screen. Hold your breath, turn blue, pass out, regain consciousness, bandage your head, and then press any key to see the application come to life.**

   I know that's a lot to remember right now, but it's a whole lot easier the second time around.

   Your application probably looks almost nothing like Figure 26-3. Then again, my application probably looks nothing like yours, either. I guess we're even.

9. **To make your creations go away and leave you in peace, click Close or select File⇨Quit from the application menu.**

   When you're psyched up enough to run it again, select Run⇨Application, and then double-click the application's name.

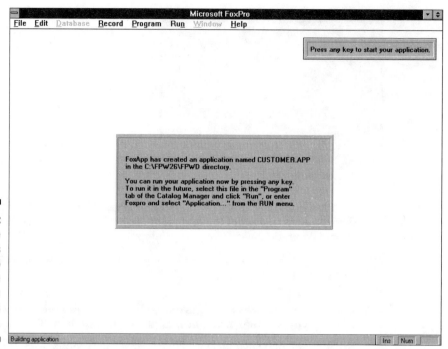

**Figure 26-2:**
Shhh! The
curtain's
ready to go
up on the
newest little
application
in FoxPro.

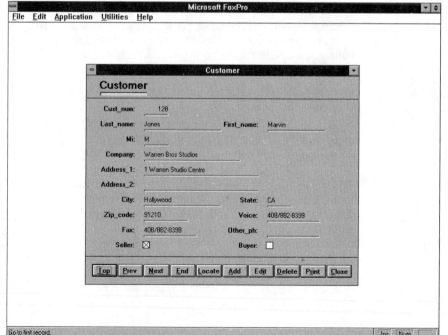

**Figure 26-3:**
The
Customer
table shur
looks nice
all gussied
up in a
purdy new
screen,
don't it?

# *Applications with Two Linked Tables*

FoxApp still has one more trick up its sleeve to amaze and amuse you: It can build applications with *linked* tables. Yes, not only does it write programs for you, it also understands one-to-many table relationships. Almost more than you can believe, isn't it?

Figure 26-4 shows what FoxApp can do with linked tables. Customer is the parent; Items is the child. I created a screen for Customer by using the Screen Wizard. FoxApp made the Items table Browse window on its own.

Using the application is a breeze. When you scroll through the parent table, FoxPro automatically lists linked child records in the other window. You can even edit the child records just as you do in Browse mode. It's pretty slick.

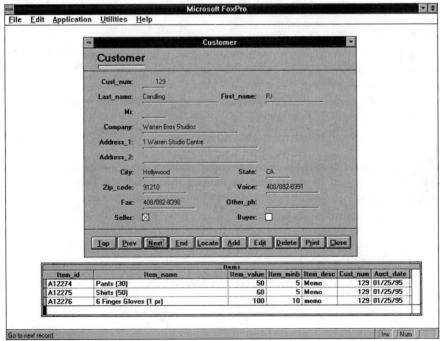

**Figure 26-4:** Yes, your linked tables can be part of an application that looks as good as this.

To create these multitable masterpieces of software design, use the preceding steps for a single table application, but add this short procedure just before Step 6:

**5a. After choosing the table file, click the Related button. This opens the Related Tables dialog box.**

Here's where the magic happens. FoxApp wants to know what other tables to include in the application — and that's just what you're going to tell it.

**5b. Click Add. The Open dialog box appears. Choose another table for the application from the list. When you find the one you want, double-click it.**

**5c. The Open dialog box is replaced by the Options dialog box. FoxApp needs to understand how these tables are related. Choose the linking fields from the dialog box's drop-down lists, and then click OK.**

If the tables have a field in common (one that has exactly the same name), FoxPro guesses that it might be the linking field and suggests using it. If it guesses wrong, just choose a different field from the pull-down lists.

The whole linking thing is covered to the point of nausea in Chapter 12. If you're a little fogged on it, take a minute to flip back there for the whole scoop.

**5d. Your chosen table appears in the Related Tables list. Click OK to get back to FoxApp.**

Pick up where you left off with Step 6.

You can add more than one table to an application, but if you're getting that advanced, I strongly suggest seeking guidance from a FoxPro guru. There might be a better way to accomplish what you need.

# Chapter 27

# The Desk Accessories: Things that Make You Go "Hmmm"

*In This Chapter*

▶ The Calculator: yup, that's what it is

▶ The Calendar/Diary: unique and fun

▶ The Filer: it beats the DOS prompt

▶ The Puzzle: built-in stress relief

There's a well known malady among software manufacturers. Very few companies (if any) manage to avoid it. I'm speaking of *multiple unrelated fluffy feature syndrome,* or MUFFS for short. It's not deadly, but it does make you scratch your head and go "hmmm" a lot.

MUFFS is a digital form of Swiss army knife envy, in which the afflicted software developer tries to pack as many features as possible into a program. Whether these features directly relate to the program's purpose is irrelevant — the point is to add for the sake of adding. I fear that FoxPro's developers have a terminal case of MUFFS.

My concern stems from the presence of four unusual options under the Help menu: Calculator, Calendar/Diary, Filer, and Puzzle. Although possibly the products of an advanced MUFFS case, they're still useful. Despite their sad origin, go ahead and use the options. You cannot help the MUFFS afflicted; the effects (sadly) are irreversible. Perhaps by using what they create, some good may still come of this whole painful tragedy.

### Why are they under Help?

All these funky accessories are in the Help menu. Why Help? Goodness, I don't know. The truth itself is forever obscured in the mists of history. But that doesn't mean the question isn't open for speculation. <sadistic grin>

Based on my own programming experience, the decision was probably made on a coin toss or some other highly scientific process. If these were average Microsoft programmers (who are generally above average themselves), they probably used a computer *simulation* of a coin toss —

you can't trust analog coins to give truly objective results for such important decisions.

Perhaps the programmers wrote the tools for themselves and included them in the final product at the last minute. Maybe the Help menu was short a few items and needed some padding. Or they thought the Desk Accessories would *help* people and placed them accordingly.

Oh, well, I guess we'll never know for sure. Maybe it's better that way.

# The Calculator: Yup, That's What It Is

You can't say much about a calculator, but I'm trying. By selecting Help⇨ Calculator, you get an on-screen representation of a $4 solar calculator, brought to you in loving detail by several thousand dollars' worth of computer equipment. Granted, this calculator handles up to 15 digits, but it's still just a calculator. It looks just like one too, as you can see in Figure 27-1. Wow; hold me back.

**Figure 27-1:**
Presenting Hmmm #1, the FoxPro calculator.

Use it by either clicking the mouse pointer on the virtual calculator keypad or by nimbly dancing your fingers over the actual keyboard keypad. Your calculator, your choice.

If you're a real keyboard aficionado, almost every calculator command works without the mouse. The non-obvious ones are / for division, * for multiplication, and C to clear the darn thing.

# The Calendar/Diary: Unique and Fun

I have a confession: I *like* this feature. Yes, despite my grousing, I really like the Calendar/Diary. It's something simple for keeping my journal, something without a lot of embellishments to get in the way. And *where* do I find it? In my *database program* for goodness' sake. Who'd have thought it?

Start the routine by selecting <u>H</u>elp⇨Calendar/Diary. Figure 27-2 shows Calendar/Diary in action. It has a perpetual calendar, so you won't run out of days. Likewise, the diary section just keeps expanding as you type.

**Figure 27-2:**
A normal day in the life of someone who keeps a journal in the Calendar/Diary.

| | | | Calendar/Diary | | | | |

It was a good day. The meals went well, the kids were good; seems like the everything just flowed. What a pleasant change!

Things are back to normal since the birthday party. Having all those four year olds at once was quite a treat. I finished cleaning up the playroom and found the cat. Must remember to use the old icing recipe next year; the new one dries hard. It came out of the carpet, but not Fritzie. She looks like a waxed pink rat, but her fur grows fast so she'll be

April 1995
Su Mo Tu We Th Fr Sa
                  1
2  3  4  5  6  7  8
9  10 11 12 13 14 15
16 17 18 19 **20** 21 22
23 24 25 26 27 28 29
30

[ < Month ]  [ Month > ]  [ < Year ]  [ Year > ]  [ <u>T</u>oday ]

To make an entry, click a day and type in the text area. FoxPro saves your work automatically. Use the buttons at the bottom of the window to move backward and forward through the months and years. If you click them enough, you can time warp forward into the next millenium or backward to the 70s. If you get back to 1976 or so and click the <u>T</u>oday button, FoxPro displays a digitized photo of Jane Pauley watching Gene Shalit dance to the strains of Saturday Night Fever on the studio desk.

I'm kidding. The <u>T</u>oday button would *never* do a thing like that — it can't stand disco music either. It takes you to the diary entry for whatever your computer thinks is the current date. (Besides, I don't think Gene Shalit ever *did* dance on the desk. Maybe Jane did, but not Gene.)

# The Filer: It Beats the DOS Prompt

Compared to the other three options, Filer is an honest-to-useful tool. I use it all the time. When you have some quick file management stuff to do, it's great to select <u>H</u>elp⇨<u>F</u>iler and finish your job without leaving FoxPro.

If you're not familiar with the terms *DOS*, *subdirectory*, or *file management*, don't mess with Filer. Instead, get a copy of *Windows for Dummies* (from IDG Books) and read all about the Windows File Manager program. You'll thank me later.

The dialog box is a little startling, as you can see in Figure 27-3. There's a lot competing for your attention, but if you concentrate, it's not (very) scary at all.

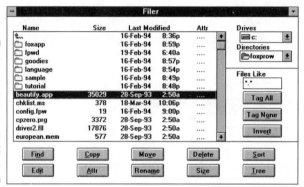

**Figure 27-3:** The Filer is a handy, powerful, and full-featured file management tool.

The big window shows the files and subdirectories wherever you are right now. Subdirectories have little manila folders next to them; files are just there. To move into a subdirectory, double-click it. To choose a file, click it. To choose more than one file, hold down the Ctrl key and keep clicking.

The buttons across the bottom perform your file management tasks. They're pretty self-explanatory, but several aren't important. Here are the ones you care about:

Copy        Copies the highlighted file (or files) wherever you choose.

Move        Moves the file instead of copying it.

Rename      Changes the name of the selected file, but leaves it in the current directory.

Delete      Forever erases the highlighted file. Treat this one with care!

Take care playing with the Tag buttons and the Files Like box on the right side of the dialog box. They give you some quick ways to work with whole great bunches of files, but you can quickly do widespread damage if they're misapplied. Like most power tools, the Filer is great if you know what you're doing, but dangerous if you're guessing.

# The Puzzle: Built-In Stress Relief

I'm actually thankful that they (whoever and wherever *they* are) threw this option in. I think more programs should include integrated games. Everyone knows the programs are more complicated than ever. All that complication raises stress levels and lowers productivity. Having an easy, fun, addictive little game available in every program would reduce stress enormously. Write your representative and senators — there ought to be a law about this!

Back in reality, the number puzzle pops up if you select Help⇨Puzzle. It's pretty simple to play. It starts out all jumbled up like the left side of Figure 27-4. Your goal is to reorganize it like the right side of Figure 27-4. What could be easier? Truth be told, a great number of things are easier. It's frustrating, addictive, and always available.

If you're deep in the middle of a puzzle attack and your boss starts into the cube, just press Esc. The puzzle immediately disappears. Select Help⇨Puzzle again, and you're right back where you started. I wonder where the programmers got the idea for that feature?

**Figure 27-4:**
To win, turn the jumbled mess on the left into the miracle of organization on the right.

| Puzzle ▼ | | | |
|---|---|---|---|
| 6 | | 1 | 10 |
| 12 | 9 | 15 | 2 |
| 3 | 4 | 11 | 8 |
| 14 | 5 | 7 | 13 |
| Shuffle | | | |

| Puzzle ▼ | | | |
|---|---|---|---|
| 1 | 2 | 3 | 4 |
| 5 | 6 | 7 | 8 |
| 9 | 10 | 11 | 12 |
| 13 | 14 | 15 | |
| Shuffle | | | |

# Chapter 28

# The View Dialog Box's Secret Buttons

*T*he View dialog box has a secret identity. Actually, it has four secret identities, but after the first one, who's counting? Yes, despite its dialog box-next-door demeanor, View is a seething cauldron of deception, intrigue, and power.

Hidden beneath its secret panel buttons is the FoxPro control room, filled with checkboxes, lists, doohickeys, and things that go *wakka-wakka-sluuurp* at night. This is the seat of power in FoxPro's world — and this chapter tells you how to get inside. Sort of like finding an unlocked entrance to Disney World's underground tunnels, isn't it?

## Buttons? What Buttons?

Although cleverly disguised as mere decorations, the secret panel buttons are almost apparent in Figure 28-1. They're the picture buttons on the left side of the dialog box. From the top, you have View, On/Off (I kid you not — that's what they call it), Files, International, and Miscellaneous. They look like an organizational chart, some boxes and squiggles, two file folders, the world, and a singing clock. Diabolically clever, isn't it?

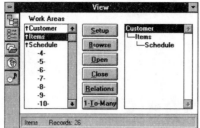

**Figure 28-1:**
The View
dialog box's
control
panels are
stacked
vertically on
the left.

The top button is pushed in; that means it's on right now. They work like radio buttons, so only one can be on at a time. When you click one, it "pushes in" and the dialog box changes to show you whatever options are available with that setting. At the same time, the old button "pops out." It's entertaining, but nothing like the Mona Lisa or an evening with your favorite film. I give it 3 stars, minus 1 for the popcorn oil on the keyboard.

Each button commands a different portion of FoxPro. Some you probably won't use much (like On/Off), but you might venture into others from time to time.

Fouling some of the settings in here can *seriously* muck up your copy of FoxPro for Windows. If you don't understand something or aren't sure whether it controls what you want to change, *don't change it!* Take your hand off the mouse, slowly put it in your lap — your hand, not your mouse — breathe deeply, and then get some professional help. Kids, don't try this at home without your parents watching. Remember: They can't learn if they're not paying attention.

# *Viewing : The Clever Cover Story*

This is the innocent, public side of View that you're already familiar with. Perhaps you thought the dialog box in Figure 28-1 was the whole View experience — it fooled me for a while, too. But now the truth is out and you see viewing for what it really is: just another option on the button panel of life.

The main sections, Work Areas on the left and the unmarked Relations area on the right, display table names. The Relations side shows you which tables are currently related to each other; Work Areas lists the open tables.

The buttons in the center of the screen manage your tables as they enter, exit, and play on FoxPro's center stage. The first four, Setup, Browse, Open, and Close, are the ones you use most of the time. Relations establishes the cool logical ties between open tables.

## Getting there from here

With the right help, anyone can conquer the View dialog box's *secret buttons*. But to do that, you have to find the View dialog box to begin with. Depending on where you are in FoxPro, this may or may not be quick and easy.

If you're hanging out with the Command window (or using FoxPro for Windows 2.5), you're practically there already. Just select Window➪View from the menu, and the View dialog box pops to attention.

If you're working with the Catalog Manager in FoxPro for Windows 2.6, though, it's another matter. Don't panic — it's not a big deal; it's just not a direct menu choice.

To get to the View dialog box from the Catalog Manager, you have to get back to FoxPro's Command Window mode (sounds impressive, doesn't it?). Select File➪Command Window. That puts away the Catalog Manager and sends you back to the classic FoxPro way of doing things. After the Command Window appears, select Window➪View, and you're finished.

When you're finished doing the View thing and ready to see the friendly Catalog Manager again, select File➪Catalog Manager. See — it wasn't *too* much of a trip.

Now, as before, leave the 1-To-Many button alone. It's nothing but trouble.

✔ Setup, being the button on top, gets a lot of use. Use it to build or change filters and indexes, to modify a table's structure, or just to find out what index is in charge at the moment.

✔ Open and Close are pretty self-explanatory. They open and, uh, close things. Yeah, that's it — open and close.

✔ For more information about the View buttons, see Chapters 7, 11, and 12. To reach an operator, please stay on the line.

✔ Along the bottom is a message area that tells you the name and number of records for the current table. It's a nice touch.

# On/Off Options

It's the most mysterious, powerful, and dangerous option in the dialog box. Look at all those controls in Figure 28-2. Awe-inspiring view, isn't it? No? Well, it didn't do a thing for me either.

There are only a few settings in here that you should *ever* be concerned with — and even some of those are kinda long shots.

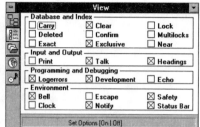

**Figure 28-2:** They could call this "Ali Onoff and the 21 Checkboxes". Nah, sounds like a 50's big band.

Please, please, *puh-leeese* don't make random changes in here. Pretty please?

✔ Now that you're warned, to change anything in this section, just click the desired checkbox. They're all checkboxes — every one of them. Think of them as little electronic "clappers" for FoxPro. "Click on, click off. The checkbox!" (No, I *don't* write jingles professionally. Why do you ask?)

✔ The Deleted checkbox (in the Database and Index section) is normally off. If it's on, records marked for deletion don't show when you're browsing, searching, or querying a table. FoxPro treats them like they're already gone, even though they aren't. Try it if this sounds like a good idea to you. You can always turn it off if you don't like it.

All the remaining options are in the Environment section, so look there before telling me they aren't on your system.

✔ Bell is what FoxPro calls the obnoxious, grating *beep* you hear every time the program is the least bit upset. Why they don't call it "Beep" or "Tone" or "Stupid Noise" is beyond me, but they don't. If you've had enough of FoxPro's alleged Bell, turn this off.

✔ The Clock appears on the status bar. If you turn the Status Bar off, you gain an extra quarter inch or so along the bottom of the screen. You lose your info (or should I say "status") bar, key lock display, and, yes, the clock in the exchange. If you're feeling time-crunched and have all the clocks you need, just turn off the clock and it slinks away but leaves the status bar in place and happy.

✔ Make sure that Safety is turned on. This tells FoxPro to ask before over-writing any files already on your disk or network. If it's turned off, FoxPro portrays the title role in the disk-based drama "Rampaging Bull and the Digital China Shop." It's not a pretty sight.

# File Selection

Here's another place to generally steer clear of. Most of the buttons you see in Figure 28-3 are things to leave alone — particularly the ones toward the bottom of the dialog box. The one (and only) friendly face is the Working Directory button near the top of the dialog box.

**Figure 28-3:**
Think of the
File and
Path items
as little on-
screen
landmines
and treat
them
accordingly.

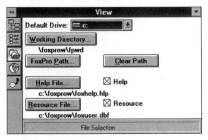

There is *one* really useful option, though: the great big Working Directory button. A click on this button lets you tell FoxPro what directory you're using for this work session. That means no more clicking here and clicking there to find your stuff. If it's all in one place, point the Working Directory there and forget about it (until next time, of course).

To set the working directory, click the button. The Select Directory dialog box appears. Using the controls in the dialog box, choose the directory of your dreams (or at least your working nightmares). If you simply *must* change disk drives, use the Drive list box and do your thing. After you're all set, click Select so that FoxPro remembers the results of your labors.

This setting only lasts until you exit FoxPro. The next time you run the program, it goes back to the old default directory.

# International Values

In a last minute blush of multiculturalism, the International settings received their own icon. As Figure 28-4 shows, the settings for your country are in place by default. The interesting things here are Show Century (which adds "19" in front of the current year) and Date Delimiter to change the punctuation that separates the date digits. That way, you can make the date "12.4.95" instead of "12/4/95." That's been keeping you up nights, hasn't it?

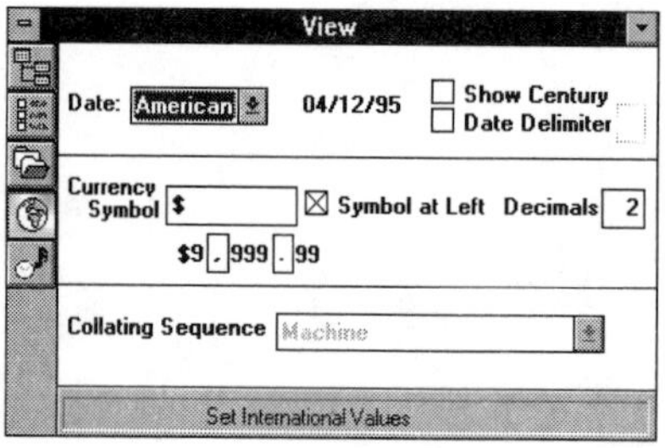

**Figure 28-4:**
A fun, international romp of a dialog box.

| | View | |
|---|---|---|
| Date: American ⬦ | 04/12/95 | ☐ Show Century |
| | | ☐ Date Delimiter |
| Currency Symbol $ | ⊠ Symbol at Left | Decimals 2 |
| $9 . 999 . 99 | | |
| Collating Sequence Machine | | ⬦ |
| Set International Values | | |

Likewise, in the Currency section you can change the currency symbol, control where it goes (in front of or behind the number), mess with the default number of decimal places, and continue fiddling with punctuation by exchanging commas and decimals for other fascinating marks. Play with the Currency section to give those foreign currency reports that much more flavor of the old country.

If the Collating Sequence box isn't grayed, don't change it. Period. If it *is* grayed, you can't change it anyway, but you can try if your frustration level is a little low for the day.

To get the British Pound symbol (£), click the Currency Symbol box, hold down the Alt key, and type **156** on the numeric keypad. For Japanese Yen (¥), do the same thing but type **157**. If your cursor runs all over the place or something else weird happens, press the Num Lock key on your keyboard and try again.

## Miscellaneous Stuff

Finally, some safe fun. Here, the options of interest are the Clock and Bell settings (the top two areas in Figure 28-5).That's right — you have *another* opportunity to torture the Clock, plus the chance to get fully even with the Bell. Is this a great dialog box or what?

**Figure 28-5:**
The fun box, where you can get even with the bell and make the clock do tricks.

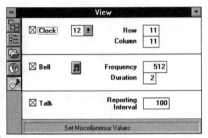

First, consider what you can do to — er, with — the clock. Clicking in the Clock checkbox merely turns the clock on or off. Want to see it do tricks? Try clicking the "12" list box. That lets you choose between 12 and 24 hour format — a boon for the international business folks, military experts, and amateur radio operators in the crowd. The Row and Column settings let you move the clock anywhere on-screen, just for kicks. Try clicking in the boxes and typing some different numbers there (usually limited to rows less than 26 and columns less than 80, please!). It's a gas!

If you manage to completely lose the clock, just double-click the Clock checkbox. Your time-enslaved friend reappears right back on the status line.

As for the Bell settings, you can (as you probably guessed) turn the darn thing off by clicking the Bell checkbox. The musical note (another cruel joke) plays a sample of the current "Didn't I *tell* you not to do that!??!" error tone for your listening pleasure. The Frequency and Duration boxes let you customize your own error tone. Go ahead, play a little. It's fun to hear the range of annoying sounds your computer can generate.

# Part VI
## The Part
## of Tens

**The 5th Wave**                                          **By Rich Tennant**

Futurists predict that eventually all people will be required to do some personal computing on a regular basis. But not everyone will own a PC. As more homes and apartments come equipped with washers and dryers, we will see the inevitable conversion of laundromats into...

**DataMats***  ©RICH TENNANT

The "Amana PC" will be the leader in the field, followed by the "IBM Front-loader," with its controversial spin-cycle architecture.

Maytag will introduce a dot matrix printer that retains its commercial dryer capabilities for shrinking 5¼-inch disks to 3½-inch size.

*Please DO NOT OVERLOAD YOUR RAM CACHE*

All Datamats will have vending machines that dispense basic software.

*Software* *

WORD PROC. | SPREAD SHEET | DBMS | BLANK DISK

Datamats will, however, suffer from the reputation of occasionally losing one document from any matching pair of documents a user arrives with.

# In this part...

Being a fine, upstanding citizen of the . . . *For Dummies* line, this book simply *must* close with the classic, ever-anticipated Part of Tens. These chapters enlighten, enliven, and enrage (oops, no — how about *enrich*) your FoxPro experience with topics and tidbits from all over.

Go forth, and be enlightened, enlivened, and enriched. Just remember to be home by 9:00 p.m. — you know how Mother worries.

# Chapter 29

# Ten Useful Things to Type in the Command Window

*T*his chapter is about the Command window, a refugee from a time when computing meant typing and mice lived in walls. You cannot permanently get rid of it, but you *can* at least be entertained by its quaint command-driven way of doing things. Treat it nicely, and it does tricks and mutters a lot. Sometimes it reminds you of a grouchy expert who wishes these young graphical whippersnappers would learn to do things the right way (that is, the "old" way).

Believe it or not, there *are* some things the Command window is good for — hey, it surprised me, too. This chapter explores the ten best commands I found. Most are the typing equivalents of menu choices elsewhere in the book.

# APPEND

This switches to Change mode and adds a new record to the current table. It's the same as selecting Record⇨Append.

# BROWSE

To see the current table in my favorite way, type this into the Command window. Of course, you *could* select Browse⇨Browse, but you already knew that. This command is handy if your table is open, but not in a window yet. The BROWSE command opens the window *and* puts the table in the right mode. What a deal!

Wait — it gets better. If you type **BROWSE FIELDS** and then some of the table's field names, FoxPro creates a Browse window *with only those fields.* Now how much would you pay for it? Just kidding. It's free; it comes with the program at no extra charge.

# CHANGE

CHANGE is the evil twin brother of the preceding command. It's the same as selecting Browse⇨Change. Like BROWSE, if your table isn't yet in a window, it creates one and displays the table in it.

# CLEAR

You use this command to clear the big work area where the FoxPro logo appears when the program starts. It's most handy after a DIR, DISPLAY FIELDS ALL *xxx*, or DISPLAY STRUCTURE command, because they scribble their answers right onto the screen. CLEAR doesn't affect windows, though. Perhaps someday they'll come up with a CLEAN command for that. Anyway, the menu version of this is available under Window⇨Clear.

# DIR

This is pretty cool — and you can't do it from the menus. It's mostly the equivalent of the DOS directory command, but with some important twists. When you type **DIR** and press Enter, FoxPro lists all the database files in the current directory, just as you expect it to. The neat thing is that, in addition to showing you the table name, it also tells you the number of records, the last date that the table changed, and the size in characters (or bytes, for you techies out there).

You also can use the wildcard characters ? and * to list nondatabase files. To see all the report files, type **DIR *.FRX** and press Enter. To find all the queries, type **DIR *.QPR.** For more than you really want to know about using the wildcard characters, see *DOS for Dummies*, 2nd Edition, from IDG Books.

# DISPLAY ALL FIELDS xxx

Like the super-cool BROWSE FIELDS command, this one shows just the fields you're interested in, but it doesn't put them in a window. Instead, it types them in the workspace. It's not as nice as a window, but at least it pauses every time the screen is full. Use this when you just want a quick browse or want to show off for that cute person in your life. To make it work, type **DISPLAY ALL FIELDS** and then the fields you want to see — don't type the *x*s. Press Enter to make FoxPro go forth and do.

# DISPLAY STRUCTURE

Another command that qualifies as cool is DISPLAY STRUCTURE. This tells FoxPro to show you a brief but highly informative report about your current table. Among other things, it tells you the exact path to the little guy, the number of records, and the date it last changed.

Most important (and most impressive, if I do say so myself), it shows the table's structure — all the fields, including their name, type, size, and whether they're indexed or not. This is useful. By using the DISPLAY STRUCTURE command, you can *see* the structure without worrying about accidental changes. The only way to get close to this information via the menus is by selecting Database⇨Setup.

See the CLEAR command for a way to make the workspace all nice and clean again.

# ERASE

Unless you're familiar with DOS commands, stay away from this. ERASE is another DOS escapee. It works just like the regular DOS command, too. I'm not going to elaborate, but for those of you with DOS in your blood, ERASE is out there awaiting your call. If you're really bent on learning more (there he goes again!), pick up *DOS for Dummies,* 2nd Edition.

# PACK

Nothing much to say here, except that it's the same as the Database⇨Pack command. See Chapter 7 for a quick informational recharge. Better yet, see the "Packing your socks, packing your tables" sidebar, because it's a lot more fun.

# SELECT

Here's another neat command that isn't the clone of a simple menu selection. When you open a database, you put it in a temporary workspace. To change workspaces, you open the View dialog box by selecting Window⇨View, and then you click your choice in the Work Areas section. No more — the tyranny of the View dialog box is broken!

Sorry, I got a little carried away again. Instead of opening the View dialog box and clicking away, just type **SELECT** and the number of the work area you're interested in, and then press Enter. Work areas are numbered consecutively from 1 to 255. To switch to area 4, for example, the command is **SELECT 4.** If you don't know the number of the workspace, that's a problem. Refer to the slightly less tyrannical View dialog box for that information.

# SET DEFAULT TO

As a special gift to you (primarily because I ran out of those never-needs-sharpening steak knives), here's a bonus command to further your FoxPro pleasure.

SET DEFAULT TO is the absolute quickest way to change your current directory in FoxPro. Instead of dealing with one of those obnoxious buttons in the View dialog box, issue this speedy command and get on with your work.

As commands go, it's pretty easy to use. Well, it's easy if you understand directories. And if you know all the punctuation that goes into a DOS directory path. And if you know how to type. Hmmm.

First, you need to know about directories. For that, see Chapter 4. If you need to know more than that, it's time for a one-on-one with IDG's *DOS for Dummies,* 2nd Edition, by Dan Gookin.

Having conquered the generalities, it's time for the details. Next, you need to know the official DOS name of the directory you want to use. That's the full name, complete with colons and slashes. If your directory is called INVOICES and it's inside the DATA directory on your computer's hard disk drive, the full DOS path would be *C:\DATA\INVOICES.*

Now you're ready for some typing. In the Command window, type **SET DEFAULT TO** and then your directory name. You don't need any fancy quotation marks or things like that — just a simple (ha!) DOS directory name does the trick.

(In case you want to change directories the old-fashioned way, see "File Selection" in Chapter 28.)

# Chapter 30

# Ten Top Operators from Mr. Boole's Amazing School of Logic

* * * * * * * * * * * * * * * * * * * * * * * * * * * * * * * * *

## In This Chapter

▶ Equal To (=)

▶ Greater Than, Less Than (>, <)

▶ Greater Than or Equal To, Less Than or Equal To (>=, <=)

▶ Not Equal To (<>)

▶ .NOT.

▶ .AND. and .OR.

▶ BETWEEN( )

* * * * * * * * * * * * * * * * * * * * * * * * * * * * * * * * *

*I*t's time for a visit with Mr. Boole, that remarkable gentleman whose legacy lives on in a decidedly logical fashion. Thanks to his work in mathematical logic, you get to work with the quaint symbols and concepts outlined in this chapter. This whole area of computerdom is called Boolean logic in his honor (or, perhaps, so everybody remembers who's to blame).

Briefly, Boolean logic means building an expression that always comes out either true or false. For example, 5>2 is a valid Boolean expression, but 5+2 isn't because 7 isn't true or false. If you change that to 5+2>9, it becomes Boolean, even though it's false. FoxPro for Windows uses Boolean logic in filters, indexes, sorts, and queries, so you can't turn around without running into it.

# Equal To (=)

It doesn't get more basic than this. The equals sign is a simple, but exact, comparison. To be true, both sides of the equation must match *exactly*.

| | |
|---|---|
| "JENNY" = "JENNY" | True — both sides are exactly the same. |
| "Joseph" = "Joey" | False — despite their similarities, to FoxPro they're completely different. |
| 742 = 741.9957 | False — close doesn't count with FoxPro. |

# Greater Than, Less Than (>, <)

One step up from the venerable equals sign are greater than and less than. It took me two years of elementary school before I could get them straight, but once I tattooed them on my hands, I was fine (oops — sorry, that was right and left). As long as you remember that the sign points at the smaller side of the equation, they work wonders. Equations with these signs only come out true if the sides are *different* in a particular way.

| | |
|---|---|
| "Chocolate" > "Asparagus" | True — both alphabetically and by taste. |
| 3 < 20 | True — numbers compare with simple arithmetic. |
| "3" < "20" | False — when numbers are treated like letters, the alphabetizing rules, not mathematical rules, apply. The *character* 2 is alphabetically smaller than the *character* 3, so "20" comes before "3." Strange, but true. |

# Greater Than or Equal To, Less Than or Equal To (>=, <=)

Time to roll up your sleeves — things are getting stranger. These operators give your expression two ways to win: either be equal or be different in the right way, and you get a "true" from FoxPro.

| | |
|---|---|
| 6 >= 6 | True — it passes because the numbers are equal. |
| 3 >= 6 | False — 3 is neither greater than nor equal to 6. |
| "BECKY" <= "becky" | True — computers think that uppercase letters are "smaller" than lowercase letters, so the all caps word is smaller than the all lowercase word. |

# Not Equal To (<>)

The last symbolic operator is an easy one. Although it looks weird, not equal to is pretty straightforward: It's true if the sides *are not* equal.

| | |
|---|---|
| "cassette" <> "compact disc" | True — even the most uneducated ear knows this one. |
| 4981 <> 4981.001 | True — the smallest difference counts, as usual. |
| "BECKY" <> "becky" | True — FoxPro is case-sensitive, so these things matter. |

# .NOT.

.NOT. is a rather contrary operator. It's so contrary that it turns expressions completely around and makes them mean the opposite of what they say.

| | |
|---|---|
| .NOT. 5 > 3 | False — the 5 > 3 part is true, but .NOT. makes it false. |
| .NOT. 3 < 5 | True — it *was* false, but now it's true. |
| .NOT. "paycheck" < "taxes" | True — even though it's a close call in real life, .NOT. saves the day from the expression's point of view. |

# .AND. and .OR.

In my opinion, .AND. and .OR. are the two most powerful logical operators. Each one lets you create complicated expressions by connecting two or more simple expressions together, but they measure success differently.

.AND. likes consistency and truth. It wants *everything* to be true before it decides to be true as well.

| | |
|---|---|
| 5+2 > 4 .AND. "JENNY" = "JENNY" | True — individual expressions are true, so the whole expression is true. |
| 5+2 > 4 .AND. "JENNY" = "jenny" | False — the "JENNY" = "jenny" expression is false, so the party's over. |
| 5+2 < 4 .AND. "JENNY" = "jenny" | False — if nothing is true, the whole expression is false. |

.OR. prefers dissension, but is okay with complete agreement. As long as *something* is true, .OR. is happy and reports the whole expression as true. It's even pleased if everything is true. .OR. is just that kind of operator.

| | |
|---|---|
| 5+2 > 4 .OR. "JENNY" = "JENNY" | True — both sides are true, so the whole shebang is true. |
| 5+2 > 4 .OR. "JENNY" = "jenny" | True — because one side is true (5+2 > 4), the expression is true as well. |
| 5+2 < 4 .OR. "JENNY" = "jenny" | False — both sides are false, leaving .OR. to wallow in abject falseness. |

# BETWEEN ( )

Although it's not *really* a Boolean operator, it's cool enough to deserve a mention. BETWEEN( ) compares something to a range of values. If it (whatever *it* is) falls inside the range, BETWEEN( ) is true; otherwise, it's false.

The order of things inside the parentheses is important. First, put whatever you're testing, and then the smallest boundary, and finally the largest boundary. If you get them out of order, BETWEEN( ) won't work right.

| | |
|---|---|
| BETWEEN("M", "A", "Z") | True — M is alphabetically between A and Z. |
| BETWEEN(15, 1, 10) | False — 15 falls outside the 1 to 10 range. |
| BETWEEN("person", "blankets", "sheets") | True — it's alphabetical and (yawn) really sounds good right now. |

# Chapter 31

# Ten Things that Sometimes Go Wrong

● ● ● ● ● ● ● ● ● ● ● ● ● ● ● ● ● ● ● ● ● ● ● ● ● ● ● ● ● ● ● ● ● ● ● ● ● ● ●

## In This Chapter

▶ The foxy little icon is gone

▶ FoxPro won't start

▶ Corrupt tables

▶ Tables that just don't relate

▶ Bad index — bad, naughty index

▶ Forgetting a field

▶ Restructuring gone awry

▶ Deleting the wrong file

▶ Mixing up .AND. and .OR.

▶ The backup's dead, Jim

● ● ● ● ● ● ● ● ● ● ● ● ● ● ● ● ● ● ● ● ● ● ● ● ● ● ● ● ● ● ● ● ● ● ● ● ● ● ●

*N*othing in life goes completely right. No matter how hard you try, there's always some little hitch or sundry crisis to enhance the experience. That's what gives life its flavor.

As life goes, so goes FoxPro. Yes, FoxPro for Windows has its own little hitches, but this chapter guides you through the most common ones. When things go wrong, take a deep breath, throw something at the wall, and check here to find a solution.

Some problems require guru-level help. Don't be shy about collaring your favorite support person if your problem isn't in here. There is no shame in asking for help, particularly if your data is important to you.

# The Foxy Little Icon Is Gone

You just can't trust those Program Manager icons, can you? Turn your back on them and (poof!) they're gone. It's no big deal, because it's easy to bring them back:

✔ If you're not particularly familiar with the Windows Program Manager (where the icons live), get some help before doing this on your own. Replacing a lost icon isn't a hard process, but it's confusing if you're not familiar with the territory.

✔ The entries you type in Steps 5 and 6 assume that you didn't create your own directory for FoxPro and that you're not using a network. If these steps don't work, get some techie help.

1. **In Program Manager, decide which program group you want to put FoxPro in and make it the current window by clicking it.**

2. **Select File➪New to open the New Program Object dialog box.**

3. **In the dialog box, select Program Item and then click OK. The Program Item Properties dialog box pops up.**

4. **In the Description box, type** FoxPro for Windows. **Press Tab to go to the next box.**

5. **For the Command Line, type** C:\FOXPROW\FOXPROW.EXE. **Press Tab again.**

6. **In the Working Directory box, type** C:\FOXPROW. **Press Enter when you're finished. The Program Item Properties dialog box goes away, and the foxy little icon returns.**

If Windows argues about creating the icon, either something went wrong or, for one reason or another, FoxPro isn't where I thought it would be. Sorry to say this, but if that's the case, seek out a good computer guru and try it again.

# FoxPro Won't Start

This time, the shifty little icon is there, but when you double-click it, Windows responds Cannot find file c:\foxprow\foxprow.exe (or one of its components). Well, isn't this a fine state of affairs?

There's no quick and simple answer to this, but there are some common things to check. If you're on a network, are you logged in? Is anyone else having problems (FoxPro or otherwise)? If so, it sounds like a network problem. Check with your friendly (if odd) network support people.

For the non-network-attached readers, click the FoxPro for Windows icon once, and then press Alt+Enter to open the Program Item Properties box. Do the entries in it match the ones in the preceding Steps 5 and 6? Are you sure FoxPro for Windows is actually loaded on your computer, or did someone just tell you it was? Using the Windows File Manager, or DOS for the hardy souls out there, look for the C:\FOXPROW directory (or whatever you called it if you didn't use Microsoft's default name). Is the directory still there? Are there any files in it? Will Manny Sorensen strike out or get the bases-loaded homer?

I hate to ask this last question, but I must: Did you do some disk cleaning recently and perhaps erase FoxPro? If so, it's okay. I was formatting a floppy disk once and accidentally formatted the hard drive instead. Don't be embarrassed about any file management missteps — it's just part of learning the ropes. Reload FoxPro and continue with your regularly scheduled life.

# Corrupt Tables

This section is probably not good news. If you do have a backup (good for you!), restore the dead file from your disk or tape or whatever backup medium you use. If you're not exactly sure how to do this, get some help from the guru-of-your-heart.

FoxPro may still shine one ray of hope on you. If you restructured your table recently (by selecting Database⇨Setup⇨Modify), FoxPro automatically created a backup of your old table. Look for a file in the same subdirectory with the same name as the dead table, but with a .BAK extension instead of .DBF. Granted, the backup table isn't in the new structure and doesn't contain your most recent changes, but it's still something, and that's more than you had before.

Check out "Recovering with the Automatic Backup Files" in Chapter 7 for details of the operation. Although the instructions assume the original table is mangled because of a bad restructuring experience, the steps work fine for corrupt tables, too. If you're on a network, someone else may back up your tables for you. Cross your fingers and check with the network manager. Be prepared to wait a day or two if your files are somewhere safe, because it often takes that long to arrange getting the tapes back.What if you don't have a backup and haven't restructured the ol' table in a while? It's looking pretty bleak. My best suggestion is to go for a brief walk, and then settle in and start rebuilding the table. And please start making backups — okay?

# Tables that Just Don't Relate

Sometimes, tables can't relate to each other. It's not that there's something wrong with the tables in question; they may not have anything in common.

Just like any good relationship, tables need common ground as the basis for the relationship. In table terms, that common ground is a field (or fields) that both tables share. In one table, the field must have unique values (each customer has a unique customer number, for example). In the other table, the field can be unique or not, depending on your needs.

If your tables won't relate, check the fields and make sure that you're connecting them with a field that's identical in size and type between both tables. If it's size five in one table and size seven in the other, the match won't work.

For more help patching up the digital relationship, see Chapter 12.

# Bad Index — Bad, Naughty Index

Just like leftover potato salad, good indexes go bad. Bad indexes don't turn green and fuzzy, though — they just don't point in the right direction any more. When you notice that queries and Seeks aren't working correctly, you probably have a bad index on your hands — er, disk.

You don't really fix an index — you trash it and build a new one. Chapter 11 explains the ins and outs of the whole sordid affair.

# Forgetting a Field

Hey — everyone forgets things from time to time: the car, the kids, how to ride a bicycle. The world's too busy for you to remember every little detail. Why should designing a database be any different?

Fixing the problem is a piece of cake. Chapter 7 (yes, Chapter 7 again) walks you through the whole process in the section called "Restructuring Tables."

# Restructuring Gone Awry

Restructuring sometimes doesn't work out quite the way you planned. For once, FoxPro for Windows is ahead of the game. It automatically makes a backup copy of your table before implementing any structure changes. If your table turns out like a disk-based Frankenstein, no problem — just kill it and turn back to the original.

The recipe for disposing of the monster and bringing back the backup is under "Recovering with the Automatic Backup Files" in Chapter 7.

# Deleting the Wrong File

If this happens to you, don't feel like you're alone. So many people do it that Microsoft started including an UNDELETE command in DOS beginning with version 5. If your DOS is older than that, you need a utility program like The Norton Utilities or PC Tools to recover your file. They're available at your local computer store or friendly mail-order outlet. In the meantime, don't do anything with your computer! Get the utility program of your choice and follow its instructions for emergency file recovery.

Provided that your DOS is version 5 or greater and you're familiar with the commands, here's how to recover the now-deleted file. If you're not comfortable using DOS, call your local computer guru and get out the snack food. If you want to learn this stuff, pick up a copy of *DOS for Dummies,* 2nd Edition, from IDG Books Worldwide.

1. **Quit Windows and get back to the DOS prompt (`C:\>`).**

2. **Change to the directory where the dearly deleted last lived.**

3. **Type** UNDELETE **, a space, and the name of the file that's missing.**

   Remember to include the file's extension, or DOS won't be able to find it. Computers are so silly sometimes.

4. **UNDELETE does some on-screen gyrations, hopefully ending in a line that asks** `Undelete (Y/N)?`. **If so, that's a good sign. Press Y for Yes, but don't press Enter.**

   The other thing that UNDELETE might say is something to the effect that part of the file is gone and can't be undeleted. If so, I'm very, very, sorry. If the file's really important, try restoring it from your backup, or consult your computer expert for some other recovery options.

5. **Now type the first letter of the file's name. As soon as you type, UNDELETE starts to work. If everything works, UNDELETE reports** `File Successfully Undeleted`.

6. **Get back into Windows by typing** WIN **and pressing Enter, and then continue going about your business.**

# Mixing Up .AND. and .OR.

This kind of mix-up doesn't happen much in regular language, but when you're talking computerese, even grammar is up for grabs. Worse yet, this is grammar with logic behind it. Now there's something you don't see every day.

Confusing .AND. and .OR. is frustrating (plus it makes all your answers wrong). Both of them connect two comparisons, but they do it in different ways: .AND. puts comparisons together; .OR. makes them a choice.

If you read the expression as a sentence, it's easy to decide which one to use. To make the expression depend on both this *and* that, use .AND. For something that could be either one or the other, try .OR. See, it's not much different than grammar class (I'm not sure that's a comforting way to put this).

For a complete report card on the whole logic thing, check out Chapter 30.

# The Backup's Dead, Jim

There's nothing like closing on a high note, so I saved the best for last. Few things are more traumatic than doing your backups just like you're supposed to, having a catastrophe, and finding out the backups didn't work — ever. It goes beyond simple anger and frustration into rage and betrayal. Darn it, you put a lot of work and effort into this backup thing, so it's going to work, and work *now*.

Unfortunately, technology is immune to such threats.

Making backups is the required first step to preventing problems. The little-discussed second step is to test the backups before you have an honest-to-goodness crisis. Try restoring your tables sometime. Go through the whole procedure, comfortable in the knowledge that your data is completely safe and you're performing an academic exercise. Document how the restoration works. For that matter, document any failures or shortcomings and find out how to fix them.

The key is doing the right things in the right way. Practice makes perfect, so bone up on your recovery procedure and give it a test while you still have hair.

Backups, in theory and practice, are presented for your sound reading enjoyment in Chapter 5. To get there, turn right at the front cover and proceed in about 40 pages. You can't miss it.

# Chapter 32
# Ten Places to (Hopefully) Find Help

● ● ● ● ● ● ● ● ● ● ● ● ● ● ● ● ● ● ● ● ● ● ● ● ● ● ● ● ● ● ● ● ● ● ● ● ● ● ● ● ● ● ● ● ● ● ● ●

*In This Chapter*

▶ F1 (The Help! Key)

▶ CompuServe

▶ Phone support

▶ Friends

▶ Local user groups

▶ Training companies

▶ Consultants

▶ Children

▶ Computer store

▶ FoxPro for Windows manuals

● ● ● ● ● ● ● ● ● ● ● ● ● ● ● ● ● ● ● ● ● ● ● ● ● ● ● ● ● ● ● ● ● ● ● ● ● ● ● ● ● ● ● ● ● ● ● ●

*T*his book is designed to get you through everything a normal person needs to know about FoxPro for Windows. If you're an overachiever, you may need more help than it can directly give, but at least it can point you in the right direction and send you on your way. Here are ten places to go when you're exhausted, haggard, and informationally forlorn.

## F1 (The Help! Key)

Like all good Windows programs, FoxPro for Windows has a built-in help system. It activates during your brain overloads when your forehead hits the F1 key.

Pressing F1 gives you various kinds of help, depending on your situation. If you're in the midst of a menu or dialog box, the help system chimes in with a series of one-liners about whatever you're attempting to do. If you're just hanging out, lounging around the main FoxPro for Windows screen, you get a general table of contents. If you're feeling *really* desperate, it's no help at all. Isn't that just like a machine?

The help system's main goal is to kick-start your memory when you forget something. It doesn't go into detail or give elaborate definitions — that's why you bought this book.

# CompuServe

If your job depends on FoxPro for Windows and the word "CompuServe" doesn't mean anything to you, don't worry — do something. Amble down to the local computer supermarket, plunk down $100 or so for a good modem, and pick up a book about CompuServe. It's an international information system your computer can reach over the phone. It offers product support, hobby groups, news, electronic mail, and (of course) computer games to the more than 700,000 people who use it.

Like most major software companies, Microsoft offers support for all its products through CompuServe forums. The FoxPro area, called FoxForum, has several areas catering to different topics and skill levels. It's like an electronic neighborhood, with people swapping FoxPro tips over a virtual backyard fence. Microsoft is so sold on its CompuServe forum that it even gives you a free sign-up kit. Look in the Help system's Table of Contents under the topic "product support" for details.

Prices keep coming down, so CompuServe is a downright inexpensive option for getting detailed answers to sticky problems. I personally recommend it because free phone support is rapidly becoming extinct, but electronic support through services like CompuServe is booming. Better to learn about it now and get ahead than play catch-up later.

By the way, check out IDG's *CompuServe for Dummies* to have the same kind of pleasurable, light-hearted experience with CompuServe as you're having with FoxPro.

# Phone Support

Microsoft offers good quality phone support for FoxPro users. They offer you a choice of talk-to-a-human, talk-to-a-machine, and your-fax-talks-to-their-fax support lines. All the numbers are listed in the Help system's Table of Contents under "product support." They also offer TDD and Text Telephone services for the hearing impaired. The numbers are listed along with the others in the Help system.

There are also companies (independent of Microsoft) that specialize in phone support. You call a 900 number and chat as long as your checkbook holds out. Depending on the service, they may charge by the minute (commonly $1 to $1.50 per minute) or have a flat fee per call (usually in the vicinity of $25). You can find these numbers at local computer stores or in computer magazines.

Microsoft's phone support is free (except for the phone call) for the first 90 days. After that, get out your credit card and watch the monthly bill soar. The software industry as a whole is moving to pay-per-call support lines, and Microsoft is no exception. That's why I recommend getting to know services like CompuServe and looking there for help.

# Friends

If you have some computer-savvy friends, asking them for help is always a possibility. It may cost you a box of cupcakes, a bag of nacho chips, or a large pizza (with everything), but that's not much when you consider the quality time it gives you with your friend. Before getting the pizza order, make sure that the friend in question actually knows something about FoxPro. There are a lot of "computer people" in the world, but not all of them are created equal, so be sure that your friend is more equal than the others.

One final word of caution: Sometimes, nothing costs more than free advice. People often mean well, but either don't know or can't communicate the answers. If your livelihood depends on FoxPro, get good help — even if it means paying for it.

# Local User Groups

Here's a source that most people don't even know is out there. In every major city, there are groups of software users who band together for self defense. They sponsor meetings, help each other, and even eat pizza. Granted, some members are bona-fide tech-weenies, but their hearts (and other body parts) are in the right place and they're genuinely interested in helping beginners. Membership usually costs under $50 per year, which is a small price for the services you receive. Some groups even organize free local phone support for their members. Test drive any group before joining, just to make sure that you feel comfortable and that the membership consists, at least partially, of the genus *normalcea homo sapiens non-nerdatae*.

# Training Companies

Computer training is big business. Local and national companies want your body in their classrooms, and they're giving extra benefits if you come. A popular feature is after-class phone help when you're in dire straits. So, in addition to what you learned during the session, you can pick the instructor's brain when you're in a jam.

Before getting all excited, remember that support is a free service with training companies, so don't expect the "operators are standing by" experience. It may be a few hours, or perhaps the next day, before your favorite instructor gets back with you. Even then, your question may be more than he or she can handle. Don't be disappointed if your instructor recommends that you call the manufacturer or look for a paid consultant; don't be surprised if she suggests some one-on-one training (from her company, of course) if you call too often.

# Consultants

Paying for help is always an option, but quality varies even here. The old adage "you get what you pay for" is at least partially true: A paid professional usually knows the answers you're looking for and can communicate them better than Eddie the FoxPro Hack. There is a large quantity of Eddies out there dressed up as consultants, so you still need to watch out.

Consider a consultant for one-on-one training to get you through the really rough parts or as an extra pair of eyes to watch you solve a tough problem and offer tips and hints as you go. Many consultants offer programming services as well, should you ever need such help. Expect to pay $40 to $150 per hour for this kind of help, depending on your locale and needs.

# Children

Yes, I *did* say children. Kids in the 8 to 14 age bracket often have more experience with computers than we like to accept. If you can explain your problem to young Becky or Joseph, they very possibly can help you solve it. Heck, you might even accidentally have some quality time with them. The thing that makes them so good is their willingness to try things — sometimes seemingly silly things — to see what happens. They don't know what approaches are "wrong," so they're liable to try anything. They have a refreshing creativity that you can harness with some patience, milk, and chocolate.

One tip: Make sure that you have a good backup before letting the kids loose on your system. If the "refreshing creativity" leads to some refreshing computer crisis, it's better to be prepared than not.

# Computer Store

Still looking for help? The list is dwindling fast, but here's another possibility: the local computer superstore where you bought your PC or software. Stores that specialize in computer products (not the combination stereo, computer, dishwasher, how-about-a-microwave-with-that-new-'486 type of store) usually offer training classes and maybe even some limited phone support. It's kind of rare in these days of discount warehouse selling, but it's always worth asking about.

# FoxPro for Windows Manuals

As a last resort, after exhausting all normal, friendly, and patient sources of help, there's always (*cringe!*) the manuals. Remember, this is a last-ditch effort to find help, so don't get your hopes too high, okay?

There are two manuals that Microsoft includes in every FoxPro for Windows box that could potentially help you (in the same sense that the government could *potentially* rebate your taxes). *Getting Started* is one of those "this is FoxPro for Windows in a perfect world where everything works the first time" kinds of manuals. It's a whirlwind tutorial that warps you from the "wow — they sure use a lot of plastic to seal the box" to "sure I can build a continental defense logistics system; give me 10 minutes or so."

The manual that's more likely to help (in relative terms) is the *User's Guide*. Microsoft organized the first half of this book by common menu items and the second half by writing topics on little pieces of paper and drawing them out of a hat. Microsoft did cleverly print a brief table of contents on the back cover of each manual, so you can quickly find out that the manuals won't tell you what you want to know.

One other thing to note: In the latest version of FoxPro, Microsoft *didn't rewrite the manuals* — not a single whit is different about them. They *did* include a swell reference card that's squirreled away somewhere near the diskettes. It briefly (*very* briefly) outlines the new product's features and suggests that you read the on-line Help for more information. Please do that — then call Microsoft and express your disbelief and outrage that they'd pull a stunt like this. If you're paying money for something, the least you can expect is that the manuals are current. Hmpf.

# Chapter 33
# Ten Best Keyboard Shortcuts

· · · · · · · · · · · · · · · · · · · · · · · · · · · · · · · · · · · · · · ·

## In This Chapter

▶ Esc, the universal *Go away!* key

▶ Ctrl+Z to undo that last change

▶ Ctrl+X, Ctrl+C, Ctrl+V for cut, copy, and paste

▶ Ctrl+N adds a record (and stays in Browse mode)

▶ Ctrl+PgDn opens a memo field

▶ Ctrl+F4 closes the current window

▶ Ctrl+F6 cycles through the windows

▶ Alt+Tab switches programs

▶ Alt+F4 closes FoxPro

· · · · · · · · · · · · · · · · · · · · · · · · · · · · · · · · · · · · · · ·

All right, so there *are* 11 keys in the chapter, not 10. I hit a buy-10-get-1-free sale and passed the savings on to you. Besides, if you don't like one of the keys described, ignore it; you still have the 10 you expected. Regardless of the specific number of keys involved, these are the best shortcuts available. Some even work in other Windows programs. It just doesn't get better than this.

# Esc, the Universal Go Away! Key

This is one *great* key. I use it whenever I do something silly, like opening the wrong window, clicking the wrong menu choice, or typing over some data in my table (oops!). Esc (short for "Escape") makes almost everything better. It makes windows vanish and typing disappear. Use it when you're in serious despair and want a key you can really pound on. Excess Escs don't hurt anything, so it's a good choice for forehead banging.

# Ctrl+Z to Undo that Last Change

Second cousin (once removed) from Esc is the Undo key, Ctrl+Z. It's the same as selecting Edit⇨Undo and has the same limitations. Undo mainly fixes editing problems, like typing a change into the wrong record. It's no cure-all, though; after you leave the field you're typing in, Undo *can't* undo any more. The change you made is *permanent,* so I hope you like it.

Don't let this happen to your data. Look carefully at your changes before pressing that Tab or arrow key. Undo can only help so much — the rest is (gulp!) up to you and me.

This keystroke is common to most Windows applications, so if you have a crisis somewhere else (in your word processor, perhaps), try Ctrl+Z as a quick fix.

# Ctrl+X, Ctrl+C, Ctrl+V for Cut, Copy, and Paste

These are basic Windows commands, so I won't get into lengthy explanations about them. As for why they chose these three keys, I'm not completely sure, but I think you can blame Apple. The C for Copy makes sense; Cut's X looks like scissors. The V, of course, refers to the original Russian word *pvaste* and just happened to be geographically close to the other two. What a lucky coincidence for the computing world.

All three keystrokes are sort of standard across different Windows applications, but not completely. Check the Edit menu of your favorite application to find out for sure.

# Ctrl+N Adds a Record (and Stays in Browse Mode)

Chapter 7 already talked this up quite a bit, but it's so good, it bears mentioning again. If you're adding records to your table and like to do it in Browse mode, use Ctrl+N instead of selecting Record⇨Append. The menu option automatically switches you into Change mode, whereas Ctrl+N just adds a new record regardless of your mode choice.

# Ctrl+PgDn Opens a Memo Field

This is a super-handy keystroke when you're looking through a table and want to see the memo field. With your cursor on the memo field, press Ctrl+PgDn. A window appears so that you can review the contents. As you move around the table, FoxPro automatically updates the memo field window with information from the current record.

# Ctrl+F4 Closes the Current Window

Here's another goodie that works everywhere in Windows. No matter where you are or what you're up to, press Ctrl+F4 to close the current window. This doesn't quit the program — that's Alt+F4 (discussed elsewhere in this chapter). In FoxPro, Ctrl+F4 closes table windows, memo field windows, the Command window, and the View window. Yes, friend, one keystroke does it all! Try it out in other applications too. It's a good one!

# Ctrl+F6 Cycles through the Windows

This is undocumented in FoxPro, but it works both there and in other Windows applications. To keep the FoxPro experts happy, let me quickly say that Ctrl+F1 is the official FoxPro window-cycling key. However, Ctrl+F6 works and seems to be consistent in other programs, so I suggest learning it instead of the FoxPro-centric approach.

This key moves you from window to window on a busy FoxPro screen. Each time you press it, a different window is activated. Eventually, FoxPro cycles through all the open windows and starts the sequence over again. It's particularly handy if you're flipping between lots of tables and other miscellaneous windows.

# Alt+Tab Switches Programs

Although it's actually a Windows keystroke, Alt+Tab is so handy I had to include it here. If you're running several programs at once, Alt+Tab switches you between them with ease and speed. While writing this book, I nearly wore out these keys. I always had my word processor and FoxPro running together and flipped back and forth to make sure that things worked the way I wrote. It saves a lot of wear and tear on the mousing arm, that's for sure.

# Alt+F4 Closes FoxPro

Finally, another all-Windows keystroke. Alt+F4 bids a fond "nighty-night" to FoxPro for Windows, as it does for all Windows applications. When you're tired and ready to quit, one quick press gracefully shuts the program down. All good Windows applications give you a final chance to save any unsaved changes and such, so don't let that worry you. Just give Alt+F4 a good whack and send that bothersome program packing.

# Chapter 34
# Ten Features to Explore Someday

- - - - - - - - - - - - - - - - - - - - - - - - - - - - - - - - - -

## In This Chapter
▶ The ~~spall speel~~ spell checker
▶ Those other things in the expression builder
▶ Importing and exporting your stuff
▶ Getting organized with the catalog manager
▶ Find the bottom line with database summary functions
▶ Dear digital diary
▶ Custom screens with Screen Designer
▶ The whole programming thing
▶ Say OLE! with general fields

- - - - - - - - - - - - - - - - - - - - - - - - - - - - - - - - - -

**S**ometimes, interesting features are hidden deep inside a product. You usually find them by accident or (worse) by reading the manual. Sometimes, they're time-savers; other times, they're just fun. Perhaps they have no impact on your life at all except to take up even more of your ever-shrinking hard drive.

FoxPro has its share of "things to explore when you have the time." Don't take the time right now unless you were thinking of reading the dictionary again and picked up this book instead (a back-handed compliment if ever there was one). Rather, keep these in mind for the future, when your proficiency and tolerance levels grow.

And yes, there are only nine. The chapter title lies.

## The ~~Spall Speel~~ Spell Checker

I'd be lost without a spell checker. I write the way I speak, but spelling doesn't count when you're talking. Take away my spell checker, and I'm in serious trubble, er, trouble.

Microsoft knows there are lots of people like me (and lots of people who can't spell, either), so they included a spell checker in the newest version of FoxPro for Windows. It's active whenever you're editing something, whether it's a little text file or a massive memo field. You can even add your own words to the custom dictionary, so that FoxPro knows the same misspellings you do. To make the spell checker do its thing, select Text⇨Spelling whenever you're in a memo field or using FoxPro's text editor.

# Those Other Things in the Expression Builder

The next time you have the Expression Builder open and leering at you from the screen, brave its stare and look at the stuff in the Functions box. You already use many of the things under the Logical list, but there are three other options to choose from. Granted, they're special-use tools, but when you need them, you really need them.

The Date, Math, and String lists contain advanced functions worthy of a book unto themselves. In my opinion, the most interesting (and potentially useful) are the ones in the Math list. They include functions for finance, statistics, and trigonometry. Using them isn't difficult after you've conquered the Expression Builder itself. Check out FoxPro's on-line help for the gory details of applying the function of your choice.

# Importing and Exporting Your Stuff

The days when computers lived in little isolated worlds are over. These days, data moves faster than someone cheating on the rent. If you're called on to share-and-share-alike, take comfort in knowing that FoxPro for Windows is multilingual.

FoxPro reads Paradox, Lotus, and Excel files; it can write in Lotus and Excel. Although it understands some other formats too, these are far and away the most common files on the planet. Any program worth its bytes knows how to use these. For importing, select the Database⇨Append From option. To export, select Database⇨Copy To.

Don't get the idea that just because FoxPro can handle this stuff means importing and exporting are the easiest things in the whole history of easy things. If you need to convert data, get some guru-level help for your first time or two. The process isn't difficult, provided you know where the potholes are.

# Getting Organized with the Catalog Manager

This is another foxy new feature. Rather than let your tables, reports, and other stuff just lie around on the hard drive, the Catalog Manager helps you track what belongs where. It shows you which reports are related to what tables, lets you enter brief descriptions for things, and generally puts your mind at ease by applying some organization to your previously chaotic electronic world.

Check out FoxPro's on-line help for the details of doing the Catalog Manager thing.

# Finding the Bottom Line with Database Summary Functions

Sometimes, you just want a quick number for a relatively simple question. Granted, that doesn't happen often, but it's still a possibility. FoxPro for Windows provides some quick and dirty options for just such occasions.

If you look under the Database menu, you find several options cowering there — options like Total, Average, Count, Sum, and Calculate. These quickly generate summaries for the whole table or just some part that you specify. Seek out information from the on-line help system to learn more and expand your summary horizons.

# Dear Digital Diary

Even though I covered this in Chapter 27, it's cool enough for another mention. Aside from simply being fun, the Diary can be pressed into real-world service in a variety of ways.

If you find yourself doing lots of fascinating things in FoxPro, consider using the Diary for the dreaded "D" word: documentation. Leave yourself a digital trail of notes and contemplations so that you can rebuild things that go awry. Keep notes of accomplishments and time-savings to impress the socks off the boss during your next review. Ramble consistently for years and years, and then sell the printout as your Collected Thoughts on the World. The possibilities boggle the mind, don't they?

# Custom Screens with Screen Designer

If you thought the Screen Wizard did great things, hang on to your mouse, 'cause you ain't seen nothing yet. For some super-custom stuff (like special buttons, lists, and checkboxes), introduce your Wizard-generated screen to FoxPro's Screen Designer. It has the tools you need to adapt, adjust, augment, and accommodate anything you want a screen to do.

It's not all menu choices and happy dust, though. Screen Designer requires some (*gasp!*) programming to really make those screens sing. If you're up to the challenge, check out the next section, "The Whole Programming Thing." Tread lightly, though — once word gets out that you're programming, for goodness' sake, people never look at you the same way again. They think it's like a communicable disease, so they don't get too close for fear of wanting to program, too.

# The Whole Programming Thing

Many generations survived their time on Earth without ever programming a computer. You, too, can avoid this trauma by simply skipping to the next section heading. If you're so inclined, don't worry — I won't be upset at all. If you're still with me, I hope you have lots of patience and a good health plan available. You're entering an aspect of computer use often (favorably) compared to the gentle art of beating your head on the wall, but lacking the opportunities for growth. FoxPro for Windows, deep in its digital heart, is a programmer's paradise, a complex tool capable of almost anything. Its language is compatible with Borland's dBASE product, so your new development skills are somewhat general (and even reasonably valuable).

The FoxPro for Windows manuals teach you some simple programming techniques. That much gets your toes wet and helps you decide whether this "writing code" thing is really for you. If it is, check out the FoxForum on CompuServe for more direction, or talk to your local FoxPro guru.

# Say OLE! with General Fields

*Object linking and embedding* (OLE) is one of the self-proclaimed "super cool" things that Windows does. Almost every Windows application does OLE, and FoxPro certainly doesn't want to be left out in the cold. General fields are FoxPro for Windows' contribution to the OLE universe. They let you store documents, graphics, spreadsheets, and even sounds in a table. An easy example to imagine is a database of Pulitzer Prize-winning photographs. The table contains the photographer's name, publication, date, perhaps a memo field with some miscellaneous background information, and a digitized copy of the photograph itself. If you click the "Photograph" field, FoxPro displays the picture on-screen for your viewing pleasure. You could even have a recording of the photographer describing what led up to the picture or how he felt taking it.

This kind of application is just emerging today. Because anything fits in an OLE field, the boundaries are limited only by your imagination (and, arguably, your time to pursue such things). Let your mind roam with the possibilities, get a guru to show you how it's done, and then amaze yourself (and your boss) with the results.

# Part VII
## Appendixes

"COMPATABILITY? NO PROBLEM. THIS BABY COMES IN OVER A DOZEN DESIGNER COLORS."

# In this part...

**O**kay, so the Part of Tens doesn't *quite* close the book. That's only because you'll have a tough time making FoxPro perform its digital miracles if you don't have it on your computer. Appendix A solves that difficulty by telling you how to install FoxPro for Windows, whether you want the full-blown, multimegabyte installation or the minimal, no-frills installation. Or even somewhere in between.

Change can be traumatic, as any long-time Coca-Cola drinker knows. Appendix B is for that special group of readers who want to — or must — make the switch from dBASE to FoxPro. What with all the new features — such as AutoMigrate, the Catalog Manager, and the Wizards — the trauma of switching isn't what it used to be. Back in my day...

# Appendix A
# Installing FoxPro for Windows

○ ● ○ ● ○ ● ○ ● ○ ● ○ ● ○ ● ○ ● ○ ● ○ ● ○ ● ○ ● ○ ● ○ ● ○ ● ○ ● ○ ● ○ ● ○ ● ○ ●

### In This Appendix

▶ The basic stuff
▶ Picking the right installation
▶ Complete installation
▶ Custom installation
▶ Minimum installation

○ ● ○ ● ○ ● ○ ● ○ ● ○ ● ○ ● ○ ● ○ ● ○ ● ○ ● ○ ● ○ ● ○ ● ○ ● ○ ● ○ ● ○ ● ○ ● ○ ●

*I*f your computer is part of a network, get your guru's help — do not attempt the installation on your own. The intricacies of networked environments go far beyond what I can tell you in this book.

If you're upgrading from a previous version of FoxPro, you still may want some help, particularly to make sure that your databases and such make it safely over to the new version.

## The Basic Stuff

The fun begins with the ceremonial shedding of the plastic wrap and continues thusly:

1. **Place the FoxPro for Windows box on a table. Sigh heavily as you consider the software before you.**

    Although often left out of software installation manuals, this is an important step. Having the right mental attitude is absolutely critical to everything in life, particularly when dealing with something as heavy as FoxPro for Windows.

    If your table shatters beneath the sheer weight of the software, just imagine what's in store for your computer's hard disk (not to mention your brain). Find a stronger table, and worry about cleaning up the mess later. There may be more to clean up by then.

2. **Inside the box are the manuals and a cardboard container containing lots of booklets, pamphlets, and other annoying things. Dig around until you find the sealed-for-your-protection program diskettes. Pull out the disks and enthusiastically free them from the plastic wrap.**

3. **Take a moment to put the disks in numeric order.**

   This is strictly a sanity-preservation step. It's an opportunity to do your part in protecting the world's endangered supply of sanity.

4. **Find the disk marked "Disk 1 — Setup" and put it into your floppy disk drive.**

   Often, this is drive A on your computer, but it may be drive B. Only the computer and your guru know for sure. If you're confused, befuddled, or just plain lonely, ask someone.

5. **From the Windows Program Manager, select File⇨Run. The Run dialog box pops up.**

6. **In the Command Line box, type the following command and press Enter when you're finished:**

   ```
   A:\SETUP
   ```

   Remember to substitute **B:** for **A:** in the command line if your computer uses drive B. If you're hungry, get a snack before continuing.

7. **If you're living right, the message** `Initializing Setup` **flashes on the screen. Sit back and wait patiently — this is not a fast process.**

   No, I don't know what it's doing in there either, but (sheesh) it certainly takes a long time to do it.

8. **The first formal communication from FoxPro is the User Information screen in Figure A-1. Type in your name and your company's name, and then click Continue or press Enter.**

9. **The next dialog box is your one and only chance to change the name entries. Check them carefully before clicking Continue.**

   The program really does store the names permanently, so look at your typing carefully. I recorded my name as "Kauflep" once because I wasn't paying attention. The worst part was the ribbing from my coworkers for the next year. Don't let this happen to you.

10. **Next, FoxPro lets you choose a directory for the program files and a program group for the icons. Unless you feel strongly about any of these settings, click the Continue button and leave them alone.**

Congratulations! You made it through the preliminaries. Now it's time for the real meat (or, if you're vegetarian, the real greens) of the installation.

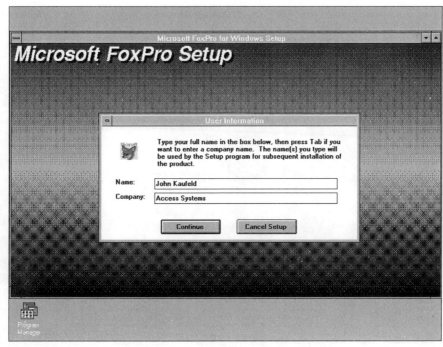

**Figure A-1:**
Here's a
chance to
see your
name on TV
(well, at
least on-
screen).
Make sure
the entries
are correct,
because
once they're
made, you
can't
change
them. Ever.

# Picking the Right Installation

You're facing a screen that looks significantly like Figure A-2: three big buttons offering three big choices. Here's a brief explanation of your options:

Complete Installation  This is the Big Fox on Computer. I'm talking about 20MB of FoxPro for Windows taking up permanent residence on your hard drive. If you have the space and the needs, this is the installation for you.

Custom Installation  Button #2 is FoxPro à la carte. Pick and choose what you want from the varied offerings FoxPro for Windows makes available. I like this option the best, particularly because you can cut FoxPro down to about 10MB of disk space without losing anything that normal humans really need.

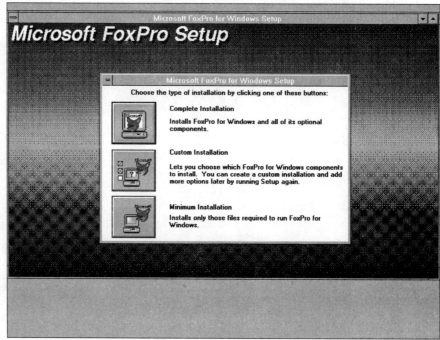

**Figure A-2:**
Is the best
installation
behind
button one,
two, or
three? My
personal
guess is
button two,
but I usually
ended up
with the
goat and
lifetime
supply of
garden
hose.

Minimum Installation   If you want the skeletal remains of FoxPro, click here.
Minimum means what it says: no help files, no
examples, no spell checking, no nothing. It just
arranges enough digital bones on the disk drive to
look like FoxPro. It's okay for laptops or a computer
that only runs a ready-made application, but I don't
recommend it for anything else.

# Complete Installation

1. **Click the Complete Installation button.**

2. **In the next dialog box, click the Windows-Style Keystrokes button.**

   If you're a dyed-in-the-DOS version type, you can click DOS-Style Keystrokes, but I don't recommend it. Make the effort to learn the Windows
   keystroke conventions. You ultimately save time, because most Windows
   applications work the same way.

3. **Sit back, enjoy the propaganda, and feed the machine a new disk whenever it whines for one.**

   Whether it's propaganda or advertising depends on your point of view, but at least Microsoft's on-screen billboard breaks up the monotony of the installation process.

4. **When you're finished, put the disks in a safe place.**

   Remember to take the last disk out of the computer.

# Custom Installation

1. **Click the Custom Installation button.**

2. **In the Setup Options dialog box, click the first two and last two checkboxes, and then click Continue.**

   When you're finished, the dialog box should look just like Figure A-3.

3. **In the dialog box that follows, click the Windows-Style Keystrokes button.**

   See Step 2 in the "Complete Installation" section for all the details.

**Figure A-3:** Here's the secret to slimming down FoxPro for Windows. By eliminating the parts you don't need, you save valuable disk space. Is this easy or what?

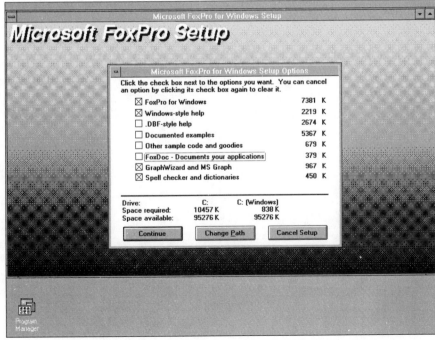

4. **You're on the installation road at last. Keep feeding it disks until it stops asking.**

Don't worry if FoxPro skips some disks during the installation process. Remember that you aren't installing the whole thing, so it's perfectly natural for FoxPro to blissfully ignore one disk or another. Make sure that you feed it the disk it asks for, and all is well.

5. **When the last disk is done (and the monitor sinks slowly into the desktop), put your disks somewhere safe.**

Don't forget the last disk. Remember to take it out of the drive and put it with the others. This note is from someone who left many, many disks in many different computers and often wondered why I — um, *he* — was perpetually missing the last one in the set.

# Minimum Installation

1. **Click the Minimum Installation button.**

2. **Continue with Step 2 in the "Complete Installation" section.**

The only difference between Complete and Minimum is the first button you click. The rest of the process works the same either way.

# Appendix B

# Migrating South from the Cold Reaches of dBASE

## Why Bother Changing?

I guess there are many reasons to switch, but I'm sure that the Microsoft Marketing Department can think of infinitely more of them than I can. There are a few things that stand out in my mind — things that you, as an ex-dBASE user, definitely want to look forward to in the new version of FoxPro for Windows:

Speed  FoxPro is supposed to be lots faster than dBASE. I say *supposed to be* because I haven't personally tested this claim, although I have complete faith in the unbiased, independent nature of the test Microsoft paid for. You don't need to do anything special to reap the speed harvest, because FoxPro looks at what you're doing and figures out how best to make it go *zoom*.

Wizards  This new FoxPro introduces several Wizards to make your life easier. They're miniprograms that actually do some work *for* you with minimal oversight. They conduct a little electronic interview to determine your needs (what salesmanship!), and then fulfill the aforementioned need as quickly and completely as they can. They're covered in the chapters with titles along the lines of "Doing Whatever at the Wave of a Wand."

| | |
|---|---|
| Windows Support | Because it's a Windows application, FoxPro delivers all the cool stuff you expect from a good Windows program. It supports TrueType scalable fonts, a multitude of printers, and all the other cutesie things that come with it. Your reports and screens will thank you for the new font togs. |
| File Sharing | If you work and play in a multicomputer world, FoxPro makes it primo easy to share files with your buddies. There are current versions of FoxPro for Macintosh, DOS, and Windows. They all read the same files, so you don't have to worry about converting your stuff and losing things (like the data) in the translation. Slick, eh? |

# Making It Easy: Catalog Manager and AutoMigrate

I have to give Microsoft five fox heads out of five for the work they did on the new FoxPro. It's a masterpiece of compatibility with dBASE. FoxPro does almost all the work for you, behind the scenes. You don't *manually* convert anything.

Say you have a dBASE table and you tell FoxPro to open it. FoxPro says, "Hey, this is a table from *that other program*. I think I'll automatically convert it to a format that is intrinsically better. Here at Microsoft, we love the people who buy our programs. We want to make life easier for them through technology, in the fervent hope that they and their children continue to purchase our products for many years to come, thus guaranteeing our jobs well into the next millennium." Actually, that's what the copy of FoxPro that I received from the Marketing Department said. I think the general distribution copy just converts the files and mutters to itself about the weather.

The Catalog Manager is at the heart of the whole compatibility thing. It *directly* reads dBASE catalog files. When you use or modify any of your dBASE things (tables, forms, reports, and such), the Catalog Manager fires up the AutoMigrate program and quickly brings your work into FoxPro. Best of all, your original files are left completely intact. If you decide switching programs was a terrible idea, everything is *still* there, just the way you left it.

There is an important exception to FoxPro's nondestructive approach. It only concerns databases with memo fields. If you don't use memo fields, you're fine. If you use memo fields but don't understand what they do, consult your FoxPro guru or Microsoft Technical Support for more information.

When FoxPro converts a table with memo fields from dBASE format, it not only converts the table but also the memo file itself. All the information in the memo fields is contained in this other file. FoxPro can have much larger memos than dBASE, so the memo file *isn't* directly dBASE compatible any more. There is a way to convert it *back* to dBASE format, but you may lose some of your data if you try it.

Before converting your tables — or anything, for that matter — make a couple of good backup copies, just in case something horrible happens. Be particularly sure to back up your tables and their associated memo fields. This is the *only* way to practice safe converting.

- The Catalog Manager directly reads your dBASE catalog files. Just tell it to open a new catalog, point it in the right direction, and you're ready to go.

- For almost everything you ever wanted to know about the Catalog Manager, see Chapter 24.

- Thank goodness, the on-line help material is a little friendlier than before. If you need to know specifics about the conversion process, press F1 in FoxPro, click Search, and look up the help topic *Converting dBASE Files*.

# Where to Go from Here

Here are the best places for a recovering dBASE user to start. They're in numerical order, so pick and choose depending on your particular needs.

# dBASE to FoxPro Dictionary

Given the fact that they're from different parts of the country, each package speaks a slightly different dialect of the language. Handy-dandy Table B-1 covers most of the common differences in usage.

| Table B-1 | Coming to Terms |
| --- | --- |
| *dBASE Term* | *FoxPro Term* |
| Catalog | Catalog |
| Database | Table |
| dBASE | That Other Program |
| Form | Screen |
| Index | Single or compound index |
| Label | Label |
| Phillippe Kahn | The Short Guy |
| Pop-up menu | Popup |
| Pull-down menu | Menu |
| Query | Query |
| Report | Report |
| That Other Program | FoxPro |
| The Thin Guy | Bill Gates |
| View | Cursor |

FoxPro has something called a View, which is different (*very* different, in fact) from a dBASE View. Just something else to remember — like you didn't have enough already.

Proceed at your own risk: The information on file extensions in Table B-2 is a borderline techno-treading ground.

| Table B-2 | | Extensions | |
| --- | --- | --- | --- |
| *dBASE Object* | *dBASE Extension* | *FoxPro Object* | *FoxPro Extension* |
| Catalog | .CAT | Catalog | .FPC, .FCT |
| Database | .DBF | Table | .DBF |
| Form | .SCR | Screen | .SCX |
| Index | .MDX | Compound index | .CDX |
| Index | .NDX | Single index | .IDX |
| Label | .LBL | Label | .LBX |
| Query | .QBE | Query | .FPQ |
| Report | .FRM | Report | .FRX |

# Index

• *N* •

*Find out why over 6 million computer users love IDG'S ...FOR DUMMIES BOOKS!*

**"I laughed and learned..."**
*Arlene J. Peterson, Rapid City, South Dakota*

### DOS FOR DUMMIES,™ 2nd EDITION
*by Dan Gookin*

This fun and easy DOS primer has taught millions of readers how to learn DOS! A #1 bestseller for over 56 weeks!

ISBN: 1-878058-75-4
$16.95 USA/$21.95 Canada
£14.99 UK and Eire

 INTERNATIONAL BESTSELLER!

### WINDOWS FOR DUMMIES™
*by Andy Rathbone*

Learn the Windows interface with this bestselling reference.

ISBN: 1-878058-61-4
$16.95 USA/$21.95 Canada
£14.99 UK and Eire

#1 BESTSELLER!

### THE INTERNET FOR DUMMIES™
*by John Levine*

Surf the Internet with this simple reference to command, service and linking basics. For DOS, Windows, UNIX, and Mac users.

ISBN: 1-56884-024-1
$19.95 USA/$26.95 Canada
£17.99 UK and Eire

 NATIONAL BESTSELLER!

### PCs FOR DUMMIES,™ 2nd EDITION
*by Dan Gookin & Andy Rathbone*

This #1 bestselling reference is the perfect companion for the computer phobic.

ISBN: 1-56884-078-0
$16.95 USA/$21.95 Canada
£14.99 UK and Eire

 NATIONAL BESTSELLER!

### MACs FOR DUMMIES,™ 2nd Edition
*by David Pogue*

The #1 Mac book, totally revised and updated. Get the most from your Mac!

#1 MAC BOOK

ISBN: 1-56884-051-9
$19.95 USA/$26.95 Canada
£17.99 UK and Eire

### WORDPERFECT FOR DUMMIES™
*by Dan Gookin*

Bestseller Dan Gookin teaches all the basics in this fun reference that covers WordPerfect 4.2 - 5.1.

ISBN: 1-878058-52-5
$16.95 USA/$21.95 Canada/£14.99 UK and Eire

 NATIONAL BESTSELLER!

### UPGRADING AND FIXING PCs FOR DUMMIES™
*by Andy Rathbone*

Here's the complete, easy-to-follow reference for upgrading and repairing PCs yourself.

ISBN: 1-56884-002-0
$19.95 USA/$26.95 Canada

 NATIONAL BESTSELLER!

### WORD FOR WINDOWS FOR DUMMIES™
*by Dan Gookin*

Learn Word for Windows basics the fun and easy way. Covers Version 2.

ISBN: 1-878058-86-X
$16.95 USA/$21.95 Canada
£14.99 UK and Eire

 NATIONAL BESTSELLER!

### WORDPERFECT 6 FOR DUMMIES™
*by Dan Gookin*

WordPerfect 6 commands and functions, presented in the friendly *...For Dummies* style.

ISBN: 1-878058-77-0
$16.95 USA/$21.95 Canada
£14.99 UK and Eire

 NATIONAL BESTSELLER!

### 1-2-3 FOR DUMMIES™
*by Greg Harvey*

Spreadsheet guru Greg Harvey's fast and friendly reference covers 1-2-3 Releases 2 - 2.4.

ISBN: 1-878058-60-6
$16.95 USA/$21.95 Canada
£14.99 UK and Eire

 NATIONAL BESTSELLER!

### EXCEL FOR DUMMIES,™ 2nd EDITION
*by Greg Harvey*

Updated, expanded—The easy-to-use reference to Excel 5 features and commands.

ISBN: 1-56884-050-0
$16.95 USA/$21.95 Canada
£14.99 UK and Eire

 NATIONAL BESTSELLER!

### UNIX FOR DUMMIES™
*by John R. Levine & Margaret Levine Young*

 NATIONAL BESTSELLER!

This enjoyable reference gets novice UNIX users up and running—fast.

ISBN: 1-878058-58-4
$19.95 USA/$26.95 Canada/ £17.99 UK and Eire

For more information or to order by mail, call 1-800-762-2974. Call for a free catalog! For volume discounts and special orders, please call Tony Real, Special Sales, at 415-312-0644. For International sales and distribution information, please call our authorized distributors:

**CANADA** Macmillan Canada
416-293-8141

**UNITED KINGDOM** Transworld
44-81-231-6661

**AUSTRALIA** Woodslane Pty Ltd.
61-2-979-5944

"**DOS For Dummies** is the ideal book for anyone who's just bought a PC and is too shy to ask friends stupid questions."

MTV, Computer Book of the Year, *United Kingdom*

"**This book allows me to get the answers to questions I am too embarrassed to ask.**"

*Amanda Kelly, Doylestown, PA on Gookin and Rathbone's PCs For Dummies*

"**If it wasn't for this book, I would have turned in my computer for a stereo.**"

*Experanza Andrade, Enfield, CT*

### CORELDRAW! FOR DUMMIES™
*by Deke McClelland*

This bestselling author leads designers through the drawing features of Versions 3 & 4.

ISBN: 1-56884-042-X
$19.95 USA/$26.95 Canada/17.99 UK & Eire

### QUICKEN FOR WINDOWS FOR DUMMIES™
*by Steve Nelson*

Manage finances like a pro with Steve Nelson's friendly help. Covers Version 3.

ISBN: 1-56884-005-5
$16.95 USA/$21.95 Canada
£14.99 UK & Eire

**NATIONAL BESTSELLER!**

### QUATTRO PRO FOR DOS FOR DUMMIES™
*by John Walkenbach*

This friendly guide makes Quattro Pro fun and easy and covers the basics of Version 5.

ISBN: 1-56884-023-3
$16.95 USA/$21.95 Canada/14.99 UK & Eire

### MODEMS FOR DUMMIES™
*by Tina Rathbone*

Learn how to communicate with and get the most out of your modem — includes basics for DOS, Windows, and Mac users.

ISBN: 1-56884-001-2
$19.95 USA/$26.95 Canada
14.99 UK & Eire

### 1-2-3 FOR WINDOWS FOR DUMMIES™
*by John Walkenbach*

Learn the basics of 1-2-3 for Windows from this spreadsheet expert (covers release 4).

ISBN: 1-56884-052-7
$16.95 USA/$21.95 Canada/14.99 UK & Eire

### NETWARE FOR DUMMIES™
*by Ed Tittel & Denni Connor*

Learn to install, use, and manage a NetWare network with this straightforward reference.

ISBN: 1-56884-003-9
$19.95 USA/$26.95 Canada/17.99 UK & Eire

### OS/2 FOR DUMMIES™
*by Andy Rathbone*

This fun and easy OS/2 survival guide is perfect for beginning and intermediate users.

ISBN: 1-878058-76-2
$19.95 USA/$26.95 Canada/17.99 UK & Eire

### QUICKEN FOR DOS FOR DUMMIES™
*by Steve Nelson*

Manage your own finances with this enjoyable reference that covers Version 7.

ISBN: 1-56884-006-3
$16.95 USA/$21.95 Canada/14.99 UK & Eire

### WORD 6 FOR DOS FOR DUMMIES™
*by Beth Slick*

This friendly reference teaches novice Word users all the basics of Word 6 for DOS

ISBN: 1-56884-000-4
$16.95 USA/$21.95 Canada/14.99 UK & Eire

### AMI PRO FOR DUMMIES™
*by Jim Meade*

Learn Ami Pro Version 3 with this friendly reference to the popular Lotus word processor.

ISBN: 1-56884-049-7
$19.95 USA/$26.95 Canada/17.99 UK & Eire

### WORDPERFECT FOR WINDOWS FOR DUMMIES™
*by Margaret Levine Young*

Here's a fun and friendly reference that teaches novice users features and commands of WordPerfect For Windows Version 6.

ISBN: 1-56884-032-2
$16.95 USA/$21.95 Canada/14.99 UK & Eire

For more information or to order by mail, call 1-800-762-2974. Call for a free catalog! For volume discounts and special orders, please call Tony Real, Special Sales, at 415-312-0644. For International sales and distribution information, please call our authorized distributors:

CANADA Macmillan Canada
416-293-8141

UNITED KINGDOM Transworld
44-81-231-6661

AUSTRALIA Woodslane Pty Ltd.
61-2-979-5944

# IDG BOOKS' ...FOR DUMMIES QUICK REFERENCE SERIES

IDG's bestselling ...For Dummies Quick Reference Series provides a quick and simple way to remember software commands and functions, written in our down-to-earth, plain English style that guides beginners and experts alike through important commands and hidden troublespots.

**Fun, Fast & Cheap!**

"Thanks for coming up with the simplest idea ever, a reference that you really can use and understand."
*Allison J. O'Neill, Edison, NJ*

## WORDPERFECT FOR DOS FOR DUMMIES™ QUICK REFERENCE
*by Greg Harvey*

With this guide you'll never have to worry about deciphering cryptic WordPerfect commands again!

ISBN: 1-56884-009-8
$8.95 USA/$11.95 Canada
£7.99 UK & Eire

## WORD FOR WINDOWS FOR DUMMIES™ QUICK REFERENCE
*by George Lynch*

End your stress over style sheets, mail merge, and other pesky Word features with this quick reference. Covers Word 2.

ISBN: 1-56884-029-2
$8.95 USA/$11.95 Canada

## ILLUSTRATED COMPUTER DICTIONARY FOR DUMMIES™
*by Dan Gookin, Wally Wang, & Chris Van Buren*

This plain English guide to computer jargon helps with even the most techie terms.

ISBN: 1-56884-004-7
$12.95 USA/$16.95 Canada
£11.99 UK & Eire

## 1-2-3 FOR DUMMIES™ QUICK REFERENCE
*by John Walkenbach*

Keep this quick and easy reference by your desk and you'll never have to worry about forgetting tricky 1-2-3 commands again!

ISBN: 1-56884-027-6
$8.95 USA/$11.95 Canada
£7.99 UK & Eire

## WINDOWS FOR DUMMIES™ QUICK REFERENCE
*by Greg Harvey*

The quick and friendly way to remember Windows tasks & features.

ISBN: 1-56884-008-X
$8.95 USA/$11.95 Canada
£7.99 UK & Eire

## EXCEL FOR DUMMIES™ QUICK REFERENCE
*by John Walkenbach*

A fast, fun and cheap way to remember bothersome Excel commands.

ISBN: 1-56884-028-4
$8.95 USA/$11.95 Canada
£7.99 UK & Eire

## DOS FOR DUMMIES™ QUICK REFERENCE
*by Greg Harvey*

A fast, fun, and cheap way to remember DOS commands.

ISBN: 1-56884-007-1
$8.95 USA/$11.95 Canada
£7.99 UK & Eire

## WORDPERFECT FOR WINDOWS FOR DUMMIES™ QUICK REFERENCE
*by Greg Harvey*

The quick and friendly "look-it-up" guide to the leading Windows word processor.

ISBN: 1-56884-039-X
$8.95 USA/$11.95 Canada/£7.99 UK & Eire

For more information or to order by mail, call 1-800-762-2974. Call for a free catalog! For volume discounts and special orders, please call Tony Real, Special Sales, at 415-312-0644. For International sales and distribution information, please call our authorized distributors:

CANADA  Macmillan Canada
416-293-8141

UNITED KINGDOM  Transworld
44-81-231-6661

AUSTRALIA  Woodslane Pty Ltd.
61-2-979-5944

# IDG BOOKS' PC WORLD SERIES

"I rely on your publication extensively to help me over stumbling blocks that are created by my lack of experience."

*Fred Carney, Louisville, KY on*
*PC World DOS 6 Handbook*

## PC WORLD MICROSOFT ACCESS BIBLE
*by Cary N. Prague &*
*Michael R. Irwin*

Easy-to-understand reference that covers the ins and outs of Access features and provides hundreds of tips, secrets and shortcuts for fast database development. Complete with disk of Access templates. Covers versions 1.0 & 1.1

ISBN: 1-878058-81-9
$39.95 USA/$52.95 Canada
£35.99 incl. VAT UK & Eire

## PC WORLD WORD FOR WINDOWS 6 HANDBOOK
*by Brent Heslop & David Angell*

Details all the features of Word for Windows 6, from formatting to desktop publishing and graphics. A 3-in-1 value (tutorial, reference, and software) for users of all levels.

ISBN: 1-56884-054-3
$34.95 USA/$44.95 Canada
£29.99 incl. VAT UK & Eire

## PC WORLD DOS 6 COMMAND REFERENCE AND PROBLEM SOLVER
*by John Socha & Devra Hall*

The only book that combines a DOS 6 Command Reference with a comprehensive Problem Solving Guide. Shows when, why and how to use the key features of DOS 6/6.2

ISBN: 1-56884-055-1
$24.95 USA/$32.95 Canada
£22.99 UK & Eire

## QUARKXPRESS FOR WINDOWS DESIGNER HANDBOOK
*by Barbara Assadi & Galen Gruman*

ISBN: 1-878058-45-2
$29.95 USA/$39.95 Canada/£26.99 UK & Eire

## PC WORLD WORDPERFECT 6 HANDBOOK
*by Greg Harvey, author of IDG's bestselling 1-2-3 For Dummies*

Here's the ultimate WordPerfect 6 tutorial and reference. Complete with handy templates, macros, and tools.

ISBN: 1-878058-80-0
$34.95 USA/$44.95 Canada
£29.99 incl. VAT UK & Eire

## PC WORLD EXCEL 5 FOR WINDOWS HANDBOOK, 2nd EDITION
*by John Walkenbach &*
*Dave Maguiness*

Covers all the latest Excel features, plus contains disk with examples of the spreadsheets referenced in the book, custom ToolBars, hot macros, and demos.

ISBN: 1-56884-056-X
$34.95 USA/$44.95 Canada /£29.99 incl. VAT UK & Eire

## PC WORLD DOS 6 HANDBOOK, 2nd EDITION
*by John Socha, Clint Hicks*
*& Devra Hall*

Includes the exciting new features of DOS 6, a 300+ page DOS command reference, plus a bonus disk of the Norton Commander Special Edition, and over a dozen DOS utilities.

ISBN: 1-878058-79-7
$34.95 USA/$44.95 Canada/£29.99 incl. VAT UK & Eire

## OFFICIAL XTREE COMPANION, 3RD EDITION
*by Beth Slick*

ISBN: 1-878058-57-6
$19.95 USA/$26.95 Canada/£17.99 UK & Eire

---

For more information or to order by mail, call 1-800-762-2974. Call for a free catalog! For volume discounts and special orders, please call Tony Real, Special Sales, at 415-312-0644. For International sales and distribution information, please call our authorized distributors:

**CANADA** Macmillan Canada
416-293-8141

**UNITED KINGDOM** Transworld
44-81-231-6661

**AUSTRALIA** Woodslane Pty Ltd.
61-2-979-5944

**...SECRETS**

"Livingston is a Windows consultant, and it is hard to imagine any tricks or tips he has ommitted from these 990 pages. True to the name, there are lots of undocumented hints that can make life easier for the intermediate and advanced user."

*Peter H. Lewis,* New York Times *on Brian Livingston's* Windows 3.1 SECRETS

"Brian Livingston has worked his magic once again. *More Windows 3.1 SECRETS* is well worth any serious Windows user's time and money."

*Stewart Alsop, Editor in Chief,* InfoWorld

"...Probably the most valuable book on computers I've ever seen, and I work in a library."

*Jacques Bourgeios, Longueuil, Quebec, on Brian Livingston's* Windows 3.1 SECRETS

"David Vaskevitch knows where client/ server is going and he tells it all."

*Dr. Robert Metcalfe, Publisher/CEO,* InfoWorld *on David Vaskevitch's* Client/Server Strategies

Over 750,000 SECRETS Books In Prints

### WORDPERFECT 6 SECRETS™
*by Roger C. Parker and David A. Holzgang*

Bestselling desktop publishing wizard Roger C. Parker shows how to create great-looking documents with WordPerfect 6. Includes 2 disks with Bitstream fonts, clip art, and custom macros.

ISBN: 1-56884-040-3; $39.95 USA/
$52.95 Canada/£ 35.99 incl. VAT UK & Eire

### DOS 6 SECRETS™
*by Robert D. Ainsbury*

Unleash the power of DOS 6 with secret work- arounds and hands-on solutions. Features "Bob's Better Than DOS" shareware Collection with over 25 programs.

ISBN: 1-878058-70-3; $39.95 USA/
$52.95 Canada/£ 35.99 incl. VAT UK & Eire

### PC SECRETS™
*by Caroline M. Halliday*    BESTSELLER!

IDG's technical support expert shows you how to optimize your PC's performance. Includes two disks full of valuable utilities.

ISBN: 1-878058-49-5; $39.95 USA/
$52.95 Canada/£ 35.99 incl. VAT UK & Eire

### MORE WINDOWS 3.1 SECRETS™
*by Brian Livingston*    BESTSELLER!

IDG's Windows guru, Brian Livingston, reveals a host of valuable, previously undocumented, and hard-to-find Windows features in this sequel to the #1 bestseller.

ISBN: 1-56884-019-5
$39.95 USA/$52.95 Canada
£ 35.99 incl. VAT UK & Eire

### HARD DISK SECRETS™
*by John M. Goodman, Ph.D.*

Prevent hard disk problems altogether with the insider's guide. Covers DOS 6 and SpinRite 3.1. Includes a disk of hard disk tune-up software.

ISBN: 1-878058-64-9; $39.95 USA/
$52.95 Canada/£ 37.99 incl. VAT UK & Eire

### WINDOWS 3.1 SECRETS™
*by Brian Livingston*    BESTSELLER!

The #1 bestselling Windows book/ disk by the renowned *InfoWorld* and *Windows Magazine* columnist. Over 250,000 in print! A must-have!

ISBN: 1-878058-43-6
$39.95 USA/$52.95 Canada
£35.99 incl. VAT UK & Eire

### NETWORK SECURITY SECRETS™
*by David Stang & Sylvia Moon*

Top computer security experts show today's network administrators how to protect their valuable data from theft and destruction by hackers, viruses, corporate spies, and more!

ISBN: 1-56884-021-7;
$49.95 USA/$64.95 Canada
£ 44.99 incl. VAT UK & Eire

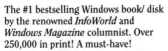

### WINDOWS GIZMOS™
*by Brian Livingston and Margie Livingston*    BESTSELLER!

The best Windows utilities, applications, and games— over 30 programs on 4 disks!

ISBN: 1-878058-66-5
$39.95 USA/$52.95 Canada
£35.99 incl. VAT UK & Eire

### CLIENT/SERVER STRATEGIES: A SURVIVAL GUIDE FOR CORPORATE REENGINEERS
*by David Vaskevitch*

An essential read for anyone trying to understand the data highways that will drive successful businesses through the '90s and beyond.

ISBN: 1-56884-064-0; $29.95 USA/$39.95 Canada
£ 26.99 incl. VAT UK & Eire

For more information or to order by mail, call 1-800-762-2974. Call for a free catalog! For volume discounts and special orders, please call Tony Real, Special Sales, at 415-312-0644. For International sales and distribution information, please call our authorized distributors:

**CANADA** Macmillan Canada
416-293-8141

**UNITED KINGDOM** Transworld
44-81-231-6661

**AUSTRALIA** Woodslane Pty Ltd.
61-2-979-5944

# IDG BOOKS

# Order Form
**Order Center: (800) 762-2974** (8 a.m.-5 p.m., PST, weekdays) or (415) 312-0650
**For Fastest Service:** Photocopy This Order Form and FAX it to: (415) 358-1260

| Quantity | ISBN | Title | Price | Total |
|----------|------|-------|-------|-------|
|          |      |       |       |       |
|          |      |       |       |       |
|          |      |       |       |       |

## Shipping & Handling Charges

| Subtotal | U.S. | Canada & International | International Air Mail |
|----------|------|-----------------------|-----------------------|
| Up to $20.00 | Add $3.00 | Add $4.00 | Add $10.00 |
| $20.01-40.00 | $4.00 | $5.00 | $20.00 |
| $40.01-60.00 | $5.00 | $6.00 | $25.00 |
| $60.01-80.00 | $6.00 | $8.00 | $35.00 |
| Over $80.00 | $7.00 | $10.00 | $50.00 |

In U.S. and Canada, shipping is UPS ground or equivalent.
For Rush shipping call (800) 762-2974.

Subtotal _____

CA residents add applicable sales tax _____

IN and MA residents add 5% sales tax _____

IL residents add 6.25% sales tax _____

RI residents add 7% sales tax _____

Shipping _____

Total _____

## Ship to:
Name _____

Company _____

Address _____

City/State/Zip _____

Daytime Phone _____

**Payment:** ❑ Check to IDG Books (US Funds Only)    ❑ Visa    ❑ Mastercard    ❑ American Express

Card# _____ Exp._____ Signature_____

Please send this order form to: IDG Books, 155 Bovet Road, Suite 310, San Mateo, CA 94402.

Allow up to 3 weeks for delivery. Thank you!

# IDG BOOKS WORLDWIDE REGISTRATION CARD

RETURN THIS REGISTRATION CARD FOR FREE CATALOG

Title of this book: **FoxPro 2.6 for Windows For Dummies**

**My overall rating of this book:** ❏ Very good [1] ❏ Good [2] ❏ Satisfactory [3] ❏ Fair [4] ❏ Poor [5]

**How I first heard about this book:**

❏ Found in bookstore; name: [6]      ❏ Book review: [7]

❏ Advertisement: [8]      ❏ Catalog: [9]

❏ Word of mouth; heard about book from friend, co-worker, etc.: [10]      ❏ Other: [11]

**What I liked most about this book:**

**What I would change, add, delete, etc., in future editions of this book:**

**Other comments:**

**Number of computer books I purchase in a year:** ❏ 1 [12] ❏ 2-5 [13] ❏ 6-10 [14] ❏ More than 10 [15]

**I would characterize my computer skills as:** ❏ Beginner [16] ❏ Intermediate [17] ❏ Advanced [18] ❏ Professional [19]

**I use** ❏ DOS [20] ❏ Windows [21] ❏ OS/2 [22] ❏ Unix [23] ❏ Macintosh [24] ❏ Other: [25]_____
(please specify)

**I would be interested in new books on the following subjects:**
(please check all that apply, and use the spaces provided to identify specific software)

❏ Word processing: [26]      ❏ Spreadsheets: [27]

❏ Data bases: [28]      ❏ Desktop publishing: [29]

❏ File Utilities: [30]      ❏ Money management: [31]

❏ Networking: [32]      ❏ Programming languages: [33]

❏ Other: [34]

**I use a PC at** (please check all that apply): ❏ home [35] ❏ work [36] ❏ school [37] ❏ other: [38]_____

**The disks I prefer to use are** ❏ 5.25 [39] ❏ 3.5 [40] ❏ other: [41]_____

**I have a CD ROM:** ❏ yes [42] ❏ no [43]

**I plan to buy or upgrade computer hardware this year:** ❏ yes [44] ❏ no [45]

**I plan to buy or upgrade computer software this year:** ❏ yes [46] ❏ no [47]

Name:      Business title: [48]      Type of Business: [49]

Address (❏ home [50] ❏ work [51]/Company name:      )

Street/Suite#

City [52]/State [53]/Zipcode [54]:      Country [55]

❏ **I liked this book!** You may quote me by name in future
IDG Books Worldwide promotional materials.

My daytime phone number is _____

**IDG BOOKS**

THE WORLD OF
COMPUTER
KNOWLEDGE

❏ # YES!

Please keep me informed about IDG's World of Computer Knowledge.
Send me the latest IDG Books catalog.

NO POSTAGE
NECESSARY
IF MAILED
IN THE
UNITED STATES

**BUSINESS REPLY MAIL**
FIRST CLASS MAIL    PERMIT NO. 2605    SAN MATEO, CALIFORNIA

**IDG Books Worldwide**
**155 Bovet Road**
**San Mateo, CA 94402-9833**